THE PENNSYLVANIA RAILROAD AT BAY

Railroads Past and Present
Edited by George M. Smerk

THE PENNSYLVANIA RAILROAD AT BAY

William Riley McKeen and the
Terre Haute & Indianapolis
Railroad

Richard T. Wallis

Indiana University Press
BLOOMINGTON · INDIANAPOLIS

This book is a publication of

Indiana University Press
601 North Morton Street
Bloomington, Indiana 47404-3797 USA

www.indiana.edu/~iupress

Telephone orders 800-842-6796
Fax orders 812-855-7931
Orders by e-mail iuporder@indiana.edu

The paper used in this publication meets the
minimum requirements of American National Standard
for Information Sciences—Permanence of Paper for
Printed Library Materials, ANSI Z39.48-1984.

Manufactured in the United States of America

Library of Congress Cataloging-in-Publication Data
Wallis, Richard (Richard T.)
The Pennsylvannia Railroad at bay : William Riley McKeen and the
Terre Haute & Indianapolis Railroad / by Richard T. Wallis.
    p. cm. — (Railroads past and present)
Includes bibliographical references and index.
ISBN 0-253-33872-7 (cl : alk. paper)
1. McKeen, William Riley, 1829. 2. Terre Haute & Indianapolis
Railroad Company—History. 3. Pennsylvannia Railroad—History.
4. Railroads—Indiana—History. 5. Railroads—Illinois—History.
    I. Series.

HE2791 .T282 2001
385'.0973—dc21
                                                    00-058073

1 2 3 4 5 06 05 04 03 02 01

For Sharon & Gramp . . . thank you both.

CONTENTS

William Riley McKeen, in a photo taken circa 1880. The 50-year-old McKeen was already a millionaire and at the height of his banking and railroad careers. Community Archives, Vigo County Public Library, Terre Haute.

AND WHERE'S AS CLEAN
A FI-NAN-SEER AS RILE' MCKEEN—
ER PUORER, IN HIS DAILY WALK,
IN RAILROAD ER IN RACIN' STOCK!
—FROM "REGARDIN' TERRY HUT" BY JAMES WHITCOMB RILEY

It must have seemed like just another day in Terre Haute, Indiana, when the wreckers finally descended upon the city's old Union Depot. Certainly few of Terre Haute's 65,000 citizens showed up to witness the first acts of destruction on that morning early in the spring of 1960; and of those who did, probably fewer still understood the significance of what they were seeing.

The edifice itself had seen better days. Though hardly an architectural master-piece, its one-time grandeur managed to elicit some mourning on the part of the more historically minded. By this date, however, the structure was just a crumbling reminder of what had once been a point of considerable civic pride, a Romanesque brick and stone pile, carried off with competence by an unremarked Cincinnati construction firm. Long since shorn of its impressive, spacious twin train sheds and allowed in later years to fall into dangerous disrepair, the old station now scarcely seemed worth saving, much less celebrating.

Yet what the few who did gather that morning failed to understand was that they were really witnessing the destruction of a monument; for, more than anything else, Terre Haute's Union Depot had stood for nearly 70 years in mute testimony to the faith and abilities of a most distinguished local banker named William Riley McKeen.

In September 1959, less than a year before its demise, Terre Haute Union Depot stands decaying and forlorn. By this time most of the upper floors of the old station had been vacated and closed off. The roof was in dire need of replacement, and the exterior required substantial repair. Instead, the Pennsylvania decided to raze the structure and announced its intention in May 1959. Demolition was supposed to take place by the end of the year, but a Clinton, Indiana, woman, who had fallen inside the building and broken her wrist, successfully sought an injunction to temporarily preserve the old station as evidence for her personal injury suit. Collection of the Vigo County Historical Society, Terre Haute.

Perhaps had the officials of the Pennsylvania Railroad, the station's final owner, fully understood what they were destroying when they consigned the structure to oblivion, they might have taken more satisfaction in the act. Their executive predecessors of seven decades past might have grimly approved, for the building of Union Depot had been the last magnanimous civic gesture by the man, and the company, that had for so long thwarted the Pennsylvania's corporate ambitions.

McKeen had been more than just the last local chief executive of the depot's original owner, the Terre Haute & Indianapolis Railroad; he had also been the control-

The Pennsylvania Railroad platform side of Terre Haute Union Depot in September 1959. All that is left of the old train sheds is the steel-framed canopy leading from the main concourse. Work will soon be under way to convert the express building in the immediate foreground into a replacement station. With the addition of a new tile floor, lowered ceilings, and air conditioning, this brick remnant of the once proud complex will carry on as Terre Haute's station for the Pennsylvania and Chicago & Eastern Illinois. After the merger of the Pennsylvania and New York Central in early 1968, all railroad traffic was diverted to the former Bee Line route two blocks to the north, and Terre Haute Union Depot finally closed. The station facility, as well as the now unused former Vandalia tracks, was sold to adjacent Indiana State University, which converted the old express building to other purposes, covering over the Vandalia name carved into the stone lintel over the door in the process. Only after the university abandoned the building did the Vandalia name reappear. But alas, not for long: The structure was leveled shortly afterward in the mid-1990s. Collection of the Vigo County Historical Society, Terre Haute.

ling owner of the Terre Haute line's stock. McKeen was the embodiment of a long heritage of local control that had begun with the formation of the company in 1847. There is some irony in the fact that Terre Haute Union Depot's official opening in August 1893 coincided almost exactly with McKeen's agreement to sell his valuable stock, bringing an end to the Pennsylvania's long, sometimes anguished quest to acquire control of the independent little railroad.

The TH&I—whose main line connected Indianapolis with Terre Haute—had operated the Pennsylvania-owned St. Louis, Vandalia & Terre Haute Railroad beyond to St. Louis ever since the latter had been opened for traffic in 1870. Moreover, it had done so with the initial blessing, encouragement, and financial guarantee of the Pennsylvania's management. When the eastern company's larger corporate interests quickly began to conflict with its own, the plucky little TH&I under McKeen usually forced the powerful Pennsylvania to yield.

Of course, the TH&I's interests had always been Terre Haute's interests, and no one had provided better stewardship of both than William Riley McKeen. It was McKeen who led the Terre Haute road into its complicated relationship with the Pennsylvania and then built up the small, local line into a highly successful regional system that was financially strong enough to resist its larger partner's strategic ambitions. But while his opposite numbers in Philadelphia and Pittsburgh might have argued bitterly to the contrary, McKeen's success came not solely at the Pennsylvania's expense. In fact, almost to the end, the Pennsylvania's proud professional managers continued to depreciate the Terre Haute banker's vision and abilities and to dismiss his road's strengths and strategic needs. It was an arrogance that nearly cost the Pennsylvania all control over its line to St. Louis.

For historians of the Pennsylvania Railroad, the Terre Haute & Indianapolis has often been an enigma. Company-sponsored histories have tended to ignore or, at best, minimize the more ambiguous relationships between the Pennsylvania and its western feeders, none more so than that with the TH&I. The very fact that the Terre Haute road remained completely independent for so long—and the extent of that independence—is often obscured. Unlike similar relationships with its other western lines, like the Indiana Central and the Pittsburgh, Fort Wayne & Chicago, the Pennsylvania's early courtship of the TH&I did not lead to the usual smothering embrace. Instead, an uneasy, arms-length partnership developed between the two vastly different organizations. It was the extent of these fascinating differences that nearly proved to be the Pennsylvania's undoing. This volume is a long-overdue attempt to shed light on that partnership and on the man who—often against all odds—kept it in balance.

There will doubtless be some who find this effort baffling to categorize. Is it a railroad history, or a biography? For the record, it is both yet neither. The fancier of tracks and trains will be quick to note its deficiencies in operating minutiae, while the reader hoping for a fuller sketch of a man's life may be left somewhat less than satisfied. But I hope not. What I have tried to do is write a railroad's history, telling the story through the life of the man who made it what it was. After all, history is really about people, not things. Of course, it helps that this is a great story to tell. And the best part for a historian is: it's true.

CAST OF CORPORATE CHARACTERS

The Bee Line. Initially the Indianapolis & Bellefontaine (in Indiana) and Bellefontaine & Indiana (in Ohio) railroads, end-to-end twins incorporated in 1848 to build the railroad between Indianapolis and Galion, Ohio, and merged together in 1864 to form the Bellefontaine Railway, from whence came the nickname: the Bellefontaine Line, or *B(ee)* Line. Merged with the Cleveland, Columbus & Cincinnati in 1868 to create the Cleveland, Columbus, Cincinnati & Indianapolis, which continued to be nicknamed the Bee Line.

The Big Four. Originally the Cincinnati, Indianapolis, St. Louis & Chicago, an 1880 reorganization of the old Indianapolis, Cincinnati & Lafayette. This Big Four merged with the Bee Line (CCC&I, see above) in 1889 to create the Cleveland, Cincinnati, Chicago & St. Louis, the "modern-day" Big Four Route.

The Fort Wayne. The Pittsburgh, Fort Wayne & Chicago, the Pennsylvania Railroad's outlet from Pittsburgh to Chicago. Built with financial support from the Pennsylvania but independent of that road, even after being leased in 1869. The Pennsylvania Railroad interests gradually acquired control, but only after a long and painfully litigious period of time.

Indiana Central. Originally the formal name of the railroad built between Indianapolis and Richmond, Indiana. Merged with the Columbus & Indianapolis Railroad (in Ohio) in 1864 to form the Columbus & Indianapolis Central. Further consolidations in 1867 and 1868 created the Columbus & Indiana Central, then the Columbus, Chicago & Indiana Central, both of which were referred to popularly in shortened form as "the Indiana Central."

Lake Shore Route. The chain of end-to-end roads extending west from Buffalo through Cleveland to Toledo, consolidated in 1868 as the Lake Shore Railway, which was then merged with its western connection in 1869 to form the Lake Shore & Michigan Southern.

Lines West. Officially: *The Pennsylvania Lines West of Pittsburgh,* the formal name given to the organization which operated all of the Pennsylvania Railroad's leased and controlled properties west of Pittsburgh and Erie, Pennsylvania. Under this management umbrella were several operating railroads and a myriad of active corporations; but the two most visible entities during the 19th century were the "Northwestern System" centered around the "Fort Wayne" (see above) and the "Southwestern System" centered around "the Pan Handle" (see below).

The Pan Handle. The Pittsburg, Cincinnati & St. Louis Railway, formed in 1868 by merger of the Steubenville & Indiana (in Ohio), and the Pan Handle railroads—the line between Pittsburgh and Columbus, Ohio. Controlled by Pennsylvania Railroad interests from the early 1860s, the Pan Handle (always two words, sometimes hyphenated) was the operating entity to which was leased other Pennsylvania-acquired properties like the Little Miami and the Indiana Central (see above). Many smaller roads were consolidated with the PC&StL in 1890 to form a "new" Pan Handle, the Pittsburgh, Cincinnati, Chicago & St. Louis.

The Vandalia Line. The name applied first to the St. Louis, Vandalia & Terre Haute Railroad during its promotional period to distinguish it from the existing Terre Haute–St. Louis railroad via Alton, Illinois. The Terre Haute & Indianapolis Railroad, which leased and operated the StLV&TH from its very beginning, assumed the nickname and by the 1880s was using it formally on maps and in advertising, as well as emblazoned on the sides of locomotives and cars. The local general public got into the habit of referring to the TH&I's system of railroads almost exclusively as *the Vandalia,* or just *the Van.* Usage of the term *Vandalia Line* on cars and locomotives continued after the 1905 merger that created the Vandalia Railroad Company.

THE PENNSYLVANIA RAILROAD AT BAY

PRELUDE

It was just a patch of Indian prairie, at first; a flat piece of land cleared of trees along the winding Wabash River. By the time Indiana became a state in 1816, Terre Haute was only a cabin or two just south of Fort Harrison. The name meant "high ground" in French. It might better have meant "high hopes," for once settlement began in earnest in the 1820s, the citizens of this frontier village were pursuing wealth and commercial advantage with single-minded devotion. It was here that William Riley McKeen entered the world on October 12, 1829, the first of five children born to Benjamin and Leatha Paddock McKeen.[1]

Benjamin McKeen had moved to Terre Haute from Kentucky in 1823, purchasing land and settling east of the little frontier village. In the early 1820s, Terre Haute was not much more than a simple farming village. Its business pursuits were confined mainly to gathering the area's crops and shipping that produce down the Wabash, Ohio, and Mississippi rivers, an activity which soon attracted Benjamin McKeen's attention. The elder McKeen went into the shipping business, building flatboats which, after loaded with the various products of the village, he then piloted down river to New Orleans to market. The Terre Haute products he shipped were inevitably flour, cornmeal, and salt pork.[2]

Riley, as the younger McKeen would come to be known, had a modest education in the village schools and spent most of his time working on the family farm. With his father often away from home on extended shipping trips, it fell to Riley as the eldest son to look after the family homestead. He chafed at being tied to the farm, but his father's imperative gave the young McKeen a front-row seat in the struggle to make Terre Haute into a town of substance, and it helped develop in the boy ambitions of his own.

Like every other town of the period, particularly those in the Old Northwest, Terre Haute made business its business. By the mid-1840s, the town had grown into an ambitious little trading center, but its commercial prospects as a river town were limited. Terre Haute's future would ultimately depend on the development of better transportation facilities.

With his father already involved in the shipping business, young Riley McKeen must have been particularly interested in the attempts to create Terre Haute's links to the outside world. First, it was the building of the National Road, an east-west thoroughfare that reached Terre Haute in the mid-1830s. This was followed by agitation for the Wabash & Erie Canal, which was gradually being extended southwestward across Indiana from Toledo, Ohio, on Lake Erie. Although the canal extension would be opened in 1849, the making of Terre Haute as a business center would truly begin with the construction of its first railroad, originally titled the Terre Haute & Richmond.[3]

To a great extent, Riley McKeen's own business career developed in step with the railroad corporation he would eventually come to dominate. McKeen became so closely identified with the railroad that biographical material written in his later years implied that Riley had been actively involved in the actual promotion and building of the road. But since he was only 17 when the company was chartered, it is unlikely that the young McKeen was much more than an avid spectator in the beginning.

Chauncey Rose, Terre Haute's commercial patriarch.
Community Archives, Vigo County Public Library,
Terre Haute.

The man credited with the actual building of Terre Haute's first railroad is also traditionally celebrated as the city's most important patriarch, Chauncey Rose. Rose had first come to Terre Haute in 1818, and within two decades he had attained the status of a wealthy local merchant and real estate baron. As one of the town's leading businessmen, Rose tirelessly promoted all the developing links in Terre Haute's transportation system, beginning with the National Road. He went on to invest in the Wabash & Erie Canal in the mid-1840s and then led the effort to secure the charter of the Terre Haute & Richmond Railroad in January 1847.[4]

By mid-century Terre Haute was a thriving town of pork-packers and retail merchants, but its business leaders dreamed of greater things. To become the important western metropolis they envisioned, Terre Haute would need better communication with the outside world than that afforded by seasonal navigation down river to the port of New Orleans or by the slow and equally seasonal canal boats plodding northeast to Lake Erie.

No one had a better grasp of the crucial commercial importance of cheap, dependable transportation than Chauncey Rose, whose first local enterprise in the early 1820s had been a combination grist- and sawmill located a dozen miles north of town. Since the miller's portion was limited in value unless it could be gotten economically to those who would pay cash for it, Rose had concentrated on sawing lumber, and eventually moved back to Terre Haute to pursue a more profitable career in retail merchandising and real estate.[5]

Indiana's pioneer railroad, the Madison & Indianapolis, had finally been completed in 1847, and its construction had provided several pointed lessons to those interested in developing a useful transportation network. The Madison line was a product of the state's disastrous attempt to provide internal improvements by fiat in the late 1830s. The railroad was built in the wrong direction and might have been a total failure had it not been turned over to private enterprise. As it was, even with citizen stockholders, the company would have only the briefest period of prosperity until it was eclipsed by its better-located rivals; but in the meantime, it demonstrated the profit potential and regional developmental power of local railroads.[6]

The Madison line's economic effect on Indianapolis was electric, and its approaching completion stimulated an epidemic of railroad charters designed to link practically every corner of Indiana with its young capital. Among them was one for a line to cross the state, from Richmond in the east to Terre Haute in the west. The new railroad was to be the central link in a proposed chain of roads between Cincinnati and St. Louis.[7]

Rose gathered around himself the cream of Terre Haute's budding business community and, with the charter of the Terre Haute & Richmond in hand, proceeded to organize the infant enterprise. The directors met for the first time on March 14, 1847, and elected Rose the company's first president. He was an excellent choice. Over the next five years, he would virtually will the road into existence.[8]

Rose began by seeking out additional on-line investors, almost all of whom came from the territory west of Indianapolis. Thus, despite the charter's intent, the line between Terre Haute and Indianapolis would be the sole focus of the TH&R's construction efforts—so much so that the Terre Haute interests would eventually be forced to solicit a separation of the company in 1851, leaving the eastern half to be rechartered and completed as the Indiana Central. It was a divorce of no great consequence, for, with the Madison & Indianapolis in operation and a number of more direct eastern connections already under construction, the TH&R's success no longer depended on the line to Richmond.[9]

The brief triumph of the Madison & Indianapolis had another happy byproduct: the pairing of the company's Madison, Indiana, banker James F. D. Lanier with New

York–based Richard H. Winslow to help float the securities of the pioneer Indiana railroad. The rise of the banking house of Winslow, Lanier & Company would help make possible an ever-widening market for the securities of a long list of midwestern railroads, the Terre Haute & Richmond included. But while Chauncey Rose would rely on Winslow, Lanier as his company's New York banker, he had even more fortuitous financial help from a very successful older brother, John.[10]

John Rose was a wealthy New York businessman whose early career had been spent as a southern cotton merchant in partnership with another Rose brother, George. As cotton brokers, the Rose brothers had made a number of influential friends who were active in British finance and business. With these contacts in the London market, John was able to help place a substantial amount of his younger brother's railroad stock with solid investors in England, Ireland, France, and Switzerland. When the railroad quickly became a profitable dividend-payer, its stock became a valuable investment worth holding onto, a circumstance which would help make the TH&R a very stable enterprise in the years ahead.[11]

Initial stock sales were strong, and the issue quickly sold out. But stock proceeds were sufficient only for acquiring right-of-way, grubbing, and grading. Like most American railroads, the company would have to borrow the money necessary to purchase iron rails and machinery. Once the required charter amendment to permit the issuance of mortgage bonds had been pried from the state legislature, Chauncey Rose was able to build and equip his railroad in a relatively short time. Construction got under way late in 1849, and the Terre Haute & Richmond was open throughout its entire 73-mile length in February 1852.[12]

Business, in the form of packed pork, farm products, and passengers, was brisk and profitable from the beginning, and the TH&R was soon hailed as a significant achievement. Terre Haute now had its ticket to future greatness.

For young Riley McKeen, the late 1840s were a time of opportunity and decision. By now his father was a man of some means and involved with friends and relatives in the pork-packing business. Riley, still tied to the family farm, had resolved to find a more congenial livelihood, and he found it in 1846 as an assistant in the county clerk's office.[13]

A hallmark of 19th-century Terre Haute was its closely knit and usually interrelated community structure. McKeen would step firmly toward the very center of that structure with his next position. In early 1848, after a single term at Asbury University in Greencastle, the young man was offered a job as bookkeeper at the Terre Haute branch of the Indiana State Bank. It proved to be the seminal moment in McKeen's career. The position not only established a firm direction but also provided unparalleled access to virtually every businessman in the community.

The bank, one of 13 semi-autonomous branches in a centrally supervised system, had been formed by practically the same group of investors that would charter the railroad; their respective boardrooms were filled with the same faces. And no wonder, since both the branch bank and the railroad were designed for the same purpose: to advance Terre Haute to the front ranks of wealth and prosperity. For a far-sighted businessman, nothing could be more personally rewarding than building up the local economy; one's own success was inextricably linked to the success of the community. This was not just rank civic boosterism, it was an article of faith, and young Riley McKeen learned it well.[14]

In 1852 McKeen received a promotion to the important position of bank cashier and took a wife, Eliza Johnston. Frail, young Eliza was the daughter of James Johnston, one of Terre Haute's most successful businessmen and a packinghouse partner of Riley's father. Eliza would bear one son, Frank. Sadly, the marriage would be cut short by Eliza's death from tuberculosis in 1855. McKeen left the state bank that same year to begin his career as a private banker, joining an older, more experienced partner named Ralph Tousey on his father's recommendation.[15]

With his railroad in operation and immediately successful, Chauncey Rose resigned the presidency of the Terre Haute & Richmond, stepping aside in favor of a more appropriate manager. It was a pattern he would repeat in a number of his commercial projects. With his brusque and sometimes impatient personality, Rose seemed temperamentally more suited to the tough tasks of starting a business than the tedious and often diplomatic requirements of its day-to-day operation. So, although he remained on the TH&R board and an active voice in the railroad's management—by virtue of being the largest stockholder—Chauncey turned over the reins to another Terre Haute business associate, Sam Crawford. Rose was far too busy for the presidency anyway, because he had already turned his attention toward extending the TH&R's reach westward to St. Louis.[16]

The Terre Haute & Richmond's completion in 1852 had given Terre Haute its railroad outlet to the state capital. There the new road connected with the Madison & Indianapolis, which in turn extended to the busy steamboat port of Madison on the Ohio River. From Madison, steamboats carried goods and passengers to and from Cincinnati, Wheeling, and Pittsburgh. By the end of the following year, however, an unbroken all-rail route was opened to the East over the Indianapolis & Bellefontaine and its Ohio twin, the Bellefontaine & Indiana. At Crestline, Ohio, this route, soon to be known as the Bellefontaine or *Bee* Line, connected with a predecessor of the Pittsburgh, Fort Wayne & Chicago to Pittsburgh and with the chain of roads which led to Cleveland, Buffalo, and—by way of the New York Central—to Albany and New York City. Pittsburgh was, of course, the western terminus of the brand new Pennsylvania Railroad to Philadelphia.

West of Terre Haute the situation was more problematic. Rose and his Terre Haute associates favored a direct link to St. Louis, and their first choice was the Mississippi & Atlantic Railroad, organized in 1850 by downstate Illinois businessmen from Greenville and Vandalia. Unfortunately, the efforts of these southern Illinois partisans had met with the organized opposition of virtually the entire rest of the state.

The Illinois legislature in Springfield, dominated by a coalition of interests including Chicago and the port towns along the Illinois and Mississippi rivers, initially refused to sanction any railroad charters that would benefit St. Louis at their expense. Specifically, this meant vigorous opposition to the Mississippi & Atlantic from Terre Haute to St. Louis and to the Cincinnati-sponsored Ohio & Mississippi from Vincennes to St. Louis. The chief beneficiary of this so-called "state policy" was the rival Mississippi River port of Alton, which would soon field its own cross-state charter for the Terre Haute & Alton Railroad.[17]

Already wounded by their loss of influence and prestige after the state capital had been removed from Vandalia, the down-staters were incensed by this heavy-handed suppression of what they considered their legitimate economic rights. With a torrid flood of political rhetoric, the on-line proponents of both the Mississippi & Atlantic and the Ohio & Mississippi rallied to each other's support, but with only partial success. The legislature would eventually, if grudgingly, allow construction of the Ohio & Mississippi. But the Greenvilleans, having had their application for a charter rebuffed once before in 1846, found their charter rejected again in 1850.[18]

With admirable tenacity, the Greenville and Vandalia crowd bypassed the legislature and went ahead to incorporate and organize their railroad anyway, following the provisions of a new Illinois General Railroad Law passed in 1849. But a problem lay with one section of the law that reserved the right of the legislature to fix the actual route and termini of a proposed railroad. Thinking this clause far too ambiguous to be effective, the Mississippi & Atlantic partisans ignored it and proceeded to survey their route and acquire the necessary right-of-way. Their opponents in Alton, feigning outrage at this flagrant disregard for state authority, hastily organized the Terre Haute & Alton, the charter for which the legislature hastily confirmed in January 1851. The battle was now joined.[19]

While the Alton forces floundered, the Mississippi & Atlantic completed its survey and secured nearly two-thirds of the right-of-way. But in attempting to condemn a piece of property in Effingham County, the railroad ran afoul of the law. The landowner sued, contending that the company, being illegally organized under the terms of the General Railroad Law, had no right to condemn. The plaintiff lost in the circuit court but won on appeal to the Illinois Supreme Court in early 1852, bringing the Mississippi & Atlantic's progress to a halt.[20]

Not content with this one legal assault, the M&A's opponents added a companion *quo warranto* action (a suit brought by government to test a franchise or charter). This suit, also decided in early 1852, actually sustained the validity of the Mississippi & Atlantic's charter, leaving the railroad in a peculiar limbo. Now, with their organization weakened in the public eye by uncertainty over its legal rights, the men from Greenville and Vandalia sought financial reinforcements from their eastern connections.[21]

One cannot say for sure that Chauncey Rose brought the Mississippi & Atlantic men together with his banker friends from Winslow, Lanier & Company, but it is certainly possible. Rose had been closely following the drama unfolding next door, since its outcome would affect his Terre Haute & Richmond; and it was definitely to Terre Haute's advantage that the Mississippi & Atlantic be completed. In any event, after obtaining eminent New York legal opinion that the company's right to build was indeed unimpaired, Winslow, Lanier signed on as the Mississippi road's bankers. They also brought their favorite railroad executive, John Brough, with them as the line's new chief executive. Brough, who was successively president of the Madison & Indianapolis and Indianapolis & Bellefontaine and, later, wartime governor of Ohio, had a genius for promotion and administration sorely needed by the Illinoisans.[22]

Winslow, Lanier agreed to take the majority of the Mississippi road's stock and, with Brough's help, managed to place a substantial portion of it with the various roads that made up the Mississippi & Atlantic's eastern connections. Among these were the Bellefontaine Line twins, the Cleveland, Columbus & Cincinnati, and predecessors of the Lake Shore Railroad, all of which were or had been Winslow, Lanier clients. Chauncey Rose also bought shares on his own account. The businessmen of Greenville and Vandalia, now reduced to minority interests in their long-anticipated railroad project, were left as helpless spectators along the sidelines.[23]

With the editorial support of Henry Varnum Poor's influential *American Railroad Journal,* Brough and his associates now set out to convince the bond-buying public of the Mississippi & Atlantic's compelling natural advantages and to try to convince Illinois itself of the line's absolute necessity. Meanwhile, with their own line at a financial and—the state's obtuse anti–St. Louis policy notwithstanding—geographical disadvantage, the promoters of the Terre Haute & Alton put as many obstacles in Brough's path as they could. As long as they could keep the legal legitimacy of the Mississippi & Atlantic organization in doubt, the Alton supporters could ruin investor confidence in the project. This they did by continuous journalistic broadsides; by instigating in 1853 another nuisance *quo warranto* proceeding testing another aspect of the Mississippi road's legal existence; and by purchasing and publishing influential *local* legal opinions, like that dated March 4, 1854, from Abraham Lincoln's Springfield firm of Stuart, Lincoln & Edwards, which argued that the Mississippi & Atlantic had no claim to any legal existence at all. While never managing to cripple the vaunted "straight line to St. Louis" with any one blow, the Alton faction's constant skirmishing became a war of attrition that the Mississippi & Atlantic forces could not possibly win.[24]

In the end it was the Terre Haute & Alton which was built, although it too had to build beyond Alton to St. Louis. Ironically, in order to attract sufficient financial support to construct its railroad, the Alton faction had to buy the charter of the Belleville & Illinoistown and use it to build a branch into what would become East St. Louis. The two companies would be consolidated in 1856 as the Terre Haute, Alton & St. Louis.[25]

Thus checked, the Mississippi & Atlantic organization gradually ran out of steam. As the Easterners lost interest, the titular leadership of the empty corporate shell reverted back to the same Greenville men who had tried so hard to bring it to life. And they too had to give up when the financial debacle of 1857 dashed all hopes of a successful resuscitation.[26]

It was an embittering experience for the Greenville businessmen, and one they vowed never to forget. Vandalia, at least, got a railroad line of its own when the Illinois Central's main line was finished in the mid-1850s. But Greenville remained landlocked and without railroad communication. The Greenvilleans tried again in 1859 with a more modest project chartered as the Highland & St. Louis, but the outbreak of war in 1861 effectively ended this second effort.[27]

Meanwhile, Chauncey Rose was aiding the construction of any and all proposed rail lines to Terre Haute, with the one notable exception of the Terre Haute & Alton. As the Mississippi & Atlantic slowly disintegrated, Rose concentrated on a railroad projected northward from Evansville to Terre Haute. Finally emerging as the Evansville & Crawfordsville with Rose and a number of other Terre Haute men represented in the directory, this company opened its line between Vincennes and Terre

Haute in October 1854. With the completion of the Ohio & Mississippi across Illinois the following summer, the Terre Hauteans finally had their connection to St. Louis, circuitous though it was. The Terre Haute & Richmond responded quickly by joining with the Ohio & Mississippi and Evansville & Crawfordsville in providing trains running "in close connection from St. Louis to Indianapolis" twice daily. A change of trains was necessary at Vincennes due to the Ohio & Mississippi's 6-foot broad gauge, but through cars were run between Vincennes and Indianapolis.[28]

The Terre Haute & Alton, soon to be the Terre Haute, Alton & St. Louis, finally wheezed into town in March 1856. It was not the direct line Rose had desired to St. Louis, but it was much better than the roundabout, multi-gauged route via Vincennes; and it became, for a time at least, the Terre Haute & Richmond's primary, if increasingly troublesome, western connection.

→►═●═◄←

The year 1855 was a good time to begin a private banking business in Terre Haute. With some assistance from his father, Riley McKeen bought a one-half interest in an existing family banking firm and became the partner of Ralph Tousey. Although there are no records available to describe the exact details and dimensions of the firm, McKeen & Tousey seems to have prospered quite well. Terre Haute was fertile ground for young McKeen's ambitions, which expanded in tandem with the town.[29]

Terre Haute was developing slowly. The raw little town on the banks of the Wabash enjoyed many natural advantages, but it was the railroad that proved to be the real engine of the city's growth. The original local industry of pork-packing continued to expand at first, along with the processing of grain and livestock. However, this agriculturally based economy gradually receded as more lucrative business pursuits became possible. Bituminous coal from the Terre Haute vicinity was dug and shipped east on the increasingly busy Terre Haute & Richmond, spurring the industrial development of Indianapolis. Still, Terre Haute's most important business activity was the railroad itself, with its busy yards and shops.

The growing success of McKeen's banking firm could not fill the void left by the loss of his young wife. Eliza McKeen had died onboard an Ohio River steamboat on Christmas day, 1855, en route home from an unsuccessful attempt to arrest the ravaging effects of her tuberculosis. The tragedy left Riley widowed at the age of only 26, but he did not remain single for long. McKeen, typical of his age, would demonstrate a particular fondness for the connubial estate, marrying three times during his lifetime. In fact, until his final years, McKeen would remain unmarried for no more than two years at a time.[30]

Marrying well seems to have been a bedrock principle to the business leadership of old Terre Haute. Not only did the community's first families intermarry from the beginning, they became almost exclusively interrelated over time. There is no doubt young Riley McKeen had married well his first time. Now, with a young son to look after, the handsome young banker began courting Ann Crawford, daughter of Sam Crawford, the president of the bustling Terre Haute & Richmond Railroad. Whether Crawford knew his prospective son-in-law well is not known, but he was, at least, certainly acquainted with the rising young banker. Unfortunately, their familial relationship would be brief, for Sam Crawford died scarcely two weeks after Ann and Riley married in March 1857, bringing an abrupt end to the couple's honeymoon in the process.[31]

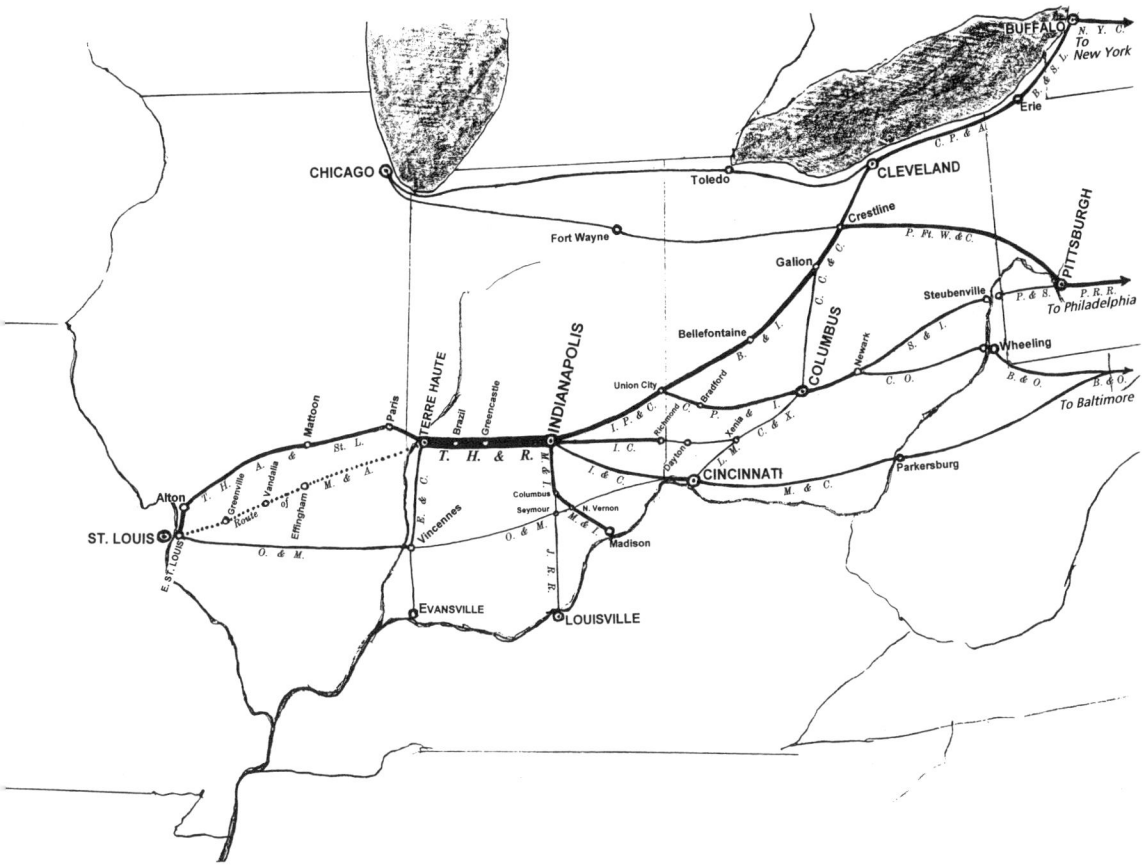

THE TERRE HAUTE & RICHMOND
and its primary connections in 1858

B. & O.	Baltimore & Ohio	J. R. R.	Jeffersonville Railroad
B. & I.	Bellefontaine & Indiana	L. M.	Little Miami
B. & S. L.	Buffalo & State Line	M. & I.	Madison & Indianapolis
C. O.	Central Ohio	M. & C.	Marietta & Cincinnati
C. P. & I.	Columbus, Piqua & Indiana	M. & A.	Mississippi & Atlantic
C. & X.	Columbus & Xenia	N. Y. C.	New York Central
C. C. & C.	Cleveland, Columbus & Cincinnati	O. & M.	Ohio & Mississippi
C. P. & A.	Cleveland, Painesville & Ashtabula	P. R. R.	Pennsylvania Railroad
E. & C.	Evansville & Crawfordsville	P. & S.	Pittsburg & Steubenville
I. C.	Indiana Central	P. Ft. W. & C.	Pittsburgh, Fort Wayne & Chicago
I. & C.	Indianapolis & Cincinnati	S. & I.	Steubenville & Indiana
I. P. & C.	Indianapolis, Pittsburg & Cleveland	T.H.A.& St.L.	Terre Haute, Alton & St. Louis

At a somber directors meeting of the Terre Haute & Richmond Railroad, Edwin J. Peck, one of the original incorporators of the company, was chosen as Crawford's successor. Peck, who lived in Indianapolis and was the only director from outside of Terre Haute, had been well known by Chauncey Rose and the rest of the city's businessmen ever since he had served as contractor for construction of the local branch of the State Bank. In fact, as a contractor, Peck had built several branch banks, including the one headed by James F. D. Lanier in Madison. More importantly, Peck had also been an early investor in and director of the Madison & Indianapolis Railroad. His participation in the creation and development of the Terre Haute & Richmond proved invaluable in generating financial support for the line.[32]

Peck assumed command of a very successful business. The Terre Haute & Richmond would have another profitable year in 1857, in spite of the short but severe recession ushered in by a financial panic in August. The company would also pay a handsome 10 percent dividend on its shares, including the 41 inherited by Ann Crawford McKeen and voted by her banker-husband.[33]

If the firm of McKeen & Tousey was affected by the financial panic, it recovered quickly. Riley was developing a healthy amount of business among the city's elite and took his partner's retirement the following year in stride. In 1858 McKeen approached the Terre Haute & Richmond board to solicit its business, and the railroad opened an account and took advantage of the young banker's offer of "low rates" and "full service." If not a coup, it was, at least, a plum, for the Terre Haute & Richmond was the city's biggest business of all, and growing bigger.[34]

The financial recession of 1857 did not have a salutary effect on the TH&R's western connection, the Terre Haute, Alton & St. Louis Railroad. Reduced earnings and tight money made the company's large load of floating debt an intolerable burden. In an attempt to remain solvent, the Alton line began to delay its payments for interline freight and accumulated a deficit in its account with the Terre Haute & Richmond. In April 1858 an angry TH&R board instructed its superintendent not to deliver any more freight to the Alton line until a specified amount of money was paid, or until he received further word from the directors. At the same time, a committee of TH&R directors was chosen to attend the next Alton line board meeting and press the company's claim. The directors apparently failed to convince their western connection to pay very much, because by year's end the TH&R board was threatening legal action if some form of regular payment was not initiated to liquidate the debt.[35]

The Alton line's misery continued into 1859, with default on its bonds and a frantic attempt by management to fund its interest payments. It was all for naught, because trustees for the company's second mortgage took possession in December 1859. For a time it seemed that the Terre Haute & Richmond would lose a substantial portion of the Alton line debt, which infuriated the company's directors and set off years of legal wrangling.[36]

Regular through business continued over the two lines, however, despite the hostile relations. In October 1859 the TH&R participated in the formation of a through freight line. The Terre Haute road joined with the Alton line, the Bellefontaine Line, and Indiana Central to provide "compromise gauge cars" to be "loaded at Buffalo, Dunkirk, Pittsburgh and Wheeling, and transported through to St. Louis, without being unloaded at each break in gauge as has been the case heretofore." Such cars were fitted with special wheels that had an extra-wide tread area so they could run on the 4-foot 10-inch gauge railroads of Ohio as well as their 4-foot 8½-inch standard gauge neighbors in Indiana and Illinois. Unfortunately, the wide-tread wheels were unstable and a safety hazard, restricting their use. This car interchange problem would remain until after the Civil War, and the resulting inconvenience and expense only intensified as business increased.[37]

Business did exactly that after the outbreak of war in 1861. On the Terre Haute & Richmond, gross revenues, which had been $378,000 in 1860, nearly doubled by the end of 1862; and the company had its first million-dollar year of gross revenues in 1864. A car shortage required a further purchase of "compromise gauge cars" in 1861.[38]

War caused the virtual closure of the Mississippi River to commercial traffic, isolating much of the Old Northwest from its traditional southern-state markets and diverting the trade of the upper Mississippi and lower Ohio valleys eastward over the new railroad network. Under this virtual floodtide of traffic, the TH&R ceased to be a small, hometown enterprise. Additional traffic required additional equipment, and more locomotives and cars meant increased shop space, more machinery, and a bigger workforce. The railroad almost throbbed with activity, pumping wealth and prosperity into Terre Haute.

Riley McKeen's bank shared in the financial rewards of the era, and the enterprising young banker also began to assume the responsibilities that accompanied his growing importance in the community. In 1861, when the initial expense of raising troops drained the Indiana treasury, McKeen responded to Governor Oliver P. Morton's request for aid by loaning the state $10,000 to help cover the interest on its debt. Though the amount was only a fraction of the total needed, McKeen's gesture elevated his stature among Terre Haute's business leaders and gained for him invaluable political recognition. Yet the real validation of his importance within the community came in January 1862, when McKeen was elected for the first time to the board of directors of the Terre Haute & Richmond Railroad. He was 32 years old.[39]

McKeen quickly displayed an interest in the details of the railroad's business. He also began to demonstrate a talent for negotiation, participating in the arrangements which led to final resolution of the claim against the Alton line, which was reorganized as the St. Louis, Alton & Terre Haute in June 1862.[40]

So involved did Riley McKeen become in the business of the railroad, and a number of lesser enterprises, that in 1863 he decided to take a new partner to help him run the bank. In some ways McKeen's relationship with his new associate, young Demas Deming, Jr., was a replay of his earlier relationship with Tousey, only this time Riley took the role of elder. Deming, who had started work in McKeen's bank office in 1857 at the age of 16, was the son of Judge Demas Deming, one of McKeen's fellow TH&R directors. As the retired first president of the Terre Haute branch of the old State Bank, Judge Deming had also been McKeen's former employer. Terre Haute was still a very small world.[41]

In contrast, the railroad world was growing decidedly larger in scope, with ever greater implications for a small, locally controlled line like the Terre Haute & Richmond. By war's end, the Terre Haute road found itself part of an increasingly important east-west trunk line, and its eastern connections were rapidly coalescing into powerful groups of interlocking interests. But for the directors and officers of the Terre Haute & Richmond, developments in the East were definitely secondary to their problems in the West.

Never completely satisfied with the St. Louis, Alton & Terre Haute as their western connection, the Terre Hauteans were becoming increasingly disenchanted with the Alton line's performance. The financially anemic road had been poorly built and remained largely unimproved. Even with the healthy traffic increases of the war years, the Terre Haute to East St. Louis main line was still almost completely unballasted, and the road was chronically short of equipment. In his annual report for 1866, the Alton line's president, Charles Butler, tried to convince his predominantly New York stockholders of the pressing need for additional investment, but his efforts were in vain.[42]

Chauncey Rose, in particular, never quite accepted the failure of the Mississippi & Atlantic and continued to encourage and support his erstwhile associates in Greenville, Illinois. Along with the Terre Haute & Richmond's president, Edwin Peck, Rose had personally helped fund the survey of the stillborn Highland & St. Louis several years earlier. It is no surprise, therefore, to find Rose's name among the southern Illinois incorporators of the new St. Louis, Vandalia & Terre Haute Railroad in February 1865.[43]

Thus, the Terre Haute & Richmond began the postbellum years with a proposed new western connection. The company also had a new name, for just one month before Lee's surrender at Appomattox, perhaps to better reflect reality, the Indiana legislature had changed the company's corporate title to the Terre Haute & Indianapolis Railroad.[44]

2

EXECUTIVE

For Riley McKeen and his fellow Terre Haute businessmen, the postwar period appeared to be full of promise. Terre Haute had been growing steadily, thanks to its importance as a railroad center, and the city's business leaders had high hopes of creating an industrial colossus in the years ahead. But they also realized that, to do so, they would have to maintain control of the primary engine of their prosperity. Events beyond their control were about to test their resolve.

As important as through business had become to the Terre Haute & Indianapolis and its connecting lines, the traffic flowing to and from St. Louis was but a fraction of the amount moving to and from the northwest via Chicago over railroads like the Pittsburgh, Fort Wayne & Chicago. St. Louis, having chosen to rely too long on Mississippi River boat traffic for its prosperity, had been left a distant second to Chicago as a gateway to the West. Yet, as a commercial center, St. Louis still had enormous strategic importance, enhanced by the city's belated efforts to tap the trans-Mississippi West with railroads of its own. Several lines were planned, one of which was intended as a branch of the transcontinental railroad project begun in 1863. The key to St. Louis's future success would be the completion of a bridge across the Mississippi River. Just such an enterprise was begun in 1865 almost simultaneously with the chartering of the St. Louis, Vandalia & Terre Haute. Like its counterparts at Keokuk and Davenport, Iowa, the St. Louis Bridge would prove to be a magnet to the railroad interests of the East.[1]

While the Terre Hauteans were preoccupied with strengthing their city's postwar commercial position, the eastern connections of the Terre Haute & Indianapolis began jockeying for position in the developing race for trunkline mastery. One of them was the Indianapolis & Cincinnati Railroad, controlled by Cincinnati interests and headed by Henry C. Lord. Lord had approached the Terre Haute & Richmond board in 1862 to solicit financial help in building a direct entry into Cincinnati for his road. Previously, the Indianapolis & Cincinnati had been dependent upon trackage rights over the Ohio & Mississippi Railroad from Lawrenceburg, Indiana. The bait was Lord's promise to exclusively interchange at Indianapolis all traffic destined to and from St. Louis, business the Indianapolis & Cincinnati was forbidden to solicit by the terms of its trackage rights contract with the Ohio & Mississippi. The Terre Haute & Richmond's board had responded generously with a loan of $50,000, and the Indianapolis & Cincinnati was able to complete its Cincinnati extension in 1863. Lord, whose hunger for financing was exceeded only by his appetite for expansion, attempted to beg additional funds from the Terre Haute road in

The great St. Louis Bridge, later called by the name of its visionary designer, Captain James B. Eads. Notable for its extensive early use of steel, the bridge took more than four years to build. This photograph was taken shortly after its completion in 1874 and appeared in the 1881 construction history written by C. M. Woodward. Photograph by Robert Benecke, 1874; Missouri Historical Society, St. Louis.

1864, but without success. By 1866 Lord was looking covetously at his highly prosperous western neighbor. He was not alone.[2]

Throughout most of 1866, the men in charge of the Terre Haute & Indianapolis Railroad's eastern connections were quietly considering their lack of control over the existing trunk line to St. Louis. These included the principal Cleveland and New York financiers who controlled the fortunes of the Cleveland, Painesville & Ashtabula, the Cleveland, Columbus & Cincinnati, and the Bellefontaine Route as well as the management of the Pittsburgh, Fort Wayne & Chicago. All relied on the independent combination of the Terre Haute & Indianapolis and the St. Louis, Alton & Terre Haute to reach St. Louis, and none could allow the route to fall into any one set of hands. Nevertheless, it appears that Lord made the first move to wrest control on behalf of the Indianapolis & Cincinnati.

Sometime in the summer or fall of 1866, Lord contacted Chauncey Rose and Edwin J. Peck and offered to buy their stock in the TH&I. Since Rose owned the controlling block of stock, this purchase alone would have been sufficient to acquire mastery of the company. Peck was certainly amenable to the arrangement, but Rose hesitated. In the meantime, the owners of the Bellefontaine Route discovered Lord's maneuvering and countered with an offer of their own.[3]

At precisely what point the management of the Pittsburgh, Fort Wayne & Chicago became aware of these developments is not clear; but as George Washington Cass, the Fort Wayne's president, subsequently reported to his stockholders, common sense prevailed and the contending parties agreed to a joint plan of action early in 1867 and invited the Fort Wayne to participate. Presumably at Cass's urging, J. Edgar Thomson, president of the Pennsylvania Railroad, which was the Fort Wayne's most important eastern connection, also became a party to these joint negotiations.[4]

Using Lord's offer to Rose and Peck for control of the TH&I as a starting point, the consortium opened negotiations with the New York management of the St. Louis, Alton & Terre Haute for a lease of that road. Here at last was a painless solution to the Alton line's financial problems, and the company's board quickly agreed to a generous lease agreement. The key to the plan was the consortium's proposed joint acquisition of the Terre Haute & Indianapolis to hold the Alton line lease and operate the combined line. Unfortunately for the collaborators, the TH&I was not for sale.

Chauncey Rose had hesitated at Henry Lord's first offer with good reason. With the St. Louis, Vandalia & Terre Haute organized and finally under contract for construction, his long-cherished direct line to St. Louis was showing every sign of becoming a reality. But there was another, more critical consideration: If he sold out, control of his Terre Haute & Indianapolis would pass from Terre Haute to a group of eastern corporations. Perhaps remembering the unhappy experience with the Mississippi & Atlantic, it was a prospect Rose preferred to avoid at all costs.

Up to this point, Rose appears to have kept his own counsel, but rumors of some kind of sale of the TH&I began to circulate early in January 1867 and were picked up by the Indianapolis newspapers. In response, on January 24 the rest of the TH&I directors jointly requested an urgent meeting with Rose and Peck. The minutes of that meeting, held four days later, do not reveal any details, but judging from subsequent events, the board must have convinced Rose that it certainly would *not* be in Terre Haute's interest for control of the company to pass to outside parties. In essence, the directors adopted the defining principle of maintaining local control of their railroad. It was a decision their one outside member and chief executive, Edwin Peck, was either unwilling or unable to accept.[5]

In his negotiations with Henry Lord and the Indianapolis & Cincinnati's leading stockholder, William Dwight, Peck had agreed to be their "agent" for soliciting and acquiring enough additional shares of TH&I stock to guarantee majority ownership. As president of the Terre Haute road, with responsibility for dealing with stockholders, Peck was in an excellent position to handle this chore. His residence in Indianapolis also kept him in closer proximity to Lord and free from close scrutiny by his fellow TH&I directors in Terre Haute. Whether by accident or design, Peck was now drawn into an act that would be interpreted by the rest of the TH&I board as the worst sort of treachery.[6]

Despite the emphatic rejection of their offer by Rose, the principals of the consortium—Lord and Dwight of the I&C (now renamed the Indianapolis, Cincinnati & Lafayette); Amasa Stone, Jr., and Stillman Witt representing the Cleveland, Painesville & Ashtabula, Cleveland, Columbus & Cincinnati, and Bellefontaine Line; and Cass of the Fort Wayne—decided to proceed with their plans. Conspicuously missing from the list of participants was J. Edgar Thomson, whose Pennsylvania Railroad withdrew from the arrangements at the last minute. In April 1867 the consortium contractually agreed to jointly purchase the Terre Haute & Indianapolis and to lease the St. Louis, Alton & Terre Haute. Control of the TH&I would now have to be accomplished by soliciting the sale of "outside" shares, which Peck had previously agreed to do. Assuming Peck's continued cooperation, the consortium executed its lease of the Alton line in May, giving the Terre Haute & Indianapolis until July 1 to exercise its responsibility as operator of the leased property, by which time the consortium planned to have full control of the TH&I.[7]

Meanwhile, a sizeable block of TH&I stock suddenly became available for sale in New York City. Whether actively negotiating on behalf of the consortium or just advising, Peck got in touch with the attorney who represented the 14 individual stockholders who were selling. The TH&I board was finally alerted to the danger when one of the affected stockholders wrote Chauncey Rose to ask for his advice.[8]

At a hastily called meeting on June 11, the Terre Haute board took swift and decisive action, and its chosen instrument was Riley McKeen. In a lengthy resolution that betrayed their emotion, the directors dispatched McKeen to New York to remonstrate with the dissident faction and, if need be, to outbid the representatives of the consortium for the 6,500 shares in question. The company treasurer was directed to supply McKeen with the necessary funds in the form of government bonds. Riley was also given one additional unpleasant chore. Convinced of Peck's duplicity, the board instructed McKeen to stop off in Indianapolis and deliver its official demand for the president's immediate resignation.[9]

Four days later in New York, McKeen had negotiated an agreement for the company to buy most of the dissident shares at a substantial premium. With the consortium thus checked, Riley rushed home for another quickly called board meeting on June 18 and got the necessary approval for his actions. At the same meeting, the board accepted Peck's resignation and then took the step which it thought would best preserve the company's independence: The board elected William Riley McKeen the new president of the Terre Haute & Indianapolis.[10]

With its collective hand now forced, the consortium, represented personally by Henry Lord, Stillman Witt, Amasa Stone, Jr., and Thomas A. Morris, came to Terre Haute on June 28 with hat in hand and attempted to negotiate directly with the TH&I board for control of the company. The directors refused and made their feelings official by vote, unanimously declining to sell any of their stock in the Terre Haute & Indianapolis.[11]

As the July 1 deadline for the TH&I to accept the lease of the St. Louis, Alton & Terre Haute came and went, the principals of the consortium proceeded with an alternate plan. Their lease agreement with the Alton line was already effective. To take the place of the Terre Haute & Indianapolis in their scheme, the Indianapolis, Cincinnati and Lafayette, the Lake Shore–Bellefontaine Line group, and the Fort Wayne organized a new operating company in September 1867, the Indianapolis & St. Louis.[12]

Although McKeen and his fellow directors had saved their company from the clutches of the consortium, they had also ensured the ultimate loss of their primary western connection and all but one of their eastern connections. It was a calculated decision, but not necessarily one to "go it alone."

The consortium represented only two of the TH&I's primary connecting lines to the east: the Bee Line–Lake Shore route to New York via Cleveland and Buffalo and

THE TERRE HAUTE & INDIANAPOLIS
and its primary connections in 1867

▬▬▬▬▬▬ **Roads of the Lake Shore-Fort Wayne Consortium**

Bee Line	Bellefontaine Railway
C. C. & C.	Cleveland, Columbus & Cincinnati
I. C. & L.	Indianapolis, Cincinnati & Lafayette
Lake Shore Route	Cleveland, Painesville & Ashtabula, and Buffalo & State Line roads
P. Ft. W. & C.	Pittsburgh, Fort Wayne & Chicago
St. L. A. & T. H.	St. Louis, Alton & Terre Haute (leased by the consortium)

▬▬▬▬▬▬ **Roads of the Pennsylvania-Indiana Central Group**

C. & I. C.	Columbus & Indiana Central
Pan Handle Route	Steubenville & Indiana, and Pan Handle roads (later merged to form the Pittsburg, Cincinnati & St. Louis)
P. R. R.	The Pennsylvania Railroad

●●●●●●●●● **Route of the St. Louis, Vandalia & Terre Haute**

▬▬▬▬▬▬ **Other Connecting Lines**

B. & O.	Baltimore & Ohio
M. & C.	Marietta & Cincinnati (affiliated with the Baltimore & Ohio)
N. Y. C. & H. R.	New York Central & Hudson River

the Fort Wayne route from Crestline, Ohio, via Pittsburgh and the Pennsylvania Railroad to Philadelphia. But a third major route east had been finished by the mid-1860s, a direct line to Pittsburgh via Columbus, Ohio; and the eastern end of this line was directly controlled by the Pennsylvania Railroad.

From its completion in 1853, the Indiana Central—the original eastern half of the Terre Haute & Richmond—had linked Indianapolis with other rail lines reaching into eastern Ohio, first to Cincinnati, then later to Dayton and Columbus. Meanwhile, the Pennsylvania had been aiding a line of roads building west from Pittsburgh in an attempt to reach Columbus and a connection to Cincinnati. This project was beset with a number of serious problems, which required an increasing amount of money and ultimately forced the Pennsylvania to take active control in order to protect its large investment. In so doing, the Philadelphia-based officers of the company began to work more closely with a number of influential Ohio investors, among whom were former Ohio Governor William Dennison and Columbus banker Benjamin E. Smith.[13]

The Pennsylvania itself was a creature of Philadelphia, intended solely as a link to Pittsburgh on the Ohio River. It was to be the medium by which Philadelphia would compete with its rival port cities of New York and Baltimore for the trade of the West. But the company's hired managers had quickly come to realize the necessity of helping to construct connecting feeder lines and were successful in convincing their merchant owners in Philadelphia to adopt such a policy. In carrying out this policy, John Edgar Thomson, the Pennsylvania's chief executive, operated with the tacit understanding that he was to aid but not attempt to acquire his western connections. Thus, for example, the Pennsylvania would invest in and lend to the three needy predecessor companies that made up the consolidated Pittsburgh, Fort Wayne & Chicago and then dispose of its interest as soon as the Fort Wayne gained solid financial health.

To compensate at least partially for his company's restrictive investment policies, Thomson developed a pattern of personal investment that would help extend the Pennsylvania's influence. Thomson led a select group of Philadelphia-based investors which usually included his vice president, Thomas A. Scott; Scott's protege Andrew Carnegie; various other officers and directors of the Pennsylvania; and business associates like George Pullman and locomotive builder Matthias Baldwin. Pooling their individual resources, the Philadelphians participated with other regional investors to help finance various projects that promised both personal profit *and* often potential traffic for the Pennsylvania. By the end of the war, these so-called "Philadelphia interests" were deeply involved in a number of promising western railroad ventures, and increasingly their primary financial partners were the group of Ohio investors led by Smith and Dennison of Columbus.[14]

The Ohioans had taken over the bankrupt Columbus, Piqua & Indiana in the early 1860s, acquired the Indiana Central, and built an intervening piece of railroad in 1863. The resulting through line between Columbus and Indianapolis was consolidated in 1864 as the Columbus & Indianapolis Central. In cooperation with the Pennsylvania-controlled Steubenville & Indiana, the consolidated road formed a new route from Pittsburgh to St. Louis that was more direct than the Fort Wayne–Bee Line route via Crestline. Understandably, given its heavy investment in the

Steubenville road, it also became the Pennsylvania's favored route to the Mississippi River.[15]

By the mid-1860s, Thomson's Philadelphia group and Smith and Dennison's Ohio group were investing together in the Union Pacific–Eastern Division, a company with transcontinental pretensions originally chartered by St. Louis interests. This involvement led to related investments, the most important of which was the St. Louis Bridge. Pennsylvania vice president Thomas A. Scott was one of the bridge company's first directors, and the Pennsylvania's former chief engineer briefly served the bridge company as a consultant.[16]

George Washington Cass was well aware of the Pennsylvania's working relationship with the Columbus & Indianapolis Central and, despite his growing irritation, understood the practical necessity of the arrangement. But it is unlikely that Cass knew anything about Thomson's far-ranging mutual commitments with the Ohioans. Thus, the Pennsylvania's abrupt withdrawal from the Alton line lease arrangements took the Fort Wayne's president by surprise. Cass registered his disappointment in his annual report to company stockholders early in 1868, even as he expressed hope for Thomson's ultimate reconsideration. It was not to be, however, for Thomson had his Ohio financial allies to consider. Anyway, by early 1868, the Pennsylvania was already making alternate plans with McKeen and the Terre Haute & Indianapolis.[17]

J. Edgar Thomson was hardly unacquainted with the existence of the St. Louis, Vandalia & Terre Haute organization. Thomson had helped float the Vandalia road's first mortgage bond issue, the arrangements for which had been made in January 1867, and his name appears in the mortgage contract along with Joseph T. Thomas, a Philadelphia lawyer, railroad promoter, and a director of Smith's Columbus & Indianapolis Central. While one can assume therefore that the Pennsylvania's president actually favored the Vandalia road over the Alton line as the best route to St. Louis, Smith and Dennison certainly had no other choice. In any event, a subscription for stock in the St. Louis, Vandalia & Terre Haute was begun in early August 1867 at the Pennsylvania's general offices in Philadelphia.[18]

While the Pennsylvania's needs and interests were still considerably hazy as the summer of 1867 came to a close, those of the Terre Haute & Indianapolis were crystal clear. If the Terre Hauteans wished to retain any of the through east-west traffic that currently moved over their line, they had to see the St. Louis, Vandalia & Terre Haute through to completion *and* forge some kind of traffic alliance with their primary connection to the east. As it happened, both "birds" would get the same "stone."

First, however, there were problems to be faced at the TH&I's offices. Riley had his hands full in the immediate aftermath of the consortium's failed raid on the company and Peck's dismissal. After the board temporarily granted him sweeping executive power, and directions to do so, McKeen purged the company of the officers most closely aligned with his predecessor. The biggest change made was the replacement of Peck's general superintendent, Jacob D. Herkimer, by longtime master mechanic Charles Peddle. Herkimer soon became superintendent of the parallel Indianapolis & St. Louis.[19]

By September McKeen had things in Terre Haute well in hand. The organization of the new Indianapolis & St. Louis company early in the month completed the consortium's arrangements and limited Riley's options. But an extraordinary opportunity was about to present itself, and McKeen's negotiating and leadership skills would help turn it into a corporate triumph for the TH&I.

On October 23 the TH&I board met and considered a joint communication from J. Edgar Thomson, Thomas Jewett of the Steubenville & Indiana, and Benjamin E. Smith of the Columbus & Indianapolis Central. The three eastern railroad presidents proposed a contract for the operation of through cars and trains over their lines and the TH&I, mentioning the pending construction of the St. Louis, Vandalia & Terre Haute. Though the TH&I board minutes contain none of the details of this proposal, it was, in the opinion of the directors, far too vague in its references to the building of the Vandalia road. McKeen was directed to respond most emphatically that, although the TH&I certainly desired such a traffic arrangement, no action would be forthcoming from its side until definite arrangements were made for the construction of the Vandalia.[20]

The Terre Hauteans had taken their stand and established a position. The response was prompt and more than satisfactory. McKeen was invited to confer with Jewett and Smith in Columbus on December 18. As Riley reported to his board on Christmas Eve, they discussed matters of mutual interest concerning the building of the Vandalia road but took no action and adjourned to meet again on December 27 with Thomson in Philadelphia. Significantly, the TH&I directors offered no special instructions, leaving McKeen free to negotiate as he saw fit.[21]

Membership in the Terre Haute & Indianapolis directorate had always been fluid but highly stable. While Chauncey Rose was the only remaining founding director, the 1867 board contained a number of members first elected in the early 1850s. Judge Demas Deming and lawyers James D. Farrington and William K. Edwards all had served ten years or more. Alexander McGregor, a local merchant and long-time friend of the McKeen family, who after a long absence from the board had just been elected to replace the departed Edwin J. Peck, had first served in 1851. Of the seven total, only Moses W. Williams had been on the board for less than five years. Williams, a Terre Haute dry goods merchant, was an interim director filling the place of Rose's close friend Firmin Nippert, another local retailer who had retired to tour his native Europe and who would return to the TH&I board in January 1868. The thread of continuity was the members' commercial interest in Terre Haute and their friendship and association with Chauncey Rose.

Rose still dominated the company, and with good reason. Using only the rough figures available, one can estimate Rose's personal TH&I stock ownership at between 6,000 and 8,000 shares. As the valued counselor of a number of smaller stockholders, Rose probably controlled by proxy an additional 2,000 to 3,000 shares. Therefore, it is likely that he personally controlled little more than one-quarter of the total of just under 40,000 TH&I shares.

But the company's purchase of the dissident New York shares in June had brought about the opportunity to buy back additional stock, and by the end of 1867, the TH&I treasury would contain almost 7,000 of the company's own shares. The board-designated trustee for this stock was Chauncey Rose. With another 3,000 to 4,000 shares in local, mostly friendly hands, and from one-quarter to one-third of the company's stock held by European owners who never exercised their right to vote, Chauncey Rose and his Terre Haute associates had a most effective grip on the TH&I. It was this Rose-dominated board of Terre Haute merchants and lawyers that dispatched 38-year-old Riley McKeen to Philadelphia as steward of its collective interests.[22]

When the parties gathered at the Pennsylvania Railroad's Philadelphia headquarters on December 27, 1867, they began to negotiate the agreements which would bind them together, for better or worse, over the next 25 years. Given his board's absolute insistence on the completion of the St. Louis, Vandalia & Terre Haute, McKeen must have pressed hard for a stronger effort to that end. Certainly the necessity for such action was clear.

The Vandalia company had already contracted with Edward F. Winslow to build its railroad, and he graded nearly 50 miles of the western end of the line before running out of funds early in 1868. The 30-year-old Winslow was one of a large crop of veteran Union Army officers who turned their command experience and war-related political contacts into personal profit in the postbellum era. Winslow's connection to the Vandalia board, however, actually predated the Civil War, for the ambitious young veteran had been associated with the company's aborted predecessor, the Highland & St. Louis, in 1859. It was only natural, therefore, that the newly discharged brigadier-general be enlisted as chief contractor. Presumably, it was Winslow who, in his quest for financing, first brought the Vandalia project to J. Edgar Thomson's notice.[23]

With the restrictive investment policy of his Pennsylvania Railroad still in force, Thomson was compelled to act through the company's two subsidiaries, the Steubenville & Indiana and Pan Handle railroads, soon to be consolidated under the revealing title of the Pittsburg, Cincinnati & St. Louis. But Thomson was very much a part of the negotiations. The outline of the plan that emerged from that December 27 meeting followed an established pattern of alliance and mutual interest that the Pennsylvania's president had used before in his personal investments. A construction company would be formed by the principal parties to build the new line, and the parties would be paid in the stock and bonds of the Vandalia. The bonds would be sold to raise the necessary funds, and the stock would be retained to ensure control of the new road. Of course, to complete the transaction it would be necessary for Winslow to surrender his contract with the Vandalia company.

On January 14, 1868, the St. Louis, Vandalia & Terre Haute board created a committee to conclude a lease of its company, subject to Winslow's approval. And on February 10, with McKeen in attendance, a contract and agreement which provided for complete construction and financial arrangements was hammered out between all the parties, as was a lease of the Vandalia to the Terre Haute & Indianapolis. With payment for his previous work guaranteed, Winslow gave his approval and agreed to surrender his contract. Now all that was needed was ratification of the agreements by the parties' various boards.[24]

McKeen was the outsider among the principal parties. Jewett and his colleagues on the Steubenville & Indiana board had a long history of working with Thomson and his PRR management. Smith and Dennison were partners with Thomson's Philadelphia investment group and well acquainted with the Pennsylvania chief's methods. Only Riley was new to this world of big-time corporate finance, and like the good banker he was, McKeen deferred to the older, more experienced hands, only insisting on fair dealing and an active participation for his TH&I. It was imperative that the TH&I remain in control of its destiny for Terre Haute's sake. McKeen was fairly confident that he had gotten what he needed, but since he had received no specific instructions from his own board, he had no way of knowing what its response would be.

Riley called the TH&I board together on Friday afternoon, February 21, and presented the bundle of contracts and agreements, the most important of which were the construction contract, the lease, and the operating agreement between the TH&I, Indiana Central, the Steubenville & Indiana, and the Pan Handle that spelled out financing arrangements and responsibilities and set down the rules which would govern relations between the interested parties. The individual directors raised objections almost immediately, and the afternoon was spent in heated debate.[25]

The crux of the problem was the Terre Hauteans' latent distrust of the Easterners. After all, Rose might have reasoned, similarly fancy footwork concerning the Mississippi & Atlantic had failed the TH&I once before. Especially thorny was the issue of the construction contract and the financial arrangements contained in the operating agreement, which must have looked like sleight-of-hand to the conservative Terre Haute merchants. Riley's board much preferred the more straightforward arrangement of actually purchasing the Vandalia's stock and jointly dividing control of the company between the several parties. The board was also suspicious of the lease arrangement and annoyed at what seemed like the Pennsylvania's reluctance to actively participate. By day's end the board had decided to rewrite the operating agreement and adjourned until the following Monday, leaving the matter in the hands of McKeen and the company's attorney, Richard W. Thompson, with its concerns and instructions duly noted.

The board reassembled on February 24 at 9 A.M. and promptly went to work. By unanimous resolution, the TH&I directors rejected the construction contract and offered their own drastically revised version of the operating agreement, directing McKeen to submit it to the principal parties with their prior approval along with their objections to the lease. In accordance with their wishes, the revised operating agreement called for a greater reliance on capital stock for the necessary construction funds and called for the joint endorsement of the Vandalia's bonds by all the various parties, including the Pennsylvania. Moreover, the TH&I directors insisted on active Pennsylvania participation in the joint stock purchase. In their view the Pennsylvania was gaining a great deal by the completion of the Vandalia route, while unfairly shielding itself from responsibility by acting through the Steubenville & Indiana and the Pan Handle. Since both of these weak roads were in precarious financial condition and in the process of being merged together, the TH&I board also demanded that the Pennsylvania itself specifically guarantee their endorsements.[26]

Having completely restructured the arrangement, the Terre Haute men adjourned, leaving McKeen to take their unequivocal answer back to Philadelphia that very night. Whether or not he agreed with his fellow directors, at least now McKeen had a much better picture of what they wanted. It was not clear where Riley stood, since the president usually did not vote unless required to break a tie; but as the board's chosen chief executive, he would try his best to do its bidding.

Two days later Riley laid his board's revised agreements before the assembled parties in Philadelphia. Their response was anything but positive. McKeen tried to convey the Easterners' objections with as much clarity as he could fit into the lengthy telegram he dispatched to Chauncey Rose later that evening. Rose called an emergency TH&I board meeting for the following morning, February 27, where he read McKeen's telegram to the directors. The Pennsylvania, McKeen had been informed, was unable to directly endorse bonds issued out-of-state or subscribe to the Vandalia company's stock. But it could indeed offer to guarantee the performance of the Steubenville & Indiana's and Pan Handle's obligations. As for relying on the issuance of a large amount of capital stock for the necessary funds, Thomson and Dennison saw no point in it, especially since the bonds would provide quite enough money for construction; Jewett and Smith had concurred.[27]

Whether or not he knew it at that point, McKeen was being finessed. Thomson had been less than frank in stating the reasons for the Pennsylvania's coyness. It was not because he was legally *prevented* from buying the Vandalia's stock, but because he was extremely reluctant to tie up his company's precious capital in an uncontrolled and distant connection. To do so would have brought the Pennsylvania's president into direct conflict with his board, which frowned on such purchases.

There was a much more compelling reason for Thomson, Dennison, Smith, and Jewett to resist actually *buying* the Vandalia's stock. Unlike the bonds, the stock could not be sold by the participants without giving up control, and it was desirable to raise most of the capital from outsiders.

Riley also telegraphed Chauncey Rose that Smith was willing for the Indiana Central to join the TH&I in the Vandalia lease, but that the lease was seen as necessary to protect the joint endorsements and to "avoid future misunderstanding between the parties." Unspoken at the time, but as subsequent events would prove, the Pennsylvania's men also considered a lease necessary for the efficient and economical operation of a line which they saw as essentially an extension of the TH&I.[28]

Discussion that morning in Terre Haute was probably brief and to the point. The TH&I board was adamant: It would not accede to any terms but its own. McKeen, who received the terse reply later that day at Philadelphia's Continental Hotel, must have felt terribly frustrated by the board's stubborn decision. Still, this was a new game for Riley, one he was beginning to like better the more he learned, and he still had one card left to play.

That card was played just two weeks later. On March 11, 1868, the obdurate TH&I board was treated to some friendly intimidation from Riley's eastern conferees, who had graciously traveled all the way to Terre Haute to turn the screws. In attendance at that meeting in the parlor of Chauncey Rose's plush Prairie House Hotel were Thomas A. Scott and George B. Roberts of the Pennsylvania, Governor William Dennison and Benjamin E. Smith of the Indiana Central, and Judge Thomas L. Jewett of the Steubenville & Indiana and Pan Handle roads. The visitors were charming but firm, and their hosts finally capitulated. When the meeting came to a close, the TH&I board directed McKeen to sign all the agreements, including the unamended lease.[29]

The agreements signed were almost identical in detail to those originally negotiated early in February. Aside from now dividing the Vandalia's second mortgage bonds into two classes, the only major difference was that the Pennsylvania now officially guaranteed the performance of its two Ohio subsidiaries. Together, the parties would build and equip the St. Louis, Vandalia & Terre Haute, and the TH&I would lease and operate the finished road for the benefit of all. Construction funds would be raised by the sale of newly issued second mortgage bonds, a significant portion of which would be purchased by the participating companies in agreed allotments. Bonds offered for sale to the public would be endorsed jointly by the various companies, but only those purchased by the interested parties would be convertible into capital stock, thus ensuring control of the completed Vandalia road.[30]

Most important was the division of responsibilities among the participating companies, for the operating agreement specified exactly how the potential profits would be divided or losses shared. The lease provided that 65 percent of the Vandalia's gross earnings would go to the Terre Haute & Indianapolis as lessee for the expenses of operation, leaving the balance to the St. Louis, Vandalia & Terre Haute for paying interest on its bonds, taxes, corporate expenses, and dividends. This proportional split was soon changed to a more equitable 70–30 percent division by the Vandalia company's board. Any profits earned by the TH&I as lessee from its allotted 70 percent of the Vandalia's gross, any loss incurred in operating the Vandalia by the TH&I, or any deficiency in the amount necessary to cover the Vandalia's bond interest, taxes, or expenses from its 30 percent of the gross would be shared according to a formula based on the participants' investment in Vandalia Line second mortgage bonds. The TH&I agreed to buy two-tenths, or $200,000 worth of the $1 million in convertible bonds issued to the participating companies. Thus, the TH&I's share of any profit or loss would be two-tenths. Likewise, Smith's Indiana Central assumed a three-tenths share and responsibility, and the Steubenville & Indiana and the Pan Handle each had a two-and-one-half-tenths share, guaranteed by the Pennsylvania. The Pittsburg, Cincinnati & St. Louis, formed by a consolidation of the latter two companies one month later, would end up with a full five-tenths or one-half share of the responsibility, fully guaranteed by the PRR.

It was finally done. Within another month's time, the boards of the other participating companies would ratify the documents, and the plans would be put into operation. The construction company was formed by Jewett, Smith, Roberts, and McKeen, acting as contractors, and the actual work taken over from Winslow's company. By the end of 1868, rails would be laid between East St. Louis and Greenville and the road graded as far east as Effingham. The contractors would turn over a completed railroad for operation by the lessee in July 1870, finally fulfilling the dreams of the promoters of the Mississippi & Atlantic. The Terre Haute & Indianapolis would have its own line to St. Louis, largely built with the resources of the Pennsylvania. And for this privilege, the feisty little TH&I would only have to bear a two-tenths responsibility.[31]

It seemed like everyone involved had gotten what they needed. Unfortunately for the Pennsylvania, its whole world would change by the time the TH&I took over operation of the Vandalia road.

⊷═◆═⊶

With the future of his railroad as part of a major trunk line assured, William Riley McKeen could now direct some of his attention to other matters, including the business of his own bank. His partner, young Demas Deming, left the firm in 1868 to become president of Terre Haute's First National Bank. Immediately upon the dissolution of McKeen & Deming, Riley formed a new partnership with Deloss W. Minshall, an experienced banker and manager. With the increasing demands of his position as chief executive of the TH&I, McKeen needed a partner to manage the day-to-day operation of the bank, now more than ever. Besides, there were additional responsibilities for Riley to attend to.[32]

As a banker, McKeen functioned as a local financier, lending money and investing, as well as acting as a financial agent for local firms and individuals. In the peculiar business ethics of the era, it was not at all improper or unusual for McKeen's bank to continue in its business relationship with the railroad, and so the TH&I account grew bigger and more important as time went on. But Riley was also actively investing in a number of other Terre Haute concerns, many of which required his time as a director and, often additionally, his talents as an officer. Especially important were investments in other railroads which served the city. McKeen served with Rose and other members of the Terre Haute business elite on the board of the Evansville & Crawfordsville Railroad, and he would later be a director for other lines, including the Evansville, Terre Haute & Chicago.[33]

From his involvement with the Terre Haute Drawbridge Company and the Terre Haute Gas Works in the late 1850s to the Terre Haute Street Railway in the postwar period, many of McKeen's investments were of a public utility character—but not all. In 1868 Riley eagerly invested in an exploratory oil well organized after oil was

The Terre Haute Drawbridge. McKeen was an original stockholder of this toll-charging enterprise. Collection of the Vigo County Historical Society, Terre Haute.

accidentally discovered during the drilling of a Terre Haute water well. It was the perfect type of investment for McKeen: one which combined the potential enhancement of Terre Haute as a business center with a handsome potential for a tidy profit. Unfortunately, in this case, it resulted in neither.[34]

There were other, similar opportunities for investment. Yet none would be more symbolically important than McKeen's joint effort with his friend Chauncey Rose in reputedly sinking the first coal mine in what would become known as Seelyville, along the TH&I's tracks just east of Terre Haute.[35]

Coal had been mined in the immediate vicinity since the 1830s, but for want of adequate transportation, production had always been limited. This would begin to change with the opening of the railroad in 1852. In fact, although the initial business of the Terre Haute to Indianapolis road was primarily the transport of passengers and the hauling of agricultural products like wheat, flour, whiskey, packed pork, and livestock, the company's promoters specifically anticipated the development of a heavy traffic in coal. And coal was hauled in small quantities from the beginning, mainly east to fuel the home fires and businesses of Indianapolis.[36]

As the industrialization of America got under way in the years immediately following the Civil War, Terre Haute's close proximity to an abundant supply of coal helped spur the city's growth. With the development of Clay County's higher quality "block coal" deposits along the TH&I tracks to the east of Terre Haute, McKeen and his business associates were finally able to attract the kind of investment they craved. The opening of the Terre Haute Nail Works in 1868 by a Youngstown, Ohio, capitalist gave the city its first truly heavy industry and promoted further development, notably in iron and steel manufacturing.[37]

McKeen especially saw coal traffic as of crucial importance to the TH&I and pushed his board to develop this business. Almost simultaneous with his efforts to drag the TH&I's directors into an alliance with the eastern railroads, Riley was prodding them into a much heavier investment in coal branches and coal-hauling equipment. At the board meeting on March 31, 1868, he was given permission to survey up to five miles of branches, and in June McKeen was authorized to put the first 3½ miles under contract. By the end of 1869, the TH&I had ten miles of branches in operation to coal mines and small iron furnaces east of Brazil and north of the TH&I main line.[38]

Coal traffic revenue had jumped from $13,000 in 1860 to $61,000 in 1866, and as the development of the Clay County fields proceeded, revenue from this source would more than double by 1870. It was healthy local traffic that would provide the company with a strong financial base, and under McKeen's guidance, the business continued to grow. Riley was well aware that completion of the parallel Indianapolis & St. Louis would reduce his company's through business, and he exerted great effort to develop substantial amounts of local traffic to offset the loss.[39]

McKeen still had to deal with the I&StL organization as a connection, and with his board's authorization, he negotiated a temporary traffic contract with the yet-to-be-completed parallel line. Recognizing the need to prevent the building of a second railroad between Indianapolis and Terre Haute if they could, the TH&I directors first contemplated litigation, then decided to pursue a negotiated compromise.[40]

Cass of the Fort Wayne proposed a number of alternatives to building an all-new railroad between Indianapolis and Terre Haute, including sharing the cost of double-tracking the TH&I and purchasing a portion of the TH&I's right-of-way for another line, but McKeen and his board resisted sharing their company's property in such a generous manner. Finally, a contract to serve as the I&StL's bridge carrier at a specified charge per car was offered by the TH&I board in April 1869, but the I&StL's Fort Wayne and Bee Line owners failed to accept the offer. In the end the Indianapolis & St. Louis built an entirely new line to the north of the TH&I, closely following an alternate survey made for the original Terre Haute & Richmond for most of the distance.[41]

Even with the prospect of a new parallel competitor, McKeen had to be pleased with the TH&I's situation and accomplishments. The nation was in the midst of a postwar economic boom, not to end until the early 1870s. Perhaps there would be enough traffic for both lines. And if not, at least the TH&I shared the burden of the new Vandalia route with an extremely strong and influential partner—the Pennsylvania Railroad.

J. Edgar Thomson of the Pennsylvania must have shared McKeen's optimism, if not his enthusiasm. He had secured another potentially lucrative western feeder at relatively small cost to his company. Moreover, he had begun to assemble, theoretically at least, the pieces of a possible transcontinental line via St. Louis. But there was a fundamental flaw in Thomson's plans. He had assumed that mutual interests and shared investments would be strong enough to bind the several partners together. He was wrong.

Thomson already had ample proof to the contrary in his dealings with Cass's Pittsburgh, Fort Wayne & Chicago, on whose line the Pennsylvania depended for its heavy traffic to and from the northwest. The Fort Wayne had become disenchanted with the Pennsylvania as its sole eastern connection as early as 1863 and had made the first of what became periodic threats to secure an alternate eastern connection at Pittsburgh. Thomson responded with what became equally periodic consolations in the form of offers to negotiate some kind of binding traffic agreement. Meanwhile, both parties pursued policies designed to strengthen their respective positions. In the Fort Wayne's case, this meant attempting to secure joint control of the existing line to St. Louis. In the Pennsylvania's case, it meant ignoring the Fort Wayne's pretensions to the southwest, seeking closer ties to Thomson's Columbus allies, and building a competitive new line to St. Louis. To make matters worse, Thomson, in an effort to demonstrate economy and prudence, had sold the Pennsylvania's earlier investment in the Fort Wayne by the end of 1866 and used the proceeds to build up the Pan Handle route. The result was an increasingly strained relationship with what was supposed to be the very model of a mutually interested ally.[42]

Thomson was only acting in what he perceived to be the best interests of his Pennsylvania, but his parochial view blinded him to the real situations and needs of his allies. The same tendencies were at work in his relationship with Smith and the Ohioans and would eventually come into full flower with McKeen and the TH&I. By contrast, Jewett and the directors of the Steubenville & Indiana and Pan Handle lines, while capable of strong opinions, were essentially acquiescent, since they served in the interest of the Pennsylvania as controlling owner. It was a lesson Thomson and his Philadelphia board had so far failed to appreciate, but one they were about to learn the hard way.

Benjamin E. Smith had been busy extending the reach of his Columbus & Indianapolis Central. With Thomson's active participation, he and Dennison had been assembling another line to the Mississippi at Keokuk, where another bridge company was planning to span the great river. Like the joint involvement at St. Louis and beyond by way of Kansas City and the Union Pacific–Eastern Division (later renamed the Kansas Pacific), the Keokuk venture was an intricate, multi-part affair which included building the bridge, constructing a connecting railroad across Iowa, and aiding the New York promoters of the intervening Toledo, Peoria & Warsaw. The goal was to create another link to the transcontinental chain. Although the project was undertaken as a purely personal involvement on the part of Thomson and his Philadelphia associates, it did offer the Pennsylvania substantial future benefits. It also depended heavily on the Pennsylvania's participation as the eastern end of this proposed new trunk line.[43]

To make the route work, Smith in 1866 first acquired the Toledo, Logansport & Burlington, which extended westward from Logansport to the Illinois line, then formed the Union & Logansport to connect it with his own road at Union City. Both of these moves were made with the Pennsylvania management's approval and with personal investment by Thomson and his Philadelphia circle. In September 1867 Smith consolidated the two roads with his own to form the Columbus & Indiana Central.[44]

Smith had also secured Pennsylvania support in other projects. In 1866, jointly with the management of the Jeffersonville, Madison & Indianapolis, Smith's road had helped extend the JM&I's Rushville branch to Cambridge City, thereby opening a new short route from the East to the Ohio River at Louisville. And in the summer of 1868, Smith would induce the Pennsylvania to join with his Indiana Central and Henry Lord's Indianapolis, Cincinnati & Lafayette in helping to fund construction of the Indianapolis & Vincennes Railroad, part of a larger scheme to tap mid-south connections at Cairo, Illinois.[45]

Had he confined himself to these projects, Smith would have had more than enough to handle, but he overreached himself and strained the tenuous financial strength of the Indiana Central when he agreed to absorb the Chicago & Great Eastern late in 1867. The Great Eastern line was an amalgamation of local Indiana roads extending from Chicago southeast to Richmond, Indiana, where it connected with the Indiana Central to Columbus and lines leading to Cincinnati. It was largely controlled from New York, and a substantial proportion of its bonds were held in Europe. The Great Eastern was also financially overextended, bearing a large floating debt which made it a marginal property at best. For the Indiana Central, however, consolidation with the Great Eastern early in 1868 meant an entrance into Chicago. Smith promoted the resulting combination, titled the Columbus, Chicago & Indiana Central, as a new outlet for the Pennsylvania from Pittsburgh to Chicago.[46]

Unfortunately for Smith, the Pennsylvania had no intention of diverting any Chicago-bound business from the increasingly restive Fort Wayne. Now saddled with the Great Eastern's heavy debt as well as that of his own Indiana Central, Smith did what he could to increase the line's traffic, falling back on an agreement made in December 1867 with Henry Lord to handle the Indianapolis, Cincinnati & Lafayette's Chicago-bound traffic via the Whitewater Valley line at Hagerstown, Indiana. This was a short-lived and extremely odd arrangement which actually short-hauled Lord's own railroad. The new Indiana Central also temporarily provided a Chicago outlet for the Baltimore & Ohio in combination with the Central Ohio from Wheeling to Columbus.[47]

Smith's merger with the Great Eastern had the practical result of giving about 40 percent ownership of his Indiana Central to the Great Eastern's former New York shareholders. With pressure exerted by such a large outside ownership and the merged road's strained financial condition, it may have been impossible to resist Jay

Gould's surprise offer to lease the Indiana Central to the Erie Railway. In any event, the Indiana Central board did conclude just such a lease early in January 1869. The reaction to this bombshell in the Pennsylvania's Philadelphia headquarters was absolute shock.[48]

Much has been written about these events of the first half of 1869, particularly concerning the 180 degree turn they brought in the Pennsylvania's previously passive corporate strategies. That Thomson and his board reacted swiftly and decisively to counter Gould's threat is clear. But in the actions taken to thwart Gould's attempt to secure control of the Indiana Central, the reasons were more complex than those usually given and probably had nothing at all to do with the line to Chicago. It was the complicated series of arrangements and guarantees Thomson had made in partnership with Smith and his Indiana Central, particularly those concerning the Vandalia route, which made an Erie lease of Smith's road absolutely unacceptable to the Pennsylvania. Moreover, Thomson and his associates had invested far too much in personal speculations beyond the Mississippi to allow Gould to wreck their plans.

The resulting changes in Thomson's thinking, and in the corporate policies of his railroad, were drastic and far-reaching. By the end of January, Thomson had convinced a majority of the Indiana Central's stockholders to reject Gould's Erie lease and to accept a better offer from the Pennsylvania-controlled Pittsburg, Cincinnati & St. Louis, still known colloquially as the Pan Handle route. When Gould went after the Fort Wayne instead, Thomson and Cass first moved to protect that line's independence, then in June concluded a lease of the Fort Wayne to the Pennsylvania.[49]

The lease of the Indiana Central in January 1869 did not alter the conditions surrounding the Vandalia route arrangements, other than to render the basic philosophy which they represented obsolete. The lease of the Fort Wayne, however, and the Pennsylvania's consequent assumption of the Fort Wayne's financial commitments had rather powerful and costly implications.

Sometime early in June 1869, McKeen was summoned to Philadelphia to meet with Thomson and the Pennsylvania's officers. Riley was officially advised of the impending Fort Wayne lease and, as he later informed the TH&I board, learned that the Pennsylvania was most anxious to stop the building of the parallel Indianapolis & St. Louis, in which they would soon have a vested interest. Would the Terre Haute & Indianapolis board be willing to share the $260,000 costs so far expended on the new Indianapolis to Terre Haute line? At their meeting on June 23, the TH&I directors eagerly replied that, yes, indeed they would.[50]

Unfortunately, the two Vandalia route partners had failed to consult the other surviving half-owner of the Indianapolis & St. Louis. The Cleveland, Columbus, Cincinnati & Indianapolis Railroad, still known as the Bee Line, had shared the Fort Wayne's ownership of the parallel line after Lord's Indianapolis, Cincinnati & Lafayette dropped out of the consortium's original arrangements. It was decidedly *not* in the Bee Line's interests to abrogate either the lease of the St. Louis, Alton & Terre Haute or the contract to build the Indianapolis & St. Louis, regardless of the Pennsylvania's pain. So it was that Thomson and the Pennsylvania grimly faced the expensive prospect of supporting not one, but two competing railroads to St. Louis. For the men from Philadelphia, the events of 1869 would be costly indeed.

3

OWNER

The Pennsylvania's binge of corporate expansion continued into the early 1870s and, in the case of its two lines to St. Louis, would produce an inevitable headache for McKeen and the TH&I. But handling the increasingly grumpy Pennsylvania Railroad executives was only one of several major challenges Riley would face in the new decade. There was also a serious legal assault mounted by the state of Indiana on the TH&I's corporate existence, and the very real problem of an aging and out-of-touch board.

In a real sense, McKeen was the first true leader of the Terre Haute & Indianapolis Railroad. While previous TH&I chief executives had been adequate administrators, content to carry out the directives of the company's merchant board, none of McKeen's predecessors had displayed any real vision of the enterprise as an organic entity which needed to expand if it were to flourish. In his dealings with the Pennsylvania, Riley had seen corporate power at work. He now realized that his own road must become something more than just a profitable local business if it were to survive in its changed environment. With the arrangements of 1868, the little TH&I had jumped into a much bigger pond with much bigger fish.

The problem was that the board itself had no leadership or vision. Chauncey Rose, while holding the largest individual block of stock, had always encouraged a highly democratic atmosphere. Directors were free to speak their minds as equals, and more than once the majority vote overrode a Rose minority. He seemed to care little about daily operations, so long as they produced an annual profit. His usual motions concerned the regular declaration of dividends and the company's periodic real estate purchases (most often with Rose himself as the seller). The prevailing direction was always cautious, conservative, prudent, and protective.

In that spirit McKeen's board procrastinated in extending their road west to the state line to meet the new St. Louis, Vandalia & Terre Haute. Not until April 1, 1869, was the president formally authorized to survey and construct the seven-mile extension, and the directors dallied almost three months longer before approving the necessary financing, provoking a rebuke from the anxious Vandalia company board. Even then, a few TH&I directors continued to oppose building the extension, probably because it would require an issue of bonds to pay for it. Presumably, the recalcitrant faction wanted the Vandalia itself to build into Terre Haute, despite their own company's contractual agreements. Riley patiently persisted and negotiated the needed contracts, one of which was awarded to Carnegie's Keystone Bridge Company for the crossing of the Wabash River.[1]

An unidentified TH&I locomotive at an unidentified location, posing with a long train of White Line boxcars, in a photograph probably dating to the 1870s. The White Line was one of the fast freight lines operating over the railroad with its own rolling stock. The engine appears to be one of the railroad's 14 American types built by the Baldwin Locomotive Works in Philadelphia in the period from 1869–73. Matthias W. Baldwin, the locomotive works proprietor, was an enthusiastic member of J. Edgar Thomson's Philadelphia investment circle and, as such, received the perquisites of membership. Like another Thomson intimate, Andrew Carnegie—whose Keystone Bridge Company received the contract to bridge the Wabash for the TH&I—Baldwin also was favored with TH&I business and supplied all of the St. Louis, Vandalia & Terre Haute's engines until later in the 1870s. Collection of the Vigo County Historical Society, Terre Haute.

The board finally agreed to a new mortgage, grudgingly issuing $800,000 in bonds, a little more than half of which paid for the state line extension, with the balance intended to cover coal branch construction. The company had been relatively debt-free since the end of the war, by which time it had paid off or converted most of its original bond issue. Only with great reluctance did the directors now authorize a new mortgage, symptomatic of the board's suffocating conservatism. While increasingly frustrated by their stubborn resistance, McKeen could only push harder and try to exercise his executive leadership.[2]

The threat posed by the state was much more dangerous to the TH&I's health, for it involved the potential loss of the company's charter. Here, Riley's growing voice in the councils of the Indiana Republican Party served as a double-edged sword, both provocative and defensive.

The trouble had its source in the company's original charter of 1847. The legislature, as was its custom at the time, had inserted a standard clause claiming a proportion of the company's profits in excess of a certain percentage, after a specified cumulative amount of dividends had been declared. This excess profit was to go to the state's common schools fund. It was a worthy idea for a predominantly agricultural state whose income was limited and whose credit had been damaged by profligate spending on internal improvements. Largely ignored during the company's first decade and a half of operation, the clause drew renewed legislative attention following the war, a conflict which had been exceedingly expensive for the state.[3]

The original charter had given the company 15 years to complete its line, and it had apparently met that deadline. But the chartering of the St. Louis, Vandalia & Terre Haute in February 1865 created the possible necessity of extending the TH&I west to the state line to connect with the new Illinois corporation. So the TH&I petitioned the Indiana legislature for an act to amend its original charter and grant an extension of time to "complete" its line. The resulting enactment of March 6, 1865, which also changed the company's original name, provided an additional seven years to complete the line. The political activity which surrounded the act's passage also put the company and its charter under close political scrutiny and raised questions concerning the monetary implications of the charter's excess profits clause.[4]

In a state famous for its 19th-century political partisanship, it was only natural that such a question would become the stuff of politics, especially considering the high Republican profiles of the TH&I's chief executive and the company's general counsel, Richard W. Thompson. And the question did come up with rising intensity at each succeeding legislative session, with committees inevitably formed to investigate the company and ascertain whether there was money due the state. McKeen and his officers usually cooperated but also mounted a spirited defense of the company's position.

Especially provocative was the fact that the company had previously declared two sizeable stock dividends, one of 20 percent in 1856 and another of 25 percent in 1864. After the company began purchasing its own shares in 1867, scrutiny was focussed on the railroad's dissipation of surplus profits on that and other outside investments. Each time, McKeen, Thompson, and a number of other directors were able to pilot the company safely through these treacherous shoals by adroit political maneuvering.

Finally, the company's frustrated political opponents sought a new avenue of attack in the form of a *quo warranto* suit to test the charter, brought by the Putnam County prosecutor in the late fall of 1872. The company fought back with high-powered legal talent that included a future president of the United States, Benjamin Harrison. After a change of venue to Owen County and a hung jury there, the case wound up by mutual agreement in Marion Superior Court in Indianapolis, where the company won on a technicality—an embarrassing filing error by a state clerk. The state's ambitious Attorney General appealed to the Indiana Supreme Court, but state justices let the lower court ruling stand in 1878, finally removing this political monkey from the company's back, or so it was thought. Unfortunately, the case would come back to haunt the TH&I almost 20 years later.[5]

The St. Louis, Vandalia & Terre Haute was finally finished and officially opened on June 12, 1870. The TH&I's extension to the state line had been rushed to completion in May, just in time. It had been an expensive undertaking for the Terre Haute company's conservative board; the seven-and-a-half miles of new track, built through the hilly high ground west of the Wabash River, had cost just under half a million dollars.

A postcard view of the Troy, Illinois, depot. This large, two-story design was used in larger towns up and down the St. Louis, Vandalia & Terre Haute at the time of its construction in the late 1860s. Housing the station agent's family on the second floor, this same combination freight and passenger station type could also be found at Greenville and Casey. Collection of Kevin Keaggy, Greenville, Illinois.

McKeen was present at the St. Louis, Vandalia & Terre Haute board meeting on July 26, held in a celebratory setting at the Cresson Springs, Pennsylvania, resort frequented by the Pennsylvania Railroad's top officers. There, high in the sylvan Allegheny Mountains, the Vandalia company officially accepted its new road from the contractors and then requested the TH&I to take possession as lessee. It was all formality, for the TH&I had been operating the line since July 1. If glasses were raised in toast to their mutual accomplishment, it would be the last time such good cheer would prevail between the parties.[6]

Already the Pennsylvania's executives were suffering intense pangs of regret. In the press of events, they had managed to acquire two parallel and competing lines from Indianapolis to St. Louis, both of which placed significant financial responsibilities on the Pennsylvania or its subsidiaries. Therefore, two issues became paramount for the Pennsylvania's management: costs and control.

Since the Indianapolis & St. Louis and the TH&I-Vandalia route were competing for the same business in a territory able to comfortably support only one line, costs of operation would have a critical bearing on financial performance for both. And the only effective way to assure control over the costs of operation was to have active control of the two companies.

In the case of the Indianapolis & St. Louis, fairly effective control was already in place by virtue of an aggressively exercised half-ownership acquired with the Pennsylvania's lease of the Fort Wayne. Thanks to the TH&I's lease, however, the same was not true of the Vandalia route. Even the Pennsylvania's financial control over the St. Louis, Vandalia & Terre Haute company was being frustrated. Hampered by the terms of a new Illinois State Constitution, the Pennsylvania interests had been struggling to organize the St. Louis, Vandalia & Terre Haute board in their favor. The problem was that, by law, a majority of the directors of all Illinois-chartered corporations had to be citizens residing within the state. To the Pennsylvania men, for their company to have provided the bulk of the money needed to build the Vandalia and not have a board majority was outrageous.[7]

Early in 1871 George B. Roberts, the Pennsylvania's newly appointed fourth vice president with responsibility for the company's lines west of Pittsburgh, opened a close correspondence with Richard W. Thompson, the TH&I's general counsel. Roberts had grown to respect Thompson's legal judgement and especially appreciated the well-connected politician's close friendship with McKeen and the members of the TH&I board. At this point Roberts was primarily interested in gaining as much control over the Vandalia company as possible and sought to use Thompson's influence with the Vandalia's original incorporators to gain control of the directorate. The Pennsylvania wanted a majority on the board and custody of the books. It would take a few months, but eventually Thompson helped work out a board representation that suited the Pennsylvania's young executive and gave Roberts the presidency of the St. Louis, Vandalia & Terre Haute. The books, and actual control over the railroad, were another matter.[8]

Like it or not, as a leased line, the Vandalia company had surrendered control of its property to the TH&I. This made the Vandalia's corporate organization dependent upon the TH&I as lessee for all operational data, and Roberts chafed at both the amount and quality he was getting from Terre Haute. The Pennsylvania Railroad under J. Edgar Thomson had innovated much of the modern corporate management structure, the most crucial element of which was the flow of accurate, detailed information. Roberts was a consummate organization man, well-schooled in the Pennsylvania's methods; and as president of the St. Louis, Vandalia & Terre Haute, he felt greatly handicapped by the deficiencies in the data he was receiving. However, as far as the Pennsylvania was concerned, there were additional and much more serious problems with the Vandalia route arrangements.

Largely to keep his own board of directors happy, McKeen felt the need to segregate the accounts and procedures for his company and the St. Louis, Vandalia & Terre Haute. Accordingly, a divided operating organization was set up along the lines of the two individual companies. Each of these separate "divisions" had a superintendent reporting to Charles Peddle, who had been elevated to general superintendent of the system. Peddle's 30-year-old former assistant, John E. Simpson, was made superintendent of the "Indianapolis Division." The superintendent of the "Vandalia Division" was given to John Conlogue, the former contractor's super-intendent.[9]

To the practiced eye of a Pennsylvania-trained executive, McKeen had created a needlessly expensive organization. Moreover, there seemed to be little discipline or accountability, the older Peddle leaving his young superintendents far too much freedom, particularly in the matter of spending money. Conlogue especially appeared to be wildly profligate, running up additional construction expenses of more than $355,000 during the first year of operation, even though the Vandalia's brand new line was supposed to have been completed. Because the construction accounts had been closed by the Vandalia's board at the Pennsylvania's behest, the additional expenses produced a sizeable floating debt. By March 1871 Roberts was writing Richard W. Thompson in great annoyance, practically begging him to impress on McKeen the absolute necessity for economy. The Vandalia could be self-sustaining, Roberts wrote, if McKeen would "only put his foot down and say he will not allow his Supt.[sic] to spend a dollar on [construction] or any other purpose that can be avoided." Unfortunately for Roberts, Riley did not necessarily agree.[10]

The problem was that the St. Louis, Vandalia & Terre Haute was "complete" only in that it reached both of its terminals in unbroken fashion. From an operating standpoint it was very much unfinished, requiring more ballast, more sidetracks, more facilities, and more equipment. For McKeen and his TH&I, the Vandalia road was not yet in a proper condition for them to efficiently compete for the traffic they needed and wanted. That was *their* test of economy. So McKeen had done nothing to discourage the expenditures necessary to put the Vandalia in top condition, in spite of the new road's growing floating debt.

To Roberts and his Pennsylvania superiors, of course, such flagrant disregard for ordinary economy was outrageous, especially since those who were doing the spending did not have to cover but 20 percent of the resulting loss. But it was the executive corps of the Pan Handle—the Pittsburg, Cincinnati & St. Louis—who complained the loudest. It was they, after all, who had to pay, and not just for the Vandalia. The Pennsylvania's pell-mell expansion had also loaded leases of the Indiana Central and Little Miami roads, both of which required financial support, on the Pan Handle.

Floundering around for some way to gain control, the management of the Pan Handle registered a formal complaint in the form of a resolution passed at the company's board meeting on April 27, 1871. The Pan Handle directors called for unimpeded access to all financial data and account information, directed their own comptroller to visit McKeen in Terre Haute for a complete accounting, and voiced their "opinion" that "great economies [could] be effected by the reorganization of the several departments of the Vandalia Line." They were very specific, insisting that all construction and equipment accounts be closed, and suggested a list of personnel changes. They named names, too: The divided organization should be eliminated and Simpson made general superintendent over the entire line, with his headquarters at St. Louis. Peddle should be demoted to motive power officer, and Conlogue should be fired.[11]

McKeen received the Pan Handle resolution with equanimity. He was not averse to accepting suggestions, especially if they promised to improve the situation for everyone involved. Riley was trying his best to be a good partner as well as a good executive. Though he may have disliked the thought of demoting his faithful friend, Charles Peddle, he agreed to all the operating changes that the Pan Handle board had suggested. To save face, it was first announced that Peddle had resigned his position for health reasons and, later, that he desired to devote his entire attention to his particular specialty of motive power. McKeen also had a complete financial report prepared on the operation of the St. Louis, Vandalia & Terre Haute under the lease.[12]

Meanwhile, the Pennsylvania-controlled Vandalia board had been busy, meeting April 29 to authorize an issue of income bonds. Since all the mortgage money had been spent, the new bonds were needed to pay off the floating debt, most of which had been advanced by the TH&I. The Vandalia directors were particularly annoyed because, shortly after turning over their road to the lessee the previous summer, they had specifically resolved to spend no more on construction or equipment without the formal approval of both their own president and the president of the Pennsylvania, neither of whom had ever been consulted. After approving the new income bonds, the Vandalia board appointed a committee of directors to "reform" the lease, an effort which failed to bear fruit but revealed the depth of the Pennsylvania's dissatisfaction.[13]

At another board meeting spread over two days late in June 1871, the Vandalia directors heard McKeen's report on operations under the lease then referred it to committee. The committee's response on the second day expressed obvious irritation at the lessee's handling of the Vandalia property and suggested that, given its previous resolution forbidding unapproved expenditures, the board would be fully within its right to reject the lessee's claims for additional construction. Even so, the committee recommended that the proper approval be sought, and only then should the lessee's claim be paid. The full Vandalia board took the claim under advisement and adjourned without action, forcing the TH&I to wait a while longer to be reimbursed.[14]

It was the first of many conflicts, small at first, that would become a running skirmish of escalating intensity between the TH&I and the Pennsylvania organization. It also highlighted the fundamental differences between the two parties, suggesting a clash of cultures as much as corporate ambitions.

J. Edgar Thomson had been quick to grasp the challenge of administration in the Pennsylvania's rapidly expanded system. His answer was to create a second, largely separate organization entitled the Pennsylvania Company. This new wholly owned subsidiary of the Pennsylvania Railroad owned and managed all of the Pennsylvania-controlled lines west of Pittsburgh. After 1874 the president of the Pennsylvania Railroad would automatically serve as president of the Pennsylvania Company. The directorate of the latter was filled with members of the staff and directorate of the former, but the Pennsylvania *Company* functioned on its own. More importantly, the management of this so-called "Lines West of Pittsburgh" organization bore sole accountability for the operation and results of the railroads in its care.[15]

The Pennsylvania Company's Lines West organization took over the lease of the Fort Wayne and assumed direction of the Pan Handle in April 1871. Top management of the Pennsylvania Company and the Pan Handle was identical, and it was this group of executives that also staffed the St. Louis, Vandalia & Terre Haute company. As a result, Lines West officers had to face and deal with the maddening contradictions of the Pennsylvania's irreconcilable situation concerning the twin routes to St. Louis.

For George Roberts and his Lines West officers, the fundamental problem was obvious: The situation they had inherited was predicated on a corporate strategy that was no longer valid. The Pennsylvania had concluded its joint-participation arrangements concerning the Vandalia route on the very eve of its quantum leap into a new era of system-building acquisitions. The very lease it had so vigorously insisted upon was now a painful liability.

The TH&I's counsel, Richard W. Thompson, was quick to discern Roberts's problem and suggested the ultimate solution to his new friend in January 1872. Roberts, in turn, shared Thompson's thoughts with his boss, J. Edgar Thomson, and William Thaw, first vice president of the Lines West organization. They were all in agreement, Roberts replied to Thompson on January 24, and would be pleased if Thompson would purchase any available TH&I stock for the Pennsylvania's account. It was a preliminary move, Roberts confided, writing that "We take this step now looking to the gradual obtaining [of] a majority of the stock." Thompson was also advised to keep an eye on Chauncey Rose's intentions concerning his large interest in the company and to approach Rose on the Pennsylvania's behalf at the first appropriate opportunity. Unfortunately for Roberts, McKeen was about to foreclose the Pennsylvania's options in that direction.[16]

By 1872 Riley McKeen had attained the top echelon of Terre Haute's elite. Besides his important position as president of the Terre Haute & Indianapolis, McKeen was generally acknowledged as the young city's leading banker. In that same year, McKeen also began his quadrennial attendance at the Republican National Convention, often serving as a district delegate or alternate. And sometime toward the end of 1872, Riley finally solved his problems with an out-of-touch board by buying Chauncey Rose's sizeable block of TH&I stock.

In the typically close-mouthed business style of the period, the unannounced transaction was revealed in the composition of the TH&I's new board, elected at the annual meeting on January 6, 1873. For the first time since the founding of the Terre Haute road in 1847, Rose's name was absent from the directorate. In fact, a number of close Rose business associates were missing, with Nippert and Deming as well as Rose replaced by Riley's friends Josephus Collett and Jonathon Hager and his brother-in-law Frank Crawford. Joining McKeen and his bank partner Deloss Minshall, the new directors gave the board a decidedly second-generational cast. Local papers reported the obvious: that McKeen had purchased the interests of Rose and Deming. It was good news, for it meant control of the railroad would remain in Terre Haute.[17]

The extent of McKeen's mastery soon became apparent. Within days the new board took steps to weaken the state's pending school fund case by surrendering the company's original charter and accepting the terms of Indiana's General Railroad Incorporation Law of 1852. Two months later, at its March 25 meeting, the new board ratified McKeen's proposal for a new general mortgage of $1.6 million to replace and thereby double the 1869 bond issue authorized so grudgingly by the old directorate. With the balance of the proceeds of the previous mortgage soaked up by its share of the Vandalia road's continuing construction expenses, the TH&I badly needed new money for additional track and equipment, and for funding McKeen's expansion in the coal fields.[18]

Over the next 12 months, McKeen placed his stamp of ownership on the Terre Haute & Indianapolis by making adjustments in its organization. Included were corporate bylaw changes which made only the top officers electable by the board, thereby eliminating the directors' involvement in such mundane matters as hiring station agents and train conductors. The board even approved a salary increase for its president on the grounds that his responsibilities had greatly increased with the lease of the Vandalia. With his hand considerably strengthened by formal control of the TH&I, Riley now turned to his problem of dealing with the Pennsylvania.[19]

The Indianapolis & St. Louis, presumably at the Pennsylvania's insistence, had offered to negotiate a traffic pooling agreement as early as the summer of 1870, shortly after construction had been completed on both its new road and the Vandalia. The TH&I board had first rejected this proposal, then reconsidered and so amended the agreement as to make it undesirable. So, at first, the TH&I was left free to compete with the I&StL for as much traffic as possible. The result was a steady and substantial falling off in the freight rates and passenger fares charged by both roads. McKeen and the TH&I were only getting a taste of the competition that would quickly become their major challenge of the new era.[20]

The TH&I's failure to cooperate with the Indianapolis & St. Louis only magnified the Pennsylvania's problems, and McKeen's acquisition of stock control over the TH&I ruined any chance for a simple solution. But a much worse situation developed when the postwar boom times officially ended in the fall of 1873, ushering in the nation's most severe and prolonged depression up to that time. As traffic and earnings plummeted, bitter and destructive competition became the norm, not only between the TH&I and I&StL, but between all railroads in the region. In consequence, the nation's supply of ready capital became so tight by the end of the year that McKeen was forced to sell a portion of the newly issued TH&I bonds at a steep discount.[21]

For the Pennsylvania, the panic and depression could not have come at a worse time. Caught at the abrupt end of five years of almost continuous expansion, the Pennsylvania was deeply in debt and perilously overextended. Under such ominous circumstances, the company's officers were in no position to temporize. Economies had to be implemented immediately, and that meant limiting losses on the Indianapolis & St. Louis and the Vandalia, so new pressure was applied to the recalcitrant Terre Haute & Indianapolis.[22]

Although the TH&I had actually ended 1873 with increased earnings over the previous year, all of its gains had been made in local traffic, particularly in the hauling of coal. Through traffic—that carried in competition with other lines to and from the St. Louis gateway—had nose-dived, and McKeen understood the implications. Accordingly, the pooling agreement with the Indianapolis & St. Louis proposed in 1870 was dusted off and finally implemented on April 1, 1874.[23]

What was mild discomfort to the prosperous Terre Haute & Indianapolis was quickly taking on the proportions of a disaster for the Pennsylvania's system of roads, particularly the Pittsburg, Cincinnati & St. Louis, or Pan Handle line. By the end of 1874, the Pan Handle was hemorrhaging internally, thanks to its leases of the Little Miami and Indiana Central. Its officers had to staunch the flow in any way possible, and their desperation is understandable. Under the circumstances, the Pennsylvania's impossible arrangements west of Indianapolis became practically unbearable.[24]

As the economic downturn settled into a severe depression, the true horror of the situation became apparent: two parallel and competing lines to St. Louis, each with a different relationship to the Pennsylvania system, and each presenting a potentially heavy liability. In one—the Indianapolis & St. Louis—the Pennsylvania had a full half-interest and relatively efficient control. Yet, bound by its Vandalia-route agreements, the Pennsylvania was unable to move any traffic over the I&StL, leaving that road dependent upon its other half-owner, the Bee Line, for all of its through business. In the other—the St. Louis, Vandalia & Terre Haute—the Pennsylvania interests had a line in whose operation it had very little say, while bearing the lion's share of the liability.

The actual figures were truly depressing. The Indianapolis & St. Louis was burdened with its expensive lease of the St. Louis, Alton & Terre Haute. What made the leased line so onerous was a clause in the contract which guaranteed the Alton line an extremely generous minimum of $450,000 per year, regardless of the road's gross earnings. The Vandalia lease to the TH&I, at least, required no minimum dollar amount. But in its Vandalia-route arrangements the Pennsylvania's Pan Handle line faced a double jeopardy, sharing eight-tenths of any loss incurred by the TH&I in operating the leased line, as well as protecting the Pennsylvania's almost sole ownership of the St. Louis, Vandalia & Terre Haute company.[25]

What made the situation particularly galling for the Pennsylvania's Lines West officers was their utter impotence when it came to the Vandalia road's operations. Thanks to the lease agreement insisted upon by the Pennsylvania in 1868, operating control was legally in the hands of McKeen and the Terre Haute & Indianapolis, in which the Pennsylvania's men had no voice at all, should McKeen choose not to listen. However, as the good banker that he was, Riley McKeen was trained to listen, and he was more than happy to hear what his esteemed colleagues at the Pennsylvania had to say, at first.

McKeen was no provincial shopkeeper. He had amply demonstrated his progressiveness as a railroad executive, busily modernizing and expanding the TH&I. He was building and extending branches throughout the Clay County coal field and buying more cars and locomotives to haul the rising tide of traffic. The company was rapidly completing the conversion of its wood-burning engines to coal-burners. McKeen had been quick to adopt steel rails as a replacement for the higher-maintenance, shorter-lived iron variety, unflinchingly accepting the high cost of relaying his main line at an accelerated pace so he could secure steel's long-term economy. And all of this was represented in the impressive figures he reported each year to his stockholders and in the handsome dividends he paid them twice annually. In fact, as the Pan Handle faltered and bled, the TH&I cheerfully disbursed 10 percent a year, and it continued to do so through most of the depression. It was a performance the mighty Pennsylvania Railroad itself could not duplicate.[26]

This very old glass-plate negative picture, likely dating from the 1880s, shows TH&I Engine No. 38 at Brazil, Indiana, where it was assigned to coal trains servicing the mines in the area. No. 38 is one of the railroad's first Mogul-type engines (2-6-0), built in 1873 by Baldwin. The TH&I would come to rely on this engine type as its heavy mainline freight haulers and would continue to buy Moguls until the end. Collection of the Clay County Historical Society, Brazil, Indiana.

From their beleaguered vantage point, it was becoming exceedingly difficult for the Pennsylvania and its Lines West organization to avoid the conclusion that they were subsidizing the TH&I's evident prosperity, particularly as operating losses gradually mounted under the Vandalia lease. Communications between the two companies grew more strident, and the Pennsylvania's suggestions took on the form of demands. Still, McKeen tried to be accommodating.

The pooling contract entered into with the Indianapolis & St. Louis in April 1874 was replaced with a much more comprehensive arrangement on November 1, 1875. Instead of dividing all through traffic, the new agreement united the two roads in joint operation. Responding to the Pennsylvania's pointed suggestions, McKeen's board approved the new arrangement on October 4. Details were hammered out at a meeting between all parties at Crestline, Ohio, on November 17, and a new organization formed with the TH&I's John E. Simpson as general manager. Beneath Simpson, each road named a general superintendent, Joshua Staples for the TH&I and Samuel Woodward for the I&StL. The remaining positions were divided among the two companies, with the TH&I's Charles Follett named as general ticket agent and his I&StL counterpart, C. C. Cobb, as assistant agent; and the I&StL's John C. Noyes as general freight agent, with Horace W. Hibbard of the TH&I as assistant.[27]

Revenue was pooled and divided, with 52 percent going to the TH&I and 48 percent to the I&StL. Authority was exercised through a Joint Executive Committee of four, two from each company, who were charged with maintaining each company's relationship with its connections. The end result was the mutual sharing of traffic and revenue and a supposed end to competition between the two parallel lines by the joint traffic solicitation arrangement. The contract was intended to run for a term of 25 years.

In practice, the joint operating organization seemed to work well enough. For some reason, all through passenger traffic was routed over the TH&I-Vandalia side. Otherwise, both lines were kept busy with their respective through freight business and local traffic. But joint operation could not remedy the general economic malaise, nor the bitter interregional rivalries it fostered. Thus, the Terre Haute & Indianapolis and the Indianapolis & St. Louis were forced to deal with sharp competition from the three other roads leading east from St. Louis, the Ohio & Mississippi, the Wabash, and the Chicago & Alton, each with a different set of competitive eastern trunkline connections.

Despite his attempts to mollify his Vandalia-route partner, McKeen's relationship with the Pennsylvania continued to deteriorate. George Roberts remained critical of McKeen's management, and the Pan Handle's officers, swamped with their own problems, kept pressing for greater economies. But McKeen and his organization were not without grounds for complaints of their own.

In January 1875 the Pittsburg, Cincinnati & St. Louis, overwhelmed by the enormous losses generated under its lease of the Columbus, Chicago & Indiana Central, repudiated that contract and surrendered control of the property. The Pan Handle's stated reason for this drastic maneuver was the Indiana Central's failure to adjust and consolidate its numerous mortgages under a supplemental lease agreement made in 1870. But the crushing financial obligations of the Indiana Central lease were threatening the very solvency of the Pan Handle and putting its management under increasing pressure from minority stockholders. Following the Pan Handle's repudiation, the Indiana Central instantly collapsed into a long and controversial receivership. Meanwhile, the judge overseeing the case ordered the Pan Handle to retain custody of the Indiana Central and to continue to operate the road for the court.[28]

Ordinarily, such a dispute, and the bitter litigation it generated, might not have mattered to McKeen and the TH&I, except that when the Pan Handle surrendered its lease of the Indiana Central, it also refused to continue fulfilling the Indiana Central's contractual obligations. To be specific, as they informed McKeen early in 1875, the Pan Handle's officers would no longer cover the Indiana Central's three-tenths proportion of the losses incurred under the St. Louis, Vandalia & Terre Haute lease.[29]

McKeen's response was simple: With the bankrupt Indiana Central's proportion in default, he would accrue any losses due. And since there was an obvious disagreement as to who was liable for the Indiana Central's portion, McKeen's TH&I as lessee ceased all rental payments to the Vandalia company, except those necessary to cover the leased road's bond interest coupons. He also made it clear that the TH&I expected to be repaid for its advances.

To the Pennsylvania's Lines West officers, McKeen's action was just one more outrageous defiance of their imperial authority. With the TH&I withholding the 30 percent of gross rental payments due the Vandalia, the Pan Handle withheld its 50 percent proportion of the shortfall from the TH&I. The resulting impasse gradually developed into open hostility.[30]

With earnings depressed on the St. Louis, Vandalia & Terre Haute, the difference between actual operating expenses and the lessee's 70 percent proportion of the gross grew much wider. Worse still for the Pennsylvania's Lines West men, without the 30 percent rental income, the Vandalia could not pay its annual fee into the first mortgage sinking fund. At their meeting on October 16, 1875, the Pan Handle board directed its officers to notify McKeen that it would cover its five-tenths of the amount due, and that it expected the TH&I as lessee to pay the balance. McKeen refused, and his relationship with the Pennsylvania interests worsened noticeably.[31]

Considering the scope of the Pan Handle management's current problems, missing a Vandalia company sinking fund payment should not have been such a major matter, as McKeen was well aware. The first mortgage agreement clearly allowed the mortgage trustee to waive the sinking fund requirement under precisely the conditions pending, *at his discretion*. But here, ironically, the Pan Handle executives had managed to burn down their own barn. The trustee for the Vandalia's first mortgage also happened to be the very same trustee for a number of the Indiana Central's mortgages, now in default as a result of the Pan Handle's lease repudiation. The Lines West men were left in a very awkward position.

McKeen was in no mood to be charitable. The year 1875 had been a costly one for the TH&I. While traffic volume was up nicely, pushing up transportation expenses, earnings were flattened by extremely low rates, a result of the brutal warfare then raging between the Baltimore & Ohio, Pennsylvania, and New York Central–Lake Shore lines. The bill for the joint operating agreement with the Indianapolis & St. Louis cost the TH&I nearly $50,000 and added another $10,500 to its share of the Vandalia's losses.[32]

If anything, 1876 was worse. McKeen ended the year with wry congratulations to his stockholders "upon the fact that your road has shown itself capable of enduring the worst that disastrous times and ruinously low rates could inflict, and through them all, of earning and paying ten percent upon its capital, of bettering its condition and adding to its value, without encroaching upon its reserve fund." Even so, the agreement with the I&StL drained another $50,000 from the bottom line.[33]

By contrast, the Pan Handle was awash in a sea of red ink, despite being freed from its responsibility for the Indiana Central. The Pennsylvania's Lines West organization also had to deal with its portion of the Indianapolis & St. Louis deficit, which was well over a quarter of a million dollars in 1876. Almost frantically, the Pan Handle's officers and directors sought to stem the tide. First Vice President William Thaw kept in close correspondence with McKeen a good part of the year, demanding that the TH&I cover the Vandalia's delinquent sinking fund payment. As Thaw reported to the Pan Handle board on October 13, 1876, McKeen had "declined" to shoulder all of the Indiana Central's defaulted share. Instead, Riley had offered to split the difference based on his original share under the lease, agreeing to absorb two-tenths of the Indiana Central's three-tenths proportion. What would result, therefore, was a new official division of two-sevenths for the TH&I and five-sevenths for the Pan Handle. But the Pan Handle's officers and directors stubbornly refused to consider McKeen's offer of compromise, and the Vandalia's sinking fund remained unpaid.[34]

McKeen seemed to bear the Pennsylvania's imperious arrogance with remarkable patience. However, the losses growing out of the TH&I's joint operations with the Indianapolis & St. Louis were becoming difficult to justify. By the end of 1877, McKeen was questioning just who was benefiting from the arrangement. After another approximate $60,000 out-of-pocket charge, he concluded it was not the TH&I. Abruptly ending the contractually required monthly account adjustments, McKeen notified the I&StL board that he could no longer live with the agreement's earnings division. The TH&I had to have an immediate increase to 55 percent of the total joint earnings, instead of its previous 52 percent.[35]

The Indianapolis & St. Louis board made its response on January 24, 1878, in a resolution framed by one of the company's Pennsylvania-interest directors, Thomas A. Scott. The I&StL could not accept the TH&I's demand but would reluctantly consent to a termination of the joint operations arrangement. McKeen's TH&I board formally accepted the contract termination on January 28, and joint operations officially ended on February 1. Once again, the Terre Haute & Indianapolis was free to compete on its own, and the Pennsylvania was left frustrated.[36]

4

THE STRIKE

Yet the TH&I was anything but free. Serving as the southwestern end of the Pennsylvania's far-flung system, the Terre Haute & Indianapolis and the St. Louis, Vandalia & Terre Haute, now referred to together proprietarily as "The Vandalia Line," were feeling the effects of the debilitating competition among eastern trunk lines. It was a situation caused primarily by the period's depressed business conditions, which reduced available traffic well below the general capacity level of the railroad industry.

As the Pennsylvania was drawn into rate-war combat with the Baltimore & Ohio, the Erie, and the Vanderbilt-controlled New York Central and Lake Shore roads, McKeen's Terre Haute & Indianapolis became a reluctant pawn. Bound by agreement and affiliation, McKeen's road was usually forced to accept its proportion of the Pennsylvania's through westbound rates, no matter how low. There was simply no alternative. And because it was in competition with other roads in the region, often functioning as the equally dependent western connections of the Pennsylvania's eastern rivals, the TH&I had to enter the same ratemaking battleground to secure eastbound traffic. It was a difficult situation that defied easy solutions.[1]

The common remedy was to seek mutual agreements between combatants and attempt to pool the available traffic at specified rates. Meetings would be called between company representatives, usually top officials, and negotiations would proceed. After everyone agreed to the new, usually lower rate and accepted their share of the traffic, the agreement would be heralded in the business press and made effective. Then, after a few months, or sometimes even just a few weeks, one company would be caught cheating, and warfare would break out anew, raging on until another round of negotiations was called. As time went on, the process took on the regularity of the tides, and rates continued their inexorable downward spiral.

McKeen, although actively involved in the process as a chief executive, tended to leave the details and hard bargaining to his youthful general manager, John E. Simpson. It was Simpson who ran the railroad on a day-to-day basis. He had McKeen's full confidence, and Riley gave him great latitude in managing the company's affairs. When the five midwestern roads leading east from St. Louis formalized a pool in April 1876, Simpson took a leading role in its organization and served as an executive. Although discontinued in November of that year, the pool was successful in maintaining rates for a time, and it would eventually be reformed later as the Central Traffic Association, providing much-needed rate stabilization in the 1880s.[2]

Fortunately, the Terre Haute & Indianapolis was magnificently situated to generate large amounts of local business, a good thing, because as through freight and passenger rates declined precipitously during the mid-1870s, captive local business became the road's sustenance. Coal traffic, especially, had become the company's lifeblood, and here McKeen's foresight and perseverance paid off handsomely. Coal was shipped in all directions and fueled Terre Haute's nascent iron and steel manufacturing industry. In counterpoint, iron ore from Missouri's Iron Mountain district was hauled eastward from St. Louis on Vandalia Line trains to feed the Indiana furnaces.

By the end of 1878, Simpson was reporting that local business had accounted for just under 75 percent of the TH&I's revenues that year. Unfortunately, the St Louis, Vandalia & Terre Haute's balance of traffic failed to keep pace, with through business still accounting for over half the company's earnings. Since through business was subject to grinding competition, the Vandalia company continued to show losses, which had to be made up by the TH&I and the Pan Handle.[3]

McKeen would also find his road's freedom circumscribed in the area of labor relations. Despite theoretical autonomy, the TH&I, in common with other members of the trunkline pool, would be lockstepped into the frightening events of the summer of 1877. In the Terre Haute road's case, being so closely bound to the Pennsylvania system practically guaranteed trouble. Yet although he was forced to deal with the Great Railroad Strike, Riley did so in a way that was both personal and at variance with his Pennsylvania partner.

By early 1877 the crippling competition was taking its toll on the nation's railroad network, physically and financially. The inability to end the rate warfare had the major trunkline systems at each other's throats and had driven the weaker lines, as well as a substantial number of western trunkline feeders, to the wall. Faced with the generally depressed levels of business and the insatiable capital demands of an industry far from maturity, railroad executives were under immense pressure to reduce expenses. The temptation to lower wages was irresistible.

J. Edgar Thomson of the Pennsylvania and his vice president and chosen successor, Thomas Scott, succumbed to the temptation soon after the depression had begun. Of course, the Pennsylvania's situation was significantly worsened by its overextended condition, a product of Thomson's stunningly rapid expansion. In the wake of the panic, the company's vast floating debt and suddenly massive size brought alarmed stockholders to the gates. The resulting investigation put additional pressure on the Pennsylvania's beleaguered executive corps, particularly Scott, who inherited the problem of saving the company when Thomson died in the spring of 1874.[4]

In fact, at first it was not at all clear that Scott would succeed his mentor, having been such an integral part of the Pennsylvania's now-criticized system-building program. To help ensure his election, and to quell the stockholder uprising once he had tenuously secured office, Scott employed the blandishment of generous dividends. As part of the painful belt-tightening necessary to pay them, the Pennsylvania's new chief kept in force the supposedly temporary 10 percent across-the-board wage cut made in December 1873. It was a strategy quickly followed by his competitors, who imposed similar wage reductions. With the need to keep his own costs in line with the competition, McKeen was forced to follow suit on the TH&I.[5]

It was not herd mentality, but basic survival. Moreover, in the TH&I's case, the

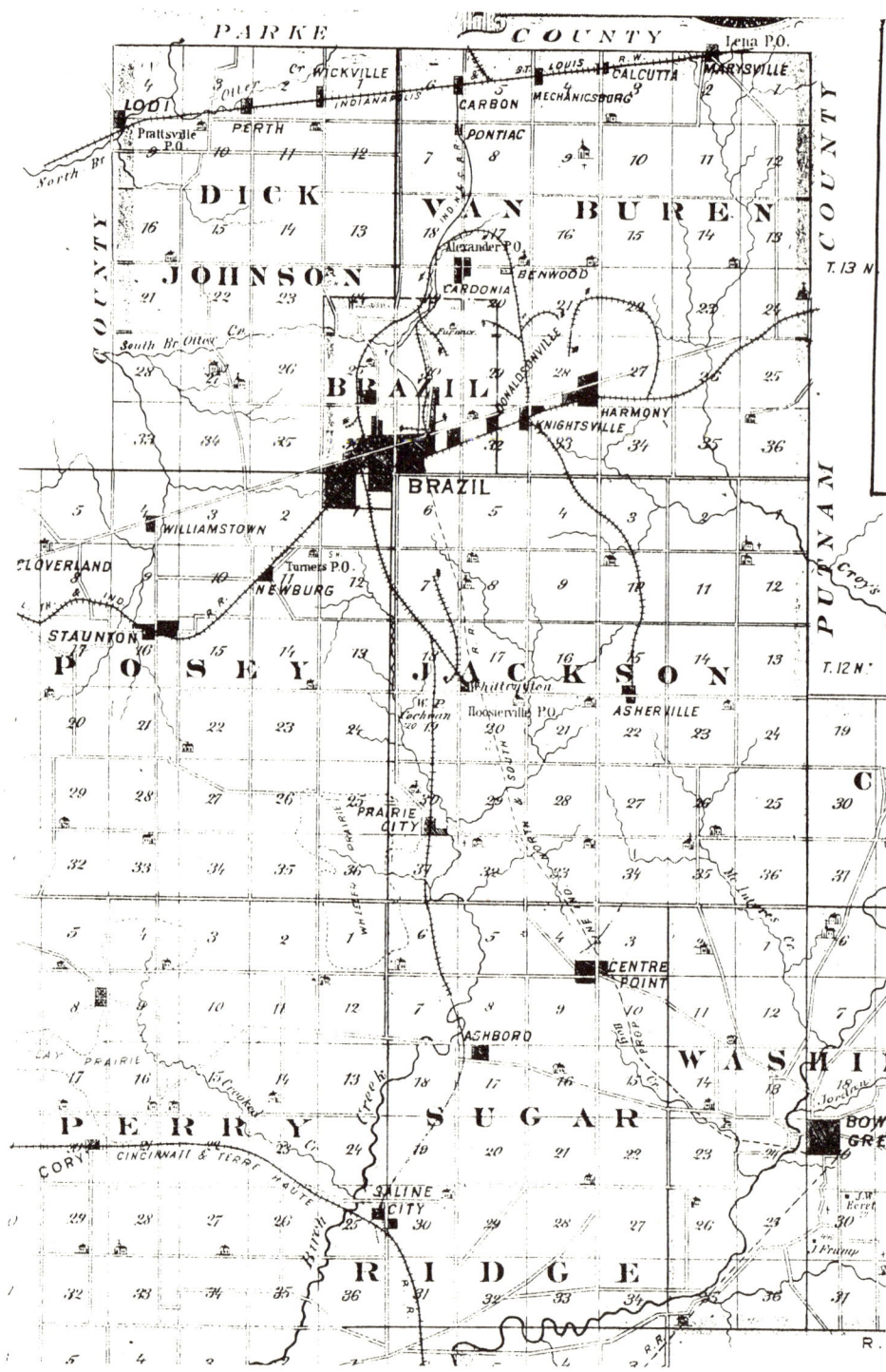

This old atlas map dating to 1876 clearly shows the extent of the TH&I's penetration of the Clay County block coal fields. The branch north from Knightsville was the first major spur, begun in the late 1860s. Later additions include the Saline City branch, and the branch which would eventually be extended all the way to Center Point from Knightsville (but which is only shown here as reaching Asherville). From *Atlas of Clay County* (Chicago, 1876).

situation was complicated by the joint-operation agreement with the Indianapolis & St. Louis that was implemented in November 1875. Once it was yoked with the Pennsylvania-controlled I&StL, the TH&I's direct control was seriously compromised.

The depression, although subject to brief rebounds, refused to go away, exacerbating the traffic situation. Lowered traffic demands put additional pressure on the labor force in the form of reduced hours and earnings. Facing the prospect of continued rate warfare and needing to improve the Pennsylvania's balance sheet, Scott chose to impose another 10 percent cut effective June 1, 1877. This time his men were faced with the very real prospect of earning incomes below subsistence level. Meanwhile, as other trunk lines indicated they would follow Scott's lead, the TH&I and I&StL announced a similar 10 percent cut to go into effect on July 1. The stage was now set for disaster, and it was not long in coming.[6]

After an unsuccessful round of petitions and appeals to their employers, railroad workers struck, beginning with the Baltimore & Ohio at Martinsburg, West Virginia, on July 16. The action quickly spread to the Pennsylvania at Pittsburgh and the Erie at Hornell, New York, and the Great Railroad Strike was suddenly under way.[7]

Railroad executives, in common with property owners everywhere, were shocked at the strikers impudence and frightened by their occasional violence. The Pennsylvania Railroad facilities in Pittsburgh, in particular, turned into a bloody battleground, raising the specter of armed insurrection. Some critics were quick to credit communistic elements, making the strike what one historian has labeled the first "red scare" in American history. It is significant to note that the Pennsylvania, in common with many politicians, chose to forever remember the event as "the Pittsburgh Riots" and rarely referred to the incident as a strike.

The same fears and concerns over the perceived threat to the fabric of society affected Terre Haute's business leaders, the "best families," as they were wont to see themselves. Riley McKeen, as a community leader, was hardly immune to such concerns, and as president of the TH&I, he was directly in the line of fire. But wealthy and influential as he was, McKeen was also unusually egalitarian in outlook. Most of all, he was a banker in the best sense of the profession. As the ambitious little city's biggest employer by far, McKeen's TH&I had a tremendous influence on the local economy. To be sure, it would not be good for Terre Haute if its largest group of workers was placed in a position of actual want; and with the latest round of wage cuts, actual want was genuinely in the offing.

As would be the case with most men of McKeen's outlook, Riley's feelings for his men tended toward paternalism. Despite his egalitarian impulses, these were his workers, and he was their employer. There were definite lines and divisions in the social structure, even if they were not always glaringly apparent. Still, McKeen's men felt free to approach him with great confidence and did so once the strike movement reached them toward the end of July.

The newspaper reports from Pittsburgh must have been as shocking to the TH&I's workers as they were to the burghers of Terre Haute, particularly in terms of the violence and bloodshed. The newspapers marked the general westward spread of the strike over the ensuing week. On Saturday, July 21, trains of the Ohio & Mississippi were stopped by strikers in Vincennes, but without violence of any kind. On

An 1880s view of the northwest corner of the TH&I's large downtown Terre Haute shops complex, with some of the men who worked there pictured beneath. The three-bay brick building shown was the coach painting shop. Beyond it is the larger coach repair building. The TH&I main line is visible at lower left, and the track curving southward just this side of the fence is the eastern approach track to the old Terre Haute Union Depot, situated at Tenth and Chestnut streets. The oldest buildings, perhaps including the ones shown, were built in the 1850s. This complex would later be superseded by a more modern facility constructed on the eastern edge of Terre Haute around 1910. Collection of the Vigo County Historical Society, Terre Haute.

Saturday night, railroad workers in East St. Louis, including Vandalia Line men, held a meeting to decide what to do. Unable to ignore the events unfolding around them, the TH&I firemen and brakemen based in Terre Haute called a meeting for Sunday, July 22, at the Engineer's Hall above Baur's Drugstore.[8]

The meeting drew a large crowd, and the men were open in their discussion. After they had organized themselves with a strike executive committee to keep order and coordinate communications, the TH&I men decided to approach McKeen directly, and a petition was drawn up to "respectfully request" a restoration of their wages, plus a slight increase as well. The resolution was very clear in stating the real need at the root of their request. On the other hand, the men insisted on an answer by 9 the next morning, informing their employer that they would stop work if their 15 percent increase were not provided and would stay off the job until they received "sufficient wages to keep our families from actual want." Most importantly, McKeen's workers promised to abstain from all use of alcohol for the duration.[9]

The petition was hand carried to McKeen's house on Seventh Street that evening. After not finding him at home, the committee tracked Riley down at his friend Deloss Minshall's house and delivered the message there. McKeen graciously heard the committee out and agreed to have an answer the next morning. Meanwhile, in Mattoon, Illinois, the Indianapolis & St. Louis workers also held a meeting and, hearing that the Vandalia Line men were organizing, voted to follow their lead.[10]

On Monday McKeen, stalling for time, put the men off for another day. Not until Tuesday, July 24, did Riley face his concerned employees. At 9:30 in the morning, the TH&I's firemen, brakemen, section men, and shop workers met with McKeen at the company's car shops. Firmly stating the universal management position that current income levels did not justify returning to the old wage rates, McKeen told them he could see no better course than to shut down the railroad. He did not mince words in placing the blame for what he considered their mutual predicament squarely on the trunk lines, saying much depended on how the big eastern roads settled their differences. And almost wistfully, Riley expressed his disappointment that the TH&I men had decided to pursue a strike.[11]

The meeting was over by 11 A.M., and the strikers, now committed, reassembled at 2 P.M. The men approved an explicit list of rules to govern their conduct during the strike, particularly emphasizing the need to keep outsiders away and to protect the TH&I's property from all harm. They recommended that their brothers in Indianapolis, Effingham, and East St. Louis take similar action. And in a resolution that revealed how they viewed their relationship to their employer, the TH&I men voted full faith and confidence in the honor and integrity of McKeen and acknowledged their belief that he would do all he could to comply with their wishes. With that, the strike began in Terre Haute.[12]

It was hardly an organized effort. Taking control of Terre Haute Union Depot that very afternoon, the strikers faced the first of a series of problems they had not been prepared for in advance. An eastbound TH&I train arrived, and the strikers mounted the vestibule steps to uncouple the coaches. Since the train was well-filled with passengers, among whom were a goodly number of women and children, the strike executive committee members who were present quickly intervened, instructing their men to allow the train to continue on to Indianapolis. The train had left St.

Louis before the strike had begun. Although an argument ensued and a large number were for turning the unsuspecting passengers out, the leadership insisted on chivalry and decorum. "Think what it would be if our wives were out from home," one fireman pleaded. "Boys, we must send them on." It was a sentiment which struck a responsive chord in McKeen's men and helped explain their restraint over the next few days.[13]

McKeen's Terre Haute forces were late in beginning their strike. Their Vandalia Line brothers in Indianapolis and East St. Louis had gone out on Monday. Riley made good his promise to shut down most operations on Tuesday, but neither side was willing to confront the federal government, so mail trains kept running as a matter of course. Since the lordly Brotherhood of Locomotive Engineers had not yet joined the strike, trains could theoretically be operated so long as the brakemen and firemen did not interfere. Only when a few company officials kept trying to maintain at least a skeletal passenger train service by attaching a coach or two to the mail cars did the angry strikers cause trouble. McKeen responded right away, informing the strike leaders that the hauling of passengers had not been done on his order and that the practice would cease immediately. The Terre Haute men were inclined to blame their lax brothers at the ends of the line, which ultimately brought about greater coordination with the strike committees in Indianapolis, Effingham, and East St. Louis. In the meantime, the Terre Haute contingent had to improvise its strike as best it could.[14]

McKeen remained a calming influence on both the strikers and the Terre Haute business community. By not reacting with bombastic threats of force, like many of his fellow railroad executives across the country, McKeen was able to keep the local situation from turning unpleasant. Riley stayed in close communication with the strike leaders, and he went to great lengths to assure the men that he would not under any circumstances call for the use of the militia. The TH&I men appreciated their employer's good judgement, especially as the combative antics of the Pennsylvania's nearly hysterical Thomas Scott reached them through sensational newspaper coverage. In fact, what was actually going on in Terre Haute seemed unremarkable when it was reported next to the frightening dispatches from Pittsburgh, Chicago, and San Francisco.

Had it been left up to McKeen and his men to work things out on the TH&I, the results might have been less damaging. But other forces were already becoming involved, most important of which was the federal judiciary. A number of the railroads being struck were bankrupt and in the hands of receivers, who now besieged the courts for help in opposing the strikers. The judges overseeing these bankruptcies naturally felt compelled to protect the property in their care and were eager to aid their charges. In Indiana and Illinois, most of the bankrupt roads were under the care of Judge Thomas Drummond of the Seventh U.S. Circuit, a distinguished but doctrinaire jurist who was offended by the striker's effrontery. Aided and encouraged by his friend and associate District Judge Walter Quinton Gresham, who sat in Indianapolis, Drummond propounded a most useful legal weapon with which to punish the striking railroaders. He would hold them in contempt of court for interfering with his receiver's trains.[15]

For the striking Vandalia Line workers, the bankrupt roads they could affect directly included the St. Louis & Southeastern and the Ohio & Mississippi in East St. Louis; the Indianapolis, Cincinnati & Lafayette and Indianapolis, Bloomington & Western in Indianapolis; and the Logansport, Crawfordsville & Southwestern in Terre Haute. The latter road was being closely overseen by Judge Gresham, who used his authority to inject himself into the TH&I strike.[16]

Gresham had very definite ideas about the propriety of the national strike and exhibited high anxiety the minute it began on the Baltimore & Ohio on July 16. As soon as the TH&I workers struck in Indianapolis on Monday, July 23, Gresham adjourned his court and called together a group of friends and law associates for consultation. Among them were Benjamin Spooner, the U.S. Marshall for the district; Benjamin Harrison; A. W. Hendricks; and former Governor Conrad Baker. Most of this august group were former Union Army officers, and all of them were part of the Indianapolis political scene. That evening strikers occupied the Indianapolis Union Depot and prevented the departure of a train on one of the local roads in receivership, namely the Indianapolis, Bloomington & Western. Incensed that Mayor John Caven and Governor James D. Williams both refused to intervene, Gresham used the IB&W incident as justification for his own action.[17]

After telegraphing Drummond in Chicago for concurrence, Gresham reconvened his group of Indianapolis associates on Tuesday and organized them into an unofficial committee of public safety. Harrison counseled against inflaming the strikers, pointing out that there were two sides to an argument, but most members of the group were for the quick and decisive use of force. Since there were virtually no troops stationed in the capital city, the group decided to form its own volunteer companies. Drawing from the large number of veterans in Indianapolis, the group was able to sign up a force nearly two hundred strong.[18]

With his hand strengthened by actual numbers, Gresham now went to see the governor and the mayor, informing them of his volunteer organization. To Gresham's disgust, neither Caven nor Williams wanted any part of his plan. Convinced that the strikers would not resort to violence unless provoked, the mayor appealed instead for a citizen's mediation committee to help settle the strike. And on Friday, July 27, Governor Williams issued a proclamation deploring the violence of the national strike and calling on citizens to desist from illegal acts.[19]

Meanwhile, the TH&I men in Terre Haute continued to wrestle with the problems associated with their actions. Meeting daily at the shops, the strike executive committee tried to keep the men and the situation in check. The strike leaders clearly understood the danger of interfering with the movement of mail and obstructing receivers of bankrupt roads, and they were bending over backward to avoid violating federal law.[20]

Inevitably, the question of halting the trains of the Logansport, Crawfordsville & Southwestern arose, since it also used the TH&I-owned Terre Haute Union Depot. On Tuesday night, shortly after the strike had begun in Terre Haute, several men had detained a Logansport road passenger train, but once they discovered that it was carrying mail, the train was quickly released. The matter of the Logansport was not fully discussed until Thursday, by which time the TH&I men recognized the danger and voted not to interfere with the bankrupt line's operations. But a report of the detention reached Gresham on Tuesday night, which the Judge immediately interpreted as a challenge to his authority. On Wednesday, July 25, Gresham wired the Logansport's receiver in Terre Haute to get the names of the guilty parties so they could later be held in contempt.[21]

What Gresham wanted most was a company of soldiers to send against the striking railroad men, and he had wired Washington to that effect on Monday. But the Hayes administration, which had already sent troops to hot spots like Martinsburg and Pittsburgh, was well enough informed to know that the situation in Indianapolis was hardly critical. It was not until Friday that Gresham finally got his detachment of regulars.[22]

The TH&I men in Terre Haute had been slow to join the national strike, and now it seemed they would be equally slow in ending their own action. By Friday, July 27, the strike was clearly over in places like Pittsburgh, Chicago, and St. Louis. Under the force of troops and police, most resistance had collapsed.

Gresham had been bombarded with requests for action by the more militant receivers in charge of the St. Louis & Southeastern and the Ohio & Mississippi. With actual U.S. troops at his disposal by late Friday, the Judge prepared to dispatch them. Gresham detailed a company of 50 men under the command of U.S. Marshall Benjamin Spooner to Vincennes to open the Ohio & Mississippi there early Saturday morning, and he sent them by way of Terre Haute. Since they were coming over his road, McKeen was alerted to this news on Friday night.[23]

Despite his continuing attempts to cooperate with the strikers, McKeen used the troop movement as a lever to bring his men back to work. On Saturday morning, McKeen announced by circular that the shops and yards would reopen that afternoon at one o'clock and asked all who wanted to work to report for duty. It was a case of poor timing.[24]

The men were meeting at that very moment to discuss the possibility of arbitration to end the strike. They also selected Riley's friend John Martin, president of the Evansville & Terre Haute Railroad, as the most likely to succeed as arbitrator. Not having joined in the last wage reduction, the E&TH had not been struck, and Martin was generally considered to be a just and fair executive. But when Martin, who was present at their meeting, addressed the TH&I men, he gravely told them that it was probably too late and that they should just go back to work. The strike was collapsing around them, he said, hinting darkly that it would have been better had they come to this decision a day earlier.[25]

It was at that point that someone rushed in and informed the TH&I men of McKeen's call to report for duty. They were suddenly stunned and angered at what seemed like duplicity on Riley's part. All discussion of compromise and arbitration came to an end, and the strikers formulated a belligerent response. They advised McKeen that they would give up custody of the company's property, but at the same time, they would no longer be responsible for protecting it. And they let him know in no uncertain terms that they considered his action an insult.[26]

McKeen felt compelled to respond that evening when he learned of the strikers' displeasure. He hastened to assure his men that he had intended no threat. No one who chose not to report to work would be punished, but those who wanted to work should be able to do so. McKeen knew that the end of the strike was near and that it was now just a matter of time. All the same, it was evident that the mood of the strikers had turned more militant.[27]

Spooner's contingent passed through the Terre Haute Union Depot on Saturday afternoon without incident. Hearing of their imminent arrival, the TH&I strikers occupying the depot prudently withdrew, making it unnecessary for the troops even to leave their coaches. Anyway, their orders were to report to Vincennes.[28]

McKeen, concerned that he had inflamed his men, now overreacted and wired Gresham that evening to ask that Spooner and his troops return to Terre Haute: "Engineers refuse to run our trains. Strikers are turbulent and men who desire to work intimidated. I trust you will let the United States soldiers remain here a few days. Please answer." It was just what Gresham had hoped for.[29]

Judge Gresham wired General Spooner in Vincennes with instructions to leave a detachment in Terre Haute when he returned, ostensibly to help keep the Logansport road open. The presence of soldiers would have "a good moral effect and be convenient for use at Vincennes or Evansville." He also told Spooner suggestively: "If the Vandalia strikers think the troops are to operate against them you will not be responsible for their mistake."[30]

Spooner and his soldiers returned to Terre Haute on Sunday night, July 29. By then the strike was all but over. Clearing the Union Depot, the troops escorted the eastbound express out of town and then bivouacked for the night.[31]

Across town at the Engineer's Hall, the strikers were voting to return to work on Monday morning. First, however, they sent for McKeen's assurance that no one would be fired for having participated. When Riley promptly agreed, the men declared the strike at an end and adjourned.[32]

The next morning, meeting with Charles Peddle, McKeen's chief mechanical officer, the strike leaders again received assurances that no one would be fired. Several men had been charged with assault on Sunday, and they would be suspended pending an investigation, but there would be no retribution from the company. However, as the executive committee reported to the men later in the day, Peddle had rejected the 15 percent wage increase. Knowing how deeply the men felt about the issue, the executive committee promised that it would continue to work "as silently as possible" for the needed increase and told the men that Peddle had assured them their request would be reconsidered as soon as freight rates rose sufficiently.[33]

Most of the men returned to work by the end of the day, Spooner and his troops headed back to Indianapolis, and train operations on the TH&I were soon nearly back to normal. But the worst was yet to come for the strike leadership.[34]

On Tuesday, July 31, Judge Gresham made good on his threat to punish the strikers, issuing warrants for the arrest of several executive committee members. The charge was contempt of court for interfering with the operation of the Logansport, Crawfordsville & Southwestern. The men, including young, 23-year-old committee chairman Mark Miller, were arrested and taken under guard to Indianapolis Tuesday night.[35]

At three o'clock, Tuesday afternoon, federal subpoenas were served on Riley McKeen, Charles Peddle, and Josephus Collett, president of the Evansville, Terre Haute & Chicago. The three were being summoned to testify against the prisoners, who would be arraigned Wednesday morning before Judge Thomas Drummond. Having played such an active role in the Indianapolis anti-strike forces, Gresham prudently disqualified himself from sitting in judgement but continued to advise Drummond throughout the proceedings.[36]

Drummond opened trial on Thursday, August 2, in Indianapolis. The strikers agreed to plead guilty to participating in the strike; but having done what they could to keep the Logansport road open, they pled not guilty to the contempt of court charge. McKeen appeared as a witness, testifying that the defendants were strike leaders and that he had dealt with them as such. But Riley refused to directly implicate them in the Logansport road interference, emphasizing that he could not say one way or the other who had actually been in control of the depot that day.[37]

Charles Peddle also testified that the defendants were members of the strike committee and generally in charge of the men at the depot, but he, too, refused to confirm the contempt charge. In fact, Peddle specifically defended his men, testifying that when others had attempted to stop the Logansport road trains, the defendants had overruled them and ordered the trains to be run without interference. Collett also refused to incriminate the TH&I men, and the trial was over by day's end.[38]

Judge Drummond delivered his verdict the next day. There was no doubt the strike leaders would be punished: Drummond was under too much pressure from Gresham and the Indianapolis political establishment not to convict. Besides, he was already predisposed to make a strict example of the strikers. Even so, most observers considered the three-month sentences meted out to be relatively light punishment. Thus ended the Great Railroad Strike on the Terre Haute & Indianapolis.[39]

In the wake of the event, it is hard to determine who won. The strikers gained nothing except bitter experience. The railroads, though they had been successful in crushing the strike, lost substantial amounts of money in unearned revenues; and the more heavily hit lines like the Pennsylvania suffered millions of dollars in damages, only adding to the burdens of depression-reduced earnings.

For McKeen, the strike had been a painful reminder of his lack of control over the TH&I's destiny. Not only was the event not of his making; once the trouble was under way, he was often at the mercy of outside forces that impeded his attempts at resolution. To be sure, McKeen was a product of his generation, with a tendency to view the rights of his employees as strictly inferior to his rights as an employer. Yet he seemed more perplexed and disappointed in his men's breech of their implied contract than offended and angered.

McKeen had promised there would be no reprisals, and there were none, further enhancing his popular image. But while his men saw him as benevolent and generous, Riley's wealthy Terre Haute business associates and neighbors tended to see his actions during the strike as being forceful and decisive. Richard W. Thompson, Hayes's Navy Secretary, who was inclined to view the strike as a communist revolution, later praised his friend McKeen's actions in a letter to the Pennsylvania's Thomas Scott, maintaining that Riley had "stood up firmly and manfully."[40]

It is definitely true that McKeen kept the interests of his company first at all times. The men won no advance and remained on a reduced wage after the strike. In fact, TH&I workers would not receive a 10 percent wage restoration until April 1880, and then only after wages had been similarly raised on the Pan Handle. Yet McKeen had shown a remarkable sensitivity, and afterward he made absolutely no attempt to destroy the union organizations. Quite the opposite happened, for in the wake of the great strike, banker McKeen lent money to a young Eugene Debs to help rebuild the shattered Firemen's Brotherhood. In recognition of his continuing support, the men often remembered McKeen with gifts. In September 1882 the firemen publicly honored Riley at their national convention. McKeen developed such an appreciation for his workers' fidelity that, in later years, he would be at a loss to remember the last week of July 1877, proudly but erroneously boasting that he had never had a strike among his employees.[41]

It can be argued that, despite the excitement of the weeklong strike, McKeen had never faced any real crisis. He never once called his directors together to provide counsel or approve an action. While the company obviously lost revenues during its closure, its earnings for the year were flat. And thanks to the restraint of its workers, there was practically no physical damage from strike activity—except for the loss of five boxcars burned in Pittsburgh on Pennsylvania rails. But there is no doubt that McKeen came away from the episode with increased resentment toward his Pennsylvania partner. He clearly placed a great deal of blame on his relationship with the Pennsylvania, and the eastern line's hotheaded management, for having dragged the TH&I into a strike situation. The strike may even have influenced his decision to end the joint operating agreement with the Indianapolis & St. Louis.[42]

5

SYSTEM BUILDER

Any resentment McKeen may have felt was fully reciprocated by the Pennsylvania's Lines West organization, especially after the joint operations west of Indianapolis came to an end in February 1878. Utterly frustrated by their inability to gain control of the line to St. Louis, the Pennsylvania men continued to monitor the TH&I's operation of the Vandalia. George Roberts, having been catapulted up to first vice president of the Pennsylvania Railroad upon the accession of Thomas A. Scott to the presidency in 1874, took every opportunity to badger McKeen about his deficient management of the Vandalia. Riley always got a lecture when the two executives met during pool negotiations at the St. Nicholas Hotel in New York City, and it must have gotten tiresome. But McKeen's dealings with Roberts were pleasant compared to the hostile treatment he was receiving from the Lines West organization.[1]

The Pennsylvania Company's top officers, the men responsible for all of the parent Pennsylvania Railroad's large interests west of Pittsburgh, had plainly had enough. Savaged by four years of economic depression during which nearly continuous rate warfare had driven their earnings practically to cost levels, loaded down with burdensome leases and costly financial guarantees, and frustrated in their repeated attempts to plug the leaky dike of their financial condition, the Lines West men suddenly turned belligerent. They determined to remedy the situation permanently, at whatever cost was required.

Their first target on this grim mission was the sickly Indianapolis & St. Louis. Although the Pennsylvania Company had never utilized the road for through traffic, it continued to honor the terms of the Fort Wayne's agreement and had advanced almost half a million dollars over the years to help the I&StL cover its deficit, a large part of which stemmed from its overgenerous lease of the St. Louis, Alton & Terre Haute. The Alton line's crushing $450,000 minimum yearly rental had originally been jointly guaranteed by three partners, but the Indianapolis, Cincinnati & Lafayette had gone bankrupt in 1870 and never actively participated in the lease. Instead, the deficiencies in meeting this large annual sum had been met jointly by the Pennsylvania Company and the Bee Line.[2]

Emboldened by their apparent success in repudiating the Pan Handle's lease of the Indiana Central, the Pennsylvania's Lines West officers decided to force a change in the I&StL's lease of the Alton line. In April 1878 they informed the Alton line's owners that, unless they agreed to reduce the minimum annual rental of their road to $300,000, the Pennsylvania Company would refuse to continue advancing its portion of the funds necessary to meet the rent. And Lines West made good on that

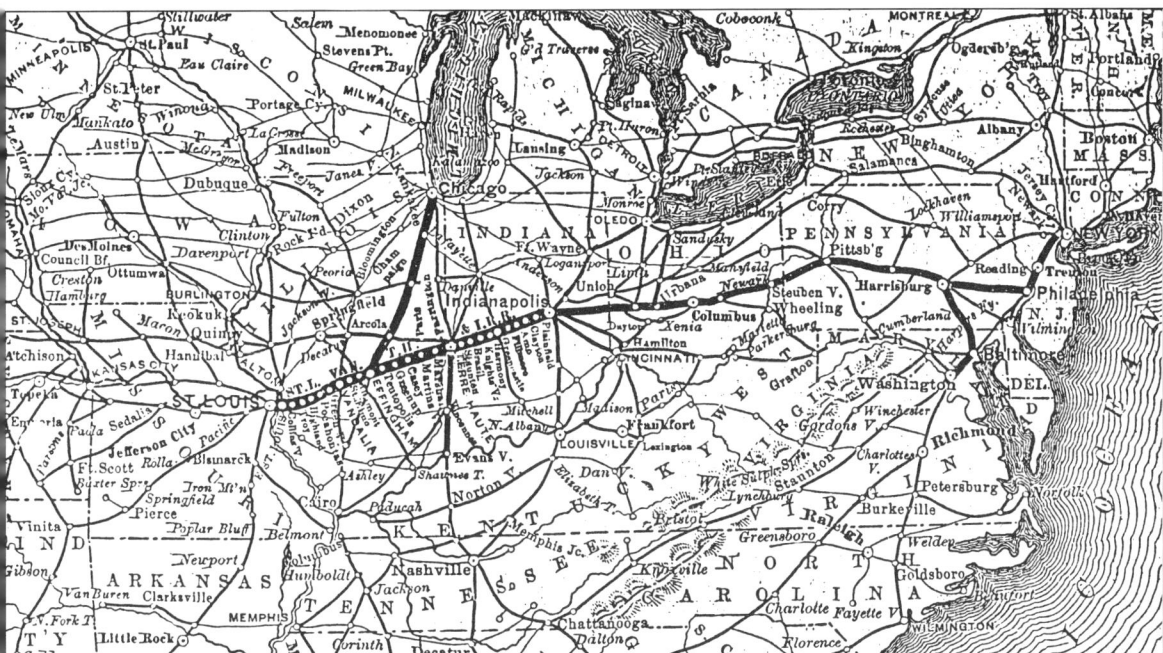

This 1881 map identifies the Vandalia Line as the St. Louis, Vandalia, Terre Haute & Indianapolis. Through interline service over the Illinois Central to Chicago was operated from the early 1870s, and by 1893 included a "solid, vestibuled" through overnight train via Vandalia and Decatur, and a day schedule with through coaches interchanged at Effingham. This passenger service ended on August 1, 1896 when the IC moved its St. Louis passenger trains to the Big Four via Pana, Illinois. Unfortunately the loss in passenger revenue was minor compared to the lost freight interchange. From *Rand-McNally Traveler's Railway Guide,* February 1881.

threat by withholding all payments beginning on June 1. In quick response, the St. Louis, Alton & Terre Haute filed suit against the Pennsylvania to compel performance of the Fort Wayne's guarantee.[3]

The Pennsylvania's solicitors were busy. All throughout 1877 Lines West officials had been worrying about the legal ramifications of the unfunded Vandalia sinking fund, and they kept after McKeen to pay the bill. Even Richard W. Thompson, whom Roberts had hired as the local counsel for both the St. Louis, Vandalia & Terre Haute and the Pennsylvania Company in 1873—a remarkable conflict of interest, since he was also counsel for the TH&I—would be involved until he resigned to become Rutherford Hayes's Secretary of the Navy. Now, with two attempts to break lease contracts wending their way through the courts, the company's attorneys were put on notice for the possibility of a third.[4]

On a director's trip west to inspect the Vandalia in the fall of 1878, George Roberts and Lines West Third Vice President Jacob Nessly McCullough made a point to corner McKeen and give him their views. They wanted nothing less than a complete operating reorganization of the entire Vandalia Line, the TH&I included.

McCullough, probably the Lines West organization's most hard-nosed and outspoken manager, was a good choice as point man, and he was quite blunt. The present arrangement was inefficient, expensive, and unacceptable, McKeen was told, and the Pennsylvania insisted on a change.[5]

Over the next several months, McKeen was treated to more conferences with McCullough and more correspondence from Roberts. Ever charming and amenable, Riley expressed a willingness to do all he could to help satisfy his friends at the Pennsylvania. Roberts mistakenly interpreted McKeen's response as "hearty concurrence," and so informed the Lines West executive committee at the end of January 1879. The Pennsylvania's Lines West officers settled back impatiently in their Pittsburgh offices to await quick action from Terre Haute. It never came.[6]

Meanwhile, in April 1879 the Pan Handle received some bad news and some good news. The court had ruled that the Pan Handle could not break its lease of the Indiana Central. On the other hand, the Indiana Central was, as the Pan Handle had claimed, in breech of the lease contract and thus liable. While not as satisfactory a decision as one might have hoped, it was technically interpreted as a victory for the Pan Handle. More importantly, it enabled the Pennsylvania men to force an eventual reorganization of the Indiana Central in their favor. Having drawn blood once, the Lines West–Pan Handle officers now moved against McKeen and the TH&I.[7]

By May 1 the Lines West executive committee, consisting of McCullough, William Thaw, and Fourth Vice President Thomas D. Messler, had lost all faith in McKeen's promises. In their meeting in Pittsburgh that morning, the committee decided to recommend stringent action when the Pan Handle board met on May 22. Thaw and Messler, who also served as president of the St. Louis, Vandalia & Terre Haute, let the pugnacious McCullough handle the details of the company's offensive. The board, in turn, voted its qualified approval and gave its officers a free hand, with the only condition being that any action taken must also be approved by the parent Pennsylvania's board in Philadelphia.[8]

McCullough wasted no time. By the end of June, he had put together a five-step plan and received the Pennsylvania board's approval. By the first week in July, Riley had the Pan Handle's formal demand in writing: The TH&I must agree to a prompt cancellation of its lease of the St. Louis, Vandalia & Terre Haute and surrender the Vandalia's property as quickly as possible. Otherwise, the Pan Handle's officers threatened legal action to compel McKeen to submit.[9]

The letter was curt and emphatic, but what was most devastating was what it did not say. The Lines West organization had also made specific plans to force the TH&I to share its through business with the Indianapolis & St. Louis, once McKeen assented to a change in the Vandalia lease. In fact, Riley would be at their mercy should he agree. And if he did not, Lines West planned to bypass the TH&I entirely by routing its through business over the I&StL, all the way to St. Louis, if necessary.[10]

Perhaps Thomas A. Scott and George Roberts of the Pennsylvania thought the Lines West plan a little too drastic. Roberts attempted to enlist Richard Thompson's help a month later, explaining the Pan Handle's position as the aggrieved party and repeating the real threat of litigation should their mutual friend McKeen not comply. Was there not something Thompson could do? Indeed, there was. Taking a mo-

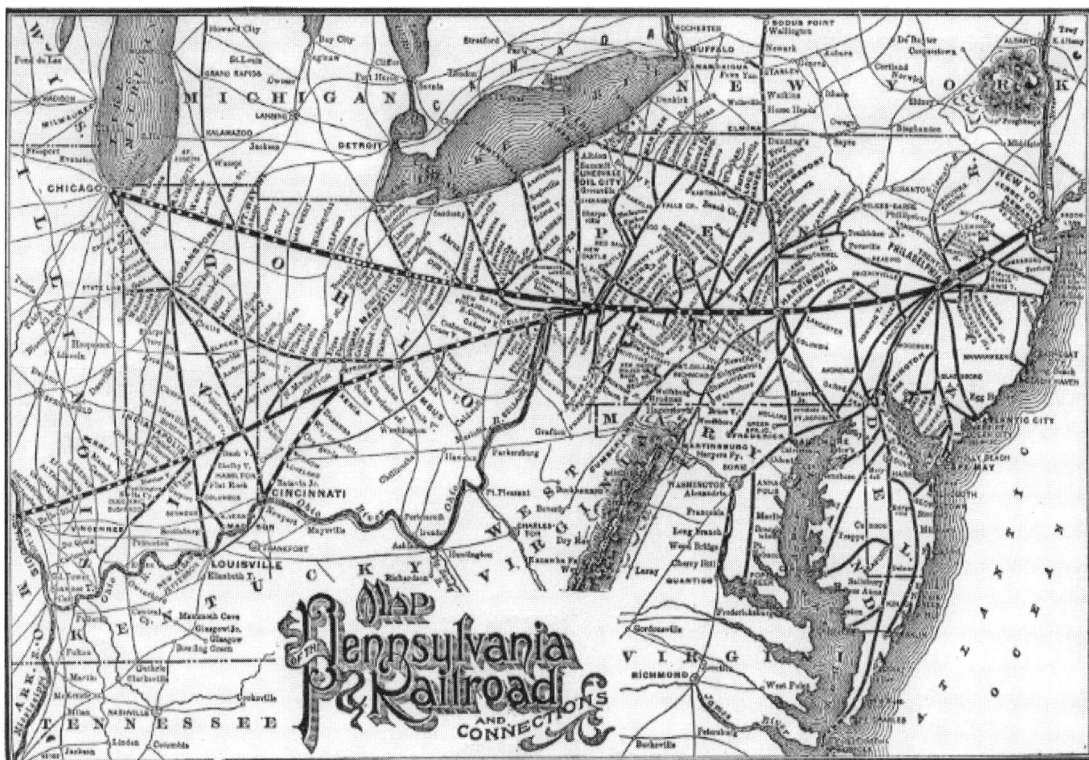

Map from *Traveler's Official Guide*, June 1893.

ment from his responsibilities as Navy Secretary, Thompson contacted McKeen and arranged for a conference between the two sides. Though it was put off several times due to scheduling difficulties, all parties finally met in Chicago in mid-November.[11]

It was a landmark meeting. For the first time since the TH&I's acceptance of the Vandalia property in the summer of 1870, Riley got to talk with the top man, in this case Pennsylvania President Thomas A. Scott. Both men were perfect politicians, the very embodiment of affability and charm, so intent on being agreeable that they managed to completely mislead each other. Both left the meeting in good spirits, with renewed confidence and false hopes.

The substance of their talk concerned the state of relations between the two companies and how to heal the breech. They both must have agreed on the natural affinity of the Vandalia Line; McKeen's TH&I and the Vandalia were complementary and belonged together, so no good could come from breaking the lease. It came down to who controlled the TH&I. Scott did his best to convince Riley that control of the entire line from Indianapolis to St. Louis ultimately belonged in the hands of the Pennsylvania. McKeen agreed. The problem was a misunderstanding as to timing.[12]

Scott informed his staff and associates that he thought he had convinced McKeen

Thomas A. Scott, the Pennsylvania's fourth president and the man who staked that company's claim on McKeen's railroad. Pennsylvania State Archives: (MG-286) Penn Central Railroad Collection.

to sell control of the Terre Haute & Indianapolis to the Pennsylvania. "Mr. McKeen . . . signified a willingness to take up the question in the manner indicated by Mr. Scott," Roberts later confided to Thompson, asking for his continued help by encouraging McKeen to do exactly that, and the sooner the better. But McKeen, although he kept up a cordial correspondence with Scott, made no attempt to close the deal. When a few weeks passed without McKeen's coming east to finish what he and Scott had discussed, Roberts began to lose hope. After a letter from Thompson mentioning Riley's plans to visit California, Roberts openly expressed his disappointment, replying, "I am just a little bit afraid that we are not going to reach the results that we had anticipated in reference to our negotiations with Mr. McKeen."[13]

The truth was that Riley was not prepared to let go of the Terre Haute & Indianapolis, not yet. His response to Scott's overtures had been forthright and positive, so Roberts's disappointment was either the result of a misunderstanding, a change of heart, or a deliberate deception. Judging from subsequent events, and McKeen's reactions and responses, it was never his intention to deceive Scott. McKeen thought he had merely promised to contact the Pennsylvania first when he finally decided to sell his TH&I stock, and he would steadfastly honor that commitment.[14]

At the time of his meeting with Scott, McKeen may have been contemplating the race for governor, which was coming up the following spring and for which he would briefly be a candidate. If he was seriously considering a political campaign, Riley most certainly would have also considered lightening his responsibilities. Given the prospect of relinquishing the bank or the railroad, McKeen would have inevitably chosen to sell the TH&I. For one thing, ownership of the railroad would have imposed a significantly greater political liability. Therefore, if McKeen's loss of enthusiasm had been due to a change of heart, it would have come much later, in the summer of 1880.

The best argument for a misunderstanding can be seen in McKeen's actions, for at the very moment he was agreeing to eventually offer his TH&I stock to the Pennsylvania, Riley was in the process of expanding the Vandalia Line system.

In his position as head of a prosperous and influential bank, McKeen regularly invested in promising ventures of all kinds. Quite naturally, his preference was to aid those enterprises that would tend to enrich Terre Haute. Since he was also a leading midwestern railroad executive, Riley was often called upon to invest in enterprises that were his particular specialty.

There was no end to the opportunities. McKeen had aided his friend Josephus Collett in his promotion of the Evansville, Terre Haute & Chicago, opened from Terre Haute north to Danville, Illinois, in 1872. This line, upon completion of the connecting Chicago, Danville & Vincennes, provided a more direct route to Chicago for TH&I coal than the previously used route via Effingham and the Illinois Central. Riley also joined Collett and William B. Tuell to finish building the Terre Haute & Southeastern to Worthington, Indiana, in the late 1870s. And McKeen had taken a leading role in the organization and construction of the Belt Railroad of Indianapolis opened in 1877, and served as the company's first president.[15]

In the summer of 1879, the end of the long receivership of the hapless Logansport, Crawfordsville and Southwestern was finally in sight. McKeen had been keeping an eye on the proceedings, partly because the TH&I was a creditor, but also because the line had possibilities for his Vandalia Line system.[16]

The Southwestern had been opened from Rockville to Logansport in 1871, a product of the era's feverishly inflated railroad-building boom. Entrance into Terre Haute was provided by leasing a section of the Evansville & Crawfordsville below Rockville. Milked by its Cincinnati promoters and New York bankers, the line quickly succumbed to the stringencies of depression and entered bankruptcy in 1874. Although the Southwestern had originally been envisioned as a feeder for the Wabash, it spent its youth as a poor agricultural road. However, it had the potentially good fortune of traversing the upper limits of Indiana's coal belt. In McKeen's way of thinking, besides whatever coal mining might develop along its own line, the Southwestern could also be of great benefit to the Terre Haute & Indianapolis by providing yet another outlet northward for the coal being mined in Clay County, thereby adding to the TH&I's local traffic base.[17]

At the court-directed foreclosure sale in Crawfordsville on September 10, 1879, the Southwestern was sold to attorney John G. Williams, representing McKeen and his associates. Williams had replaced Thompson as general counsel of the TH&I in April 1877 and was Riley's personal legal advisor. Significantly, he was also counsel for the Southwestern's receiver. On October 24 Williams incorporated the Terre Haute & Logansport Railroad, with himself, McKeen, Deloss Minshall, TH&I director Jonathon B. Hager, and TH&I Secretary George E. Farrington as directors. McKeen and Williams owned most of the stock, with Riley holding about 65 percent of the total.[18]

They got the Southwestern for a song: Williams's bid was just a half-million dollars, probably paid with greatly depreciated Southwestern bonds picked up for pennies on the dollar. With another half-million dollars in new bonds, which would be issued for improvements, McKeen and his fellow stockholders could easily afford to lease the Logansport road to the TH&I for just 25 percent of the gross earnings. The Terre Haute & Indianapolis board ratified the agreement and guaranteed the Logansport's bonds on November 22, and by year's end the Vandalia Line had a new 115-mile branch.[19]

A southbound freight on the Logansport road at Crawfordsville, Indiana, in the 1890s. Note the frail-looking 60-pound rail. The handsome depot was one of four built in 1884 to the same design, the debut of the ornate, gambrel-roofed "Vandalia style." The others were in Greenville, Illinois; up the road in Frankfort, Indiana; and in Rockville, Indiana. Sadly, only Rockville's depot survives intact, albeit in wonderfully restored glory. Historical Collection of the Crawfordsville District Public Library, Crawfordsville, Indiana.

McKeen's timing was right. Economic recovery was well under way by the summer of 1879, and by year's end the long depression was clearly over. The results showed only modestly in the TH&I's annual report, mainly because the company's fiscal year ended on October 31; but by the end of 1880, the return to prosperity provided a gratifying surge of earnings. Freight traffic—particularly high-value westbound merchandise traffic—was up substantially, easing competitive pressure by providing plenty of volume for all the trunk lines. At long last, rates rose modestly, just enough to produce a profit on through business. Unfortunately, the temporary calm was like the eye of a storm, for general profitability stimulated a return to large-scale railroad construction, from which not even McKeen would be immune. And the additional carrying capacity produced by new railroad lines would continue to drag down rates.[20]

For the Pennsylvania's Lines West officers, an improved economic situation meant some breathing room. But their problems with McKeen and the Vandalia Line remained. Consternation had replaced frustration as they watched the Pennsylvania's chief executive short-circuit their carefully planned offensive against McKeen. Now the Pan Handle's executives were left in a temporary limbo, helpless to do more than complain and wait. And yet things were about to improve by chance.

A postcard picture of the second Frankfort, Indiana, depot. This Vandalia-style design was built in 1884 to replace a smaller station constructed by predecessor Logansport, Crawfordsville & Southwestern. Collection of Leroy Good, Frankfort, Indiana.

In June 1880, worn down by the stress of guiding the Pennsylvania through the difficulties of the seventies and now seriously ill, Thomas A. Scott resigned the presidency. He was succeeded by George Brooke Roberts, whose close association with the Lines West organization could only help the latter's cause. And then, on August 2, McKeen's general manager, John E. Simpson, died suddenly in St. Louis after suffering a stroke.[21]

The loss of the TH&I's top operating officer was something of a shock; he was only 40 years old. But it presented Roberts with a golden opportunity, and the Pennsylvania's new president lost no time in contacting his old friend Richard W. Thompson with a suggestion. With such an important vacancy in his management, Roberts wrote, McKeen "could not do a wiser thing" than to appoint the Pan Handle's general manager, Darius W. Caldwell, in Simpson's place. Caldwell could supply one of his own assistants as superintendent of the TH&I, and the arrangement would provide an efficient management for McKeen. And, as Roberts put it succinctly, "It would also have the great feature in it that would be of importance, not only to Mr. McKeen's interest, but to our own, of relieving many of the raspings which take place between two managements." Roberts concluded by asking Thompson to pass along this suggestion to McKeen.[22]

McKeen found the proposal acceptable; and after negotiating details like salary and responsibilities, he implemented the arrangement on October 1, 1880. By year's end, Caldwell was in charge of both McKeen's road and the Pan Handle and had installed a former Pan Handle man, Joseph Hill, as general superintendent of the TH&I. Even though Caldwell and Hill reported to McKeen as president, the Lines West organization now at long last had some influence in the TH&I's management.[23]

The results of this corporate cross-pollination were immediate and, for the Pennsylvania men, highly satisfactory. Pennsylvania Lines West operating practices were instituted on the Vandalia Line system. All reports assumed the form dictated by Pennsylvania system operating rules. This gathering of crucial data was dramatically apparent in the greater depth and detail presented in the TH&I's annual reports beginning with the one for 1881.[24]

The movement of personnel flowed in more than one direction. As retirements and resignations occurred in the Lines West organization, the Pennsylvania occasionally took advantage of McKeen's fine executive corps, naming several TH&I men to corresponding positions with the Pan Handle and the Pennsylvania Company. In April 1881, for example, Elias A. Ford became general passenger agent for all of the Pennsylvania Lines West of Pittsburgh as well as the Vandalia Line. As management consolidation proceeded, McKeen insisted only on maintaining a completely separate freight traffic department in order to help safeguard the TH&I's considerable local business.[25]

Joint operating supervision of Lines West and the TH&I lasted only until May 1, 1882, when Caldwell left to become vice president and general manager of the newly built New York, Chicago & St. Louis, but the changes made during the period seemed to ease a great deal of the tensions, just as Roberts had predicted. When Caldwell resigned, the TH&I eliminated the position of general manager, and Joseph Hill became the top operating officer. However, the joint passenger traffic department remained in place, and many of the Pennsylvania operating and accounting practices were retained on the Vandalia Line.[26]

Even though it had not produced any useful results for the Pennsylvania, Thomas Scott's conference with McKeen had one definite effect: It had caused Riley to seriously consider the possibility of selling out. Management of the Vandalia Line system still required a large portion of his time, and it seemed more and more to be time spent on frustrating competitive details like rates and pooling. The long depression had exacted its toll through the twin pressures of having to maintain earnings and drastically reduce costs. And though he had been successful in fending them off, McKeen's relationship with the Pennsylvania's Lines West executives had no doubt become wearisome. Often, it must have seemed, he was almost powerless in defending his company's position, as in his attempts to establish a rate structure free from interference or to avoid being drawn into the crippling labor problems of the summer of 1877.

Perhaps it was time to let go, after all. The bank was busy and prosperous, yet McKeen did not have enough time to properly administer it. Minshall had retired as a partner in 1876, and Riley had brought his brother, Sam, and his eldest son, Frank, into the firm, which was reorganized as McKeen & Company. Though Riley maintained close supervision, it was up to Frank to run the bank on a daily basis.[27]

Despite the scope of his many obligations, Riley remained a thoroughly contented homebody. From all appearances, McKeen was a devoted husband and father, the genial head of a large family of seven children. He was an active Methodist layman and stayed involved in civic affairs. As a hobby, Riley indulged his fondness for racing and horses, raising fine pacers and trotters at the family's Edgewood Farm on the east edge of Terre Haute. Pedigreed cattle were raised on another McKeen-owned farm.[28]

Riley and his second wife, Ann, kept a warm and gracious home. For years the handsome brick residence at Seventh and Cherry was alive with children, and it was the site of memorable events like the McKeen's annual New Year's ball, reputedly the biggest social event of the season. Riley even had the backyard flooded every winter to provide a skating rink for family and friends.[29]

McKeen also maintained his political activities as a leader of the Indiana Republican Party. Perhaps, had he not had so many business commitments, Riley might have actively pursued his party's nomination for governor in 1880, for which, it was reputed, he could have had a majority of delegates for the asking. Instead, McKeen decided against an actual campaign and supported his friend Albert Porter.[30]

As for the railroad itself, the Terre Haute & Indianapolis was in good shape financially, its foreign and outside stockholders kept content by the maintenance of generous and regular dividends. The company had amassed an impressive cash surplus of $1 million and held a number of income-producing investments. The only areas which caused concern were the drain on earnings made by the system's leased lines and the stability of the railroad rate structure. McKeen assured his stockholders that the earnings deficiencies the company was covering under its lease agreements would be amply repaid by future profits, particularly in respect to the sizeable charges for improving the Logansport road. And the stockholders believed him, having come to trust implicitly in McKeen's Terre Haute management. The rate problem, however, continued to defy solution.[31]

If the year 1880 provided a period of peaceful contemplation for Riley, 1881 would shatter both calm and stability. By summer renewed warfare among the trunk lines would bring rates crashing downward once again. The fighting was bitter and

Ever the charming Victorians, Riley and his second wife, Ann Crawford McKeen, sat for properly painted portraits sometime in the late 1870s. Courtesy of Mr. and Mrs. William Riley McKeen, IV, Bedford, Indiana.

costly, touched off by the Erie's poaching of the New York Central's eastbound grain traffic. Long-suffering William H. Vanderbilt responded like a maddened bull in a china shop and, goaded on by New York's commercial community, also declared war on the Pennsylvania and Baltimore & Ohio over the rate differentials they maintained to the ports of Philadelphia and Baltimore. The resulting rate demoralization left no one unaffected.[32]

On a more personal note, tragedy touched the McKeen household in September with the death by illness of Riley's wife Ann. It was sudden, a shock to family and friends, and could not have helped but give Riley pause to reflect on his future.[33]

Perhaps the burdens felt much heavier as 1881 came to a close. For whatever reason, McKeen finally decided to sell his control of the Terre Haute & Indianapolis. Certainly there were opportunities to do so. Besides the standing offer from the Pennsylvania, there was one from the syndicate of eastern bankers and midwestern entrepreneurs headed by George I. Seney and Calvin S. Brice. Approached by a representative of this so-called "Seney Syndicate" sometime between late 1880 and the fall of 1881, McKeen was offered the exceptional price of 300 percent of par, or $150 per share (par value of the TH&I stock being $50). Whether the syndicate intended to use the TH&I as a branch of their Lake Erie & Western or as the St. Louis leg of their Nickel Plate project is not known, but McKeen's Vandalia Line system could have served well in either capacity by providing a through route from Frankfort, Indiana, to the Mississippi River. Though he may have been tempted by the money, Riley stood by his verbal commitment to the Pennsylvania and refused the offer.[34]

There were other considerations, of course, particularly those concerning what was best for the company and Terre Haute. Despite the gratifying development of local industry, in which McKeen had played a large part, the Terre Haute & Indianapolis remained the city's biggest single employer. With its extensive facilities, the company was crucial to the economic health of Terre Haute, and McKeen would not consciously endanger his community by putting the railroad in the wrong hands. And, as McKeen had agreed at the time of his conference with Thomas Scott, the Vandalia Line had become an integral part of the Pennsylvania's system, and removing it from that system would be unnatural and risky.

McKeen had remained in touch with the Pennsylvania's new president, George Roberts. While he must have encouraged Riley, Roberts at least stopped pressing him for a decision, conveying his continued hope for a resolution to their mutual friend Richard Thompson. It proved to be an intelligent strategy, for by early 1882

More than three years McKeen's junior, George Brooke Roberts would come to wield the power of the Pennsylvania Railroad as its fifth president. Often overlooked or, worse, dismissed as an inflexible and timid corporate bureaucrat, Roberts presided over the Pennsylvania's second greatest period of geographical expansion and arguably its most impressive era of physical development, at the same time ably defending the railroad from rate-cutting competitors and dividend-hungry British stockholders. His nearly 17 years at the helm of what was then the country's largest and most important corporation coincided with the Pennsylvania's rise as the self-proclaimed "Standard Railroad of America." George Roberts made no apology for being what some might see as corporate America's first notable "Organization Man," nor did he need to. The organization he headed spoke volumes about his executive ability. Pennsylvania State Archives: (MG-286) Penn Central Railroad Collection.

Riley had definitely decided, and he authorized his lawyer-friend Thompson to act as his agent. Thompson, in turn, wrote Roberts on March 4 to open negotiations.[35]

Ironically, Thompson's letter, and McKeen's sudden decision to sell, caught Roberts off guard. Preoccupied by far more serious matters, like the ongoing rate war with Vanderbilt, and locked in a bitter struggle with the Baltimore & Ohio for mastery of the route between Washington and New York, Roberts had little time or energy to devote to the problem of the Vandalia Line. He diverted Thompson's inquiry with a logical, if bureaucratic response. "The responsibilities of the purchase of Mr. McKeen's stock are so great that I could not undertake to make any intelligent reply to your letter without having more data before me than at present," he replied on March 6. He meant it, too. Roberts was far too cautious an executive to rush into an expensive purchase without studying the cost.[36]

George Roberts had grave concerns. As he put it to Thompson: "Since we last discussed with Mr. McKeen the question of purchasing his stock, he has made several very material changes in the property." What bothered Roberts most was the TH&I's lease of the Terre Haute & Logansport and the consequent burden it imposed. The Pennsylvania's president insisted on obtaining exact facts and figures concerning the TH&I's financial situation before he could think of entertaining a purchase, and he communicated that demand to McKeen.[37]

Although Thomas A. Scott had been gone almost two years, McKeen had never forgotten his promise to Roberts's esteemed predecessor, nor had he expected Scott's offer on behalf of the Pennsylvania to change. Yet Roberts was now demanding unimpeded access to the TH&I's books in order to weigh the offer. It was hardly in the spirit of the gentlemanly understanding Riley had made with Scott in November 1879. Considering the ongoing dispute with the Pan Handle over accounts under the Vandalia lease, it also seemed more than a little suspicious. So McKeen ignored Roberts's demand. One misunderstanding begot another, for Roberts and his Lines West organization interpreted McKeen's response as an attempt to withhold damaging secrets. The resulting impasse was an annoyance to Riley but not serious enough to force an immediate change of mind. Knowing just how badly the Pennsylvania men wanted his road, McKeen could afford to be patient.

If Roberts was put off by McKeen's lease of the Logansport road, he must have been utterly dismayed at Riley's next moves. In March 1882 McKeen offered to lease the bankrupt Illinois Midland from the line's receiver. The moribund Midland extended west to Decatur and Peoria, entering Terre Haute over TH&I tracks from a connection just across the state line in Illinois. McKeen had had financial dealings with the Midland's builder, Robert Hervey, and both the McKeen Bank and the TH&I were creditors of the company. In any event, the offer was refused by the bankruptcy judge in charge.[38]

Whatever the Pennsylvania might have thought of such a move, it was perfectly logical to McKeen. Riley's efforts at system building almost always involved extending his railroad's reach in distributing on-line coal. Despite the Midland's obvious weaknesses, it did provide access to Decatur's manufacturing industries, whose need for fuel made an excellent market for TH&I coal.

The same coal-distribution strategy was behind McKeen's decision to extend the Terre Haute & Logansport to South Bend. And in that sense, it was an even better move than the attempt to lease the Illinois Midland. South Bend, home of the extensive Oliver Chilled Plow works, had developed a substantial amount of heavy industry that consumed an increasing tonnage of coal. Unfortunately, there were no direct rail routes from the southwestern Indiana coal fields, allowing strong competition from northern Illinois and Ohio to flourish. If he could extend the Logansport road northward to South Bend, McKeen was virtually assured of a substantial amount of local business. Furthermore, tapping the industrial complex that was developing along the St. Joseph River would help cure one of the Logansport road's biggest ills: that of a largely one-way traffic flow to the north. Part of the line's poor showing was due to the expense of hauling little but empty cars south. South Bend offered a potentially large amount of high-value merchandise traffic that the TH&I could haul southward over the leased Logansport road.[39]

It was an easy decision. The economy was booming again, and the time was right for easy financing. The extension, which had been rumored as early as February, was officially approved by the stockholders of the Terre Haute & Logansport on August 26, 1882. Construction began early in 1883. The new line was opened as far north as Marmont on Lake Maxinkuckee (later renamed Culver) by September 17, 1883; to Plymouth the following June; and all the way to South Bend on November 24, 1884. Unfortunately, by the time the extension was completed, the country was again mired in a business depression.[40]

George Roberts had not pressed McKeen very hard in trying to get an accurate assessment of the financial condition of the Terre Haute & Indianapolis with good reason: At that moment he probably did not want to spend the money necessary to

In its idyllic setting on the shores of beautiful Lake Maxinkuckee, the original Culver, Indiana, depot received a constant stream of summertime day-excursionists, usually on special trains aggressively promoted in on-line newspapers. Originally called Marmont, the village was later renamed for the military academy which was built on its northerly edge. This particular depot, built in the classic Vandalia style, burned in January 1920 and was replaced in 1925 by a more modern brick station which still stands. Courtesy of *The Culver Citizen*, Culver, Indiana.

buy control of McKeen's road. By the end of 1882, it was clear that any peace established between the eastern trunk lines could not be maintained for long; there were just too many destabilizing forces at work. Vanderbilt, whose New York Central–Lake Shore Route was bracketed by the Grand Trunk to the north and Jay Gould's eastwardly expanding Wabash system to the south, was in a particularly volatile mood. And thousands of miles of new trunkline railroad were rapidly being completed. By the summer of 1883, the Nickel Plate, the Erie's Chicago & Atlantic, the Lackawanna's Buffalo extension, and the New York, West Shore & Buffalo were all operating and competing for traffic, upsetting the previous allotments assigned by the trunkline pool. As a result, rates plummeted once more.[41]

The Pennsylvania's Lines West of Pittsburgh were particularly hard hit by low rates. Despite an actual improvement in the Pan Handle's fortunes, net earnings for the entire Lines West operation declined by 55 percent in 1883; and in 1884 Lines West registered a loss of over $800,000. Roberts was in no position to add any additional burden, if he could help it.[42]

Several significant changes had been made in the Lines West family. In 1881 a suddenly competitive-minded William H. Vanderbilt, facing up to the fact that he

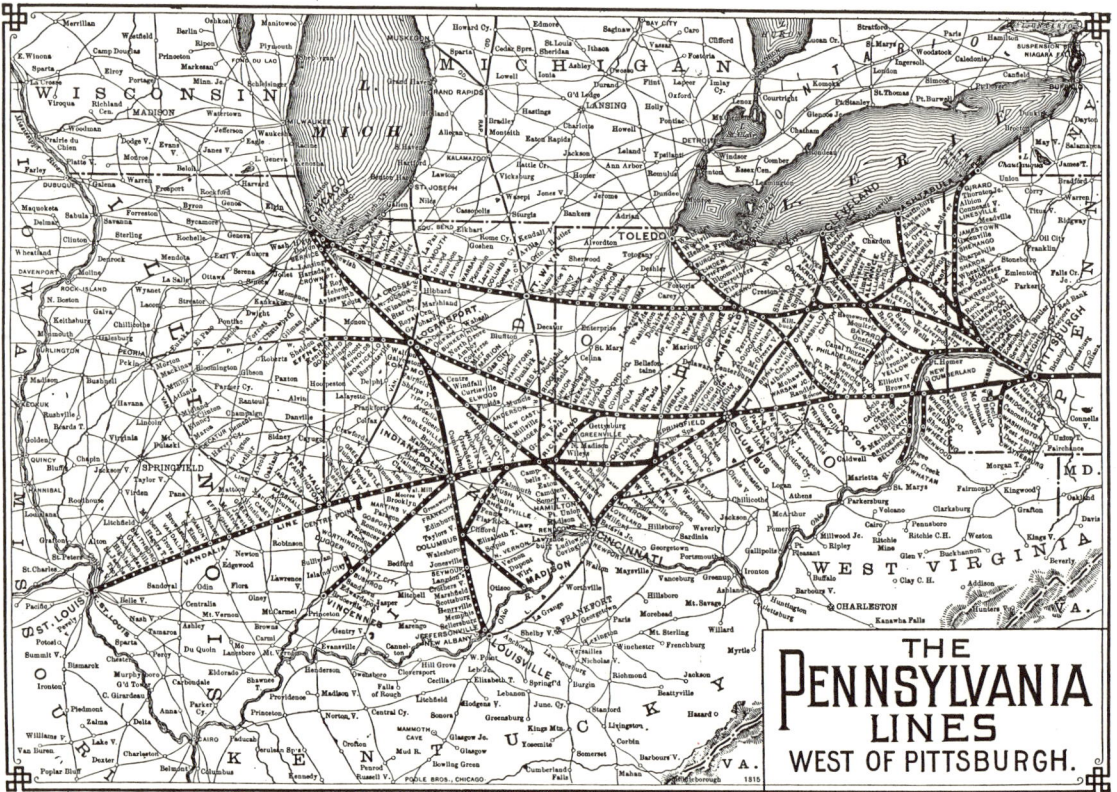

Map from *Traveler's Official Guide*, June 1893.

would never be able to depend on Gould's Wabash as his outlet to the southwest, had acquired control of the Bee Line, removing it from its previous Erie–Atlantic & Great Western affiliation. Then, in the summer of 1882, the Pennsylvania Company agreed to sell its half-interest in the Indianapolis & St. Louis to Vanderbilt's Bee Line. Having assumed by then that the entire Vandalia Line would be theirs, once McKeen got around to completing the transaction, the Lines West organization felt it could finally afford to give up the I&StL. But just to make sure they had something to fall back on, the Pennsylvania men included a clause in their agreement with the Bee Line reserving the right to use the Indianapolis & St. Louis in the future, should the need arise. The nightmare of funding two competing lines to St. Louis had finally ended. With the reorganization of the bankrupt Indiana Central into the Chicago, St. Louis & Pittsburgh in 1883, controlled and staffed by the Pennsylvania Company, the Lines West system adjustments were almost complete.[43]

For McKeen, the return to brutal competition in the mid-1880s only reaffirmed his decision to sell control of the Terre Haute & Indianapolis. Extending the Terre Haute & Logansport to South Bend had resulted in increased business for that line: ton-miles were up 23 percent in 1884 and 53 percent in 1885. But the demoralization of rates and necessary spending for improvements meant continuing losses in the Logansport road's operation.[44]

Poor crops and the business depression of 1884 caused a fall-off in through and local business on the Vandalia Line. Lowered demand closed a number of iron furnaces and mills, in particular those of the St. Louis Ore & Steel Company, resulting in decreased coal tonnage. A three-month miners' strike in the Clay County block coal fields during the spring of 1884 reduced local ton-mileage on the TH&I another 9 percent. And pooling of the coke-carrying business from Pittsburgh diverted additional tonnage.[45]

McKeen's standoff with George Roberts over an examination of the TH&I's books continued into early 1885. Finally, in February, an increasingly impatient McKeen wrote the Pennsylvania's president with a cautiously extended invitation. If it would help facilitate matters, Riley would authorize controlled access to his books so the Pennsylvania could assess the TH&I's financial condition. Roberts forwarded McKeen's letter to the Pennsylvania Company's finance committee of William Thaw, Jacob McCullough, and Thomas Messler, and they in turn received their board's authorization to send Messler to do the examination. Messler, a highly regarded accounting expert, visited Terre Haute early in March 1885 and gave the Terre Haute & Indianapolis a thorough going over. His report, dated March 17, is a detailed and astutely analyzed snapshot of the TH&I and the entire Vandalia Line system.[46]

Messler began by reassuring his colleagues that McKeen had not attempted any deception and that his reluctance to grant access was due to a complete misunderstanding of the Pennsylvania's intentions. He carefully catalogued the Terre Haute & Indianapolis company's considerable strengths, noted its several weaknesses, and tried to soften concerns regarding the Logansport road lease. And then, stressing McKeen's good faith in keeping his verbal commitment to Thomas A. Scott and noting that it would not be in the long-term interests of the Pennsylvania Company to break the Vandalia lease, Messler strongly recommended buying McKeen's stock at the price Riley had named. After all, as Messler put it, "Control of the Terre Haute

The joint Vandalia Line–Big Four depot in Colfax, Indiana, was built in 1880. This postcard view shows the Vandalia side to the left. Collection of Leroy Good, Frankfort, Indiana.

Another postcard view of the "Union Depot" at Colfax, Indiana, at the turn of the 20th century. We are looking northward on the Logansport road. The manual interlocking tower is situated beyond the crossing with the Big Four. Collection of Leroy Good, Frankfort, Indiana.

& Indianapolis Railroad company would be the solution of all our difficulties in connection with the St. Louis, Vandalia & Terre Haute Railroad."[47]

Yet it seemed to George Roberts still not an opportune time to be spending a large sum for McKeen's stock. Earnings for the entire Pennsylvania system were down, thanks to severely depressed rates; the Lines West of Pittsburgh were bleeding profusely. Roberts's contest with Vanderbilt in the West Shore–South Pennsylvania affair was reaching its climax. And the Pennsylvania's management was under increasing pressure from its sizeable contingent of British shareholders. Finally, after receiving a letter from McKeen in late April requesting a reply, Roberts reluctantly formulated an official response, passing it by Thaw and his Lines West officers first.[48]

While the specifics of Roberts's letter were never revealed, the primary reason for McKeen's rejection of this first in a series of Pennsylvania counteroffers was well known to Riley's closest associates. Roberts, probably with strong support from his Lines West management, wanted nothing to do with the Terre Haute & Logansport, which was now an integral part of the TH&I system. Although the Pennsylvania president also may have offered too little for McKeen's TH&I stock, price was negotiable; it was the rejection of the Logansport road which derailed the deal.[49]

Once McKeen had made up his mind to sell, he steadfastly maintained his minimum requirements: a price of at least $75 dollars per share for his TH&I stock— what he had paid Rose for it in 1872—and protection of his investment in the Terre Haute & Logansport. Its lease of the Logansport road gave the Terre Haute & Indianapolis virtual financial control of the Logansport company, not a problem so long as Riley maintained direction of the TH&I. But any change in the TH&I's control would threaten his ownership of the Logansport road. At the time, the Logansport's survival outside of the TH&I system was doubtful. Therefore, as a condition of any sale of his controlling block of stock in the Terre Haute & Indianapolis, McKeen also required either the purchase of his Terre Haute & Logansport stock or a substantially strengthened contract to cover the lease of the Logansport and to limit the TH&I's freedom to increase the line's capital investment. Either way, the Pennsylvania would have to commit itself to a continuing financial responsibility for the Logansport road, and Roberts balked at the prospect.

The Pennsylvania's intractability must have been annoying to Riley. In his view, reinforced by Messler's report, the Logansport road's losses were modest. Most of the funds advanced by the TH&I under the Logansport lease went for material improvements that would eventually reduce operating expenses of the railroad. McKeen felt entirely justified in his position, which led to a frustrating new standoff with the Pennsylvania. Although Roberts revised his offer at least once over the next two years, reputedly increasing the price he was willing to pay for McKeen's TH&I stock to $100 per share, the Pennsylvania president's continued opposition to the inclusion of the Logansport road made it impossible for Riley to accept.[50]

Once again McKeen demonstrated remarkable patience, knowing that ultimately the Pennsylvania must meet his terms if it were to secure complete control of the Vandalia Line. However much he might want to dispose of his interest in the TH&I, and there is much circumstantial evidence to suggest he was now eager to do so, McKeen knew he must bide his time. The company was in good physical and financial condition; Messler's report testified to that.

The Terre Haute & Indianapolis Railroad proper had a well-constructed right-of-way, its main track laid throughout entirely with 60-pound steel rails. It maintained ample terminals at each end of the line and, although not of the most modern design, substantial engine and car shops in its home city of Terre Haute. The company had been gradually upgrading its locomotive roster with heavier and more modern power and kept expanding and improving its supply of car equipment.[51]

Most of the improvements made during the past several years had been charged to expense, which, with the reduction in earnings caused by rate demoralization, had forced the TH&I to accumulate a larger than normal floating or unfunded debt. To help reduce that debt, McKeen had lowered the company's annual dividend rate to 6 percent early in 1885 from the 8 percent rate it had been since the late 1870s. Later that summer, when he began the process of refunding the company's mortgage debt at a lower interest rate, McKeen also arranged to issue an additional $600,000 in new bonds, half of which were sold to eliminate the floating debt entirely.[52]

TH&I No. 25, a typical 52-ton American-type 4-4-0 built in 1884 by the Pittsburgh Locomotive Works. The tender carried about 4½ tons of good Indiana block coal. This builder's photo was part of a collection maintained at what was originally called Rose Polytechnic Institute in Terre Haute, a school founded and endowed by Chauncey Rose to ensure there would be plenty of technically trained young men to work for his railroad. The study of locomotive engines, particularly those of the hometown Vandalia Line, was part of the curriculum. Archives of Rose-Hulman Institute of Technology, Terre Haute.

The TH&I's traffic base was solid. Despite the effects of periodic business downturns, its traffic was increasing. Rate wars kept pressure on earnings and made expense control more critical, but no more so than on the Pennsylvania's lines. Local business, mainly coal traffic, remained the company's earnings strength and provided the greatest margin of prosperity.

Still, although he did not publicize the fact, McKeen clearly had some concerns. Like Roberts, he had to be acutely sensitive to the dangerously low level of freight rates, and even more worried about their lack of stability. McKeen also had to be vigilant in protecting the TH&I's considerable coal traffic, especially since coal mining also contributed heavily to the economic well-being of Terre Haute and other on-line communities. And patient as he was, Riley's forbearance had definite limits. Ironically, the Pennsylvania's Lines West officers were, at that very moment, in the process of testing those limits.

One of the more costly lines included in the Pennsylvania's Lines West system was the Indianapolis & Vincennes, opened in 1869 as the Indiana portion of a line from Indianapolis to Cairo, Illinois. Promoted by former Union Army General (and U.S. Senator from Rhode Island) Ambrose E. Burnside, the line became a pet project of the Pennsylvania's Thomas A. Scott, who saw it as a link to a chain of Pennsylvania-controlled railroads extending from the mouth of the Ohio River to New Orleans. This complicated venture fell apart with the onset of depression in 1873, leaving the Indianapolis & Vincennes an orphan appendage to the Pan Handle. Built through largely undeveloped territory of limited agricultural value and denied the through traffic it was intended to carry, the Vincennes line operated at a constant loss and required regular infusions of increasingly scarce Lines West cash.[53]

What seemed like the solution to the Vincennes line dilemma appeared early in 1884. Approached by a syndicate of businessmen seeking to develop the known coal deposits lying just to the north of the Indianapolis & Vincennes in Greene County, Lines West management agreed to extend a short branch from Bushrod on the main line northwest to a cluster of proposed new coal mines at Island City, just south of present-day Linton. In another agreement with a second coal operator, this branch was later extended to additional mines near Dugger in eastern Sullivan County. By early 1885 the Indianapolis & Vincennes had a new source of potentially heavy traffic, and Lines West had access to a new supply of cheap locomotive coal.[54]

For Riley McKeen, the sudden appearance of a dangerous new competitor in his most important market for coal was bad enough. That the invader was one of his closest allies was intolerable, and one can safely assume that McKeen registered an angry protest with both George Roberts and the Lines West managers.[55]

The industrial development of Indianapolis had been made possible by the easy availability of TH&I coal, and the Indiana capital would continue to be the key market for Clay and Vigo County coal miners. But, inevitably, the introduction of Vincennes line coal from Greene County produced price competition and reduced earnings. The year 1886 saw a 23 percent decrease in coal tonnage and a drop of $53,286 in actual coal traffic earnings. While changes in consumption due to weather and variable business conditions may have contributed to the reduction, the new competition from Vincennes line mines was undoubtedly a major cause.[56]

Nor was Greene County coal off the Indianapolis & Vincennes the only threat to the TH&I's coal business. By 1886 the natural gas boom that had fueled phenomenal industrial development in northwestern Ohio was beginning to move into east-central Indiana, setting off a frenzy of interest all over the state, including Terre Haute. Although gas was never developed as a significant fuel in McKeen's home city, its cheapness and easy availability temporarily concentrated industrial development in gas boom towns like Kokomo and Muncie and tended to restrict the regional growth of coal consumption.[57]

Even controlling his anger over the Pennsylvania's perfidy, McKeen was losing his patience. Besides the assault on his most profitable traffic, he continued to endure cavalier treatment from the Pennsylvania's officers in matters that seriously affected their working relationship. While McKeen voluntarily continued to share his general passenger manager with the Pennsylvania's Lines West and willingly cooperated with the Lines West freight traffic management, he was definitely at a disadvantage when dealing with his eastern ally. Locked in battle with the other trunk lines, the Pennsylvania's competitive responses were naturally self-serving and, insofar as they affected the TH&I, usually delivered to McKeen and his management as a *fait accompli*. Typical of this kind of treatment was the Pennsylvania's unilateral reduction of immigrant passenger rates in January 1885. Reacting to widespread cheating under the passenger pooling agreement among the trunk lines, the Pennsylvania slashed the already low one-way rate charged to immigrants traveling from New York to St. Louis to $1. This made an essentially profitless business an active loser. As Riley pointed out to his stockholders, the TH&I's share on the haul from Indianapolis to St. Louis was reduced to a paltry 17 cents per ticket, and that on traffic which comprised almost 10 percent of the passengers carried on the TH&I that year.[58]

At the end of March 1887, in a move strongly opposed by McKeen and the TH&I, the Trunk Line Association and the Central Traffic Association jointly outlawed the paying of agent's commissions on through passenger tickets. This action was the culmination of a long campaign led by the Pennsylvania, which, with its Lines West subsidiaries, was well represented in both organizations. To the Pennsylvania men it meant the elimination of tariff abuses and ticket scalping; but to McKeen it meant another restriction on his line's ability to do business and threatened to be a drag on income. And through it all, Riley's dissatisfaction and unhappiness as a Pennsylvania Lines partner was mounting.[59]

A Vandalia Line passenger train crosses the flooded Kaskaskia River just east of Vandalia, Illinois, sometime in the late 1880s or early 1890s. Collection of Charles Barenfanger, Vandalia, Illinois.

6

IVES

By the beginning of 1887, it was becoming known outside Terre Haute that McKeen was interested in selling control of the Terre Haute & Indianapolis. Sometime early in the year, he was contacted by Melville E. Ingalls, president of the Cincinnati, Indianapolis, St. Louis & Chicago. Ingalls's Big Four Route depended on the TH&I as its outlet to St. Louis, and, if it was for sale, he was very interested in making an offer. But McKeen rebuffed the inquiry, still intent on honoring his previous commitment to the Pennsylvania. Even so, Riley's patience was wearing thin as George Roberts showed no sign of meeting his terms.[1]

On Saturday morning, May 7, 1887, while McKeen was at work in his office over the bank, Charles H. Rockwell, the general passenger and ticket agent of the Cincinnati, Hamilton & Dayton Railroad dropped by quite unexpectedly. McKeen knew Rockwell through the TH&I's relations with the CH&D and through their mutual attendance at regular Central Traffic Association meetings. But Charlie Rockwell had not come to see him on ordinary business. Instead, he inquired how much McKeen would take for control of the Terre Haute & Indianapolis. Caught off guard, McKeen hesitated, insisting his stock was not for sale. But Rockwell persisted, unaware that Riley held much less than a majority of the TH&I's shares. How much for $1 million worth of the almost $2 million in TH&I stock outstanding? After further prodding, and probably thinking hypothetically, McKeen said he would take $2 million. It was, in his conservative judgement, a fanciful figure, and he probably intended it as a put-off; yet Rockwell was still interested. So McKeen asked him who he represented. The answer was "Henry Ives."[2]

McKeen could hardly have been unacquainted with the name of Henry S. Ives, for the young man was at that very moment attracting quite a bit of attention on Wall Street. Although he was barely 25 years old, Ives had managed to acquire both the title of "Young Napoleon of Finance" and an option on Robert Garrett's controlling block of stock in the Baltimore & Ohio.[3]

Baby-faced, slight of build, and short, but every inch the unscrupulous plunger, Ives had first burst on the scene in June 1885 with a carefully contrived scheme to corner the still-listed stock of a defunct telegraph company. As punishment for his impudence, Ives was banished for a time from the stock exchange, though he was able to operate successfully on the periphery. After forming a partnership in early 1886 with a much older and more experienced broker named George H. Staynor, Ives began his railroad campaign with the capture of the Mineral Range Railroad in upper Michigan. Converting the small line's assets to his own use, Ives pyramided his holdings by going after the prosperous and conservatively run Cincinnati, Hamilton & Dayton. Thus was a pattern developed.[4]

The CH&D was a highly regarded and financially strong midwestern road which extended by ownership and lease from Cincinnati to Toledo and controlled a separate line from Hamilton, Ohio, to Indianapolis. Somehow, Ives had convinced a majority of the CH&D's stockholders, almost all of whom were the cream of Cincinnati's business establishment, to sell him their stock and to finance the purchase as part of the deal. The Cincinnatians' trust and the CH&D's sterling reputation improved Ives's standing overnight, and the railroad's considerable assets provided the young financier with a potent new source of funds. He would need all he could muster, and then some, for his next maneuver.[5]

Sometime early in 1887, Robert Garrett, son of long-time Baltimore & Ohio President John W. Garrett, had reluctantly decided to sell his family's controlling interest in the Baltimore company. The B&O, whose presidency the younger Garrett had inherited upon his father's death in 1884, was a troubled railroad, at odds with its trunkline competitors, poorly maintained, and in financial disarray. The company was burdened with unprofitable telegraph and express subsidiaries and had accumulated a crushing floating debt later reputed to be approximately $10 million. By continuing his father's contentiously independent programs, Garrett had also inherited the bitter antagonism of his competitors, the most dangerous of which was the Pennsylvania. In particular, Garrett's almost fanatical commitment to building a line to New York City ensured open combat with the Pennsylvania and simultaneously produced the potentially fatal floating debt. Weary, ill, and increasingly unstable, Robert Garrett had decided to give it all up.[6]

Early in March 1887, an option on Garrett's 80,000 B&O shares was taken by Alfred Sully, who headed a loosely organized syndicate comprised mainly of the principle investors in the Richmond & West Point Terminal and East Tennessee, Virginia & Georgia railroad systems. News of the affair sent Wall Street into a swoon as investors contemplated the prospects of the combined system. But Sully was unable to mobilize enough resources and, with the rumored opposition to the deal by some of the key members of his syndicate, had to let the option lapse. Immediately, Ives and Staynor stepped into the breech and began negotiations with Garrett. By the end of March, rumors circulated in the newspapers that the parties had an agreement.[7]

Unfortunately for Ives, the B&O would not come cheap, and he did not have the necessary funds. But the young man was nothing if not bold. While continuing to procure extensions on his option from Garrett, Ives set about to improve his bargaining position by focussing on two of the B&O's most glaring deficiencies.[8]

The Baltimore & Ohio was being thwarted in its attempt to enter the New York City terminal district by the power and superior position of the Pennsylvania Railroad. At the same time, the company was suffering from its loss of control over the Ohio & Mississippi, the B&O's connection from Cincinnati to St. Louis. The scheme that began to take shape in Ives's fertile mind had the potential to correct both problems and make his offer more desirable to the younger Garrett, who continued to think of the B&O as a monument to his dead father.

Rockwell and McKeen parted amicably after their discussion on May 7. Whether

Riley gave their conversation much additional thought is unknown. He had turned down several offers already, always honoring his verbal agreement with the Pennsylvania's Thomas Scott made back in 1879. On the other hand, McKeen may also have begun to think he had already fulfilled the terms of that agreement. His fidelity had certainly gained him nothing so far. But there was more than money at stake. Terre Haute, for which McKeen had a strong sense of *noblesse oblige,* still depended heavily on the TH&I's presence, both as a large employer and as a strategic commercial weapon. It would not do to lose either advantage. And it would certainly not be acceptable to do anything which would weaken the railroad that was Terre Haute's pride and crowning achievement.

Charlie Rockwell returned for another unannounced visit the following Tuesday morning, May 10, greeting McKeen with the news that Ives had accepted his price. Perhaps intrigued by the course of events, and never having met the man before, Riley agreed to see Ives that afternoon.[9]

Riley must have been surprised by Ives's unimpressive appearance. Small, pale, and somewhat fragile looking, possessed of boyish features poorly disguised by thick sideburns and wire-rimmed glasses, Ives looked like anything but a fearless financial titan. Rockwell introduced them and retired, leaving them alone to discuss Ives's proposal. Still not convinced he should make such a deal, McKeen listened politely but made no commitment. Riley was particularly bothered by the fact that Ives had not made a thorough investigation of the TH&I, and he suggested that the young man should know more about the condition of his road and the details of its various leases and agreements before making an offer. In any event, he told Ives as they concluded their meeting, he would make no agreement whatsoever without consulting his counsel, John Williams, who happened to be away on business.[10]

This woodcut illustration from *Harper's Weekly* is the only known picture of Henry S. Ives. The substance of his brief and scandalous career earned him scorn from his Wall Street colleagues and guaranteed historical obscurity. Ives constantly endured the undisguised enmity of his Stock Exchange colleagues—which sometimes took the humorous form of sarcastic schoolboy taunts published blindly in the personals section of contemporary business journals—and died tragically young of tuberculosis on April 17, 1894. *Harper's Weekly* 31 (August 27, 1887): 620.

A youthful John G. Williams, Riley's lawyer and his right-hand man from 1879 onward. This picture must have been taken shortly after Williams arrived in Terre Haute in 1869. He married a Terre Haute girl, Florence Turner, whose sister was married to George Farrington, scion of another influential local family and general agent for the TH&I. Williams moved to Indianapolis following his term as TH&I general manager, then served as the new Vandalia Railroad's general counsel until his retirement in 1916. A son, David Percy Williams, also a lawyer, followed his father into the Pennsylvania's legal department. Community Archives, Vigo County Public Library, Terre Haute.

Throughout his career, Riley McKeen displayed a remarkable talent for selecting skilled associates and employees. Usually a keen judge of character and ability, Riley always surrounded himself with outstanding people. Nowhere was this more evident than in his choice of John G. Williams as both his own personal lawyer and general counsel of the TH&I.

Williams, born in 1849 on his father's Mississippi plantation, studied law in Natchez and moved to Terre Haute in 1869, where he joined a well-connected local law firm. He married into one of Terre Haute's leading families and became associated with the city's business elite, including Riley McKeen, who made him the TH&I's chief counsel when Richard Thompson resigned to become Navy Secretary in April 1877. Spare-built, urbane, and reserved, Williams had an agile mind and a precise tongue and proved to be an excellent litigator and administrator. McKeen had come to trust him implicitly and relied on his judgement and legal guidance. Riley would need Williams even more in the months ahead, for he was about to make the worst mistake of his career.[11]

After exchanging telegrams, McKeen met with Ives at the Denison Hotel in Indianapolis on Monday, May 16, and the negotiations continued. This time Riley had John Williams at his side, and he let his lawyer do much of the talking. Williams explained to Ives that there were a couple of obstacles to the plan as the young financier had envisioned it. First, McKeen did not own 20,000 shares of Terre Haute & Indianapolis—the $1 million worth in $50 par value per share stock—nor was he willing to try to buy the necessary additional shares on the open market to meet that amount of stock. And second, both he and McKeen had a substantial investment in the Terre Haute & Logansport, which would have to be protected by either modifying or canceling the TH&I's lease or by having their Logansport stock included in the purchase.[12]

Somehow, in explaining the distribution of TH&I stock and how much of it actually provided control, McKeen and Williams mentioned the company's treasury stock—the 8,840 shares it had bought back beginning in 1867. This fact registered quickly with Ives, but he said nothing and continued to ask a few more questions about the Logansport road.

Williams and McKeen tried to explain how the current setup gave the TH&I complete freedom to spend the Terre Haute & Logansport's money on improvements and rolling stock, too much freedom for the Logansport road's stockholders. Ives understood the problem and inquired about the Logansport road's condition. He asked how much they thought the Logansport stock was worth, and Williams suggested 75 cents on the dollar. Then Ives returned to the subject of the TH&I stock. Was McKeen absolutely sure he could not come up with the full 20,000 shares; and if not, what about using the company's treasury stock? The question took McKeen by surprise, and he responded with severity, insisting that the treasury stock belonged to the company as invested surplus and was not his to handle. Momentarily chastened, Ives quickly moved on, asking Riley what he thought the treasury stock was worth, to which McKeen hesitantly responded, about $1.25 on the dollar, considering the number of shares involved. In the custom of the times, blocks of stock varied in price, the value increasing with the weight of the block's voting influence.

Henry Ives then lapsed into thoughtful silence. After making a few quick computations with pencil and paper, he showed Riley the sheet, pointing to two figures and asking him if he would be willing to furnish "this much stock for this much money?" Riley stared at the paper for a moment, then handed it to Williams. The figures were 11,160 shares for $1,447,500. It was a critical moment. Williams could not help but notice that the number of shares was precisely 8,840 short of the full 20,000 Ives wanted to buy—the exact number of TH&I shares held in the company's treasury. After Williams passed the paper back, McKeen looked at it again and nodded, finally answering that he could. When Ives inquired as to the terms, Riley replied that he expected cash. The younger man chuckled and said that his people in New York would be surprised to have that much drawn out all in cash. And on that pleasant note, the meeting ended, with Ives indicating that he would consult with his associates and get back to McKeen for the final arrangements.

McKeen and Williams left for Terre Haute believing everything was still up in the air, with no date set for another meeting. In the course of their brief conference, it appeared that Riley had agreed in principle to sell a specific number of TH&I shares at a specified price, but nothing had been decided about the disposition of the Terre Haute & Logansport, and no financial arrangements had been made.

It is difficult to determine McKeen's reasoning for such an astonishing change in position, especially considering the number and nature of his previous refusals to sell. Furthermore, in the light of subsequent events, McKeen's willingness now to sell to Ives seems incredible. But from McKeen's perspective, there were plausible reasons to proceed.

For one thing, whatever Ives's reputation on Wall Street, the managers and former owners of the Cincinnati, Hamilton & Dayton obviously had enough confidence in the young financier to entrust him with their railroad. The CH&D was, like McKeen's own TH&I, a well-run and profitable enterprise. The two companies complemented each other, both physically and from a traffic standpoint. And if Ives was successful in securing control of the Baltimore & Ohio, as it then appeared he would be, the TH&I would not only continue to be a part of a major trunkline system, but, by virtue of its binding contracts with the Pennsylvania Lines, would actually be an important part of two. As for his longstanding verbal agreement to sell to the Pennsylvania, McKeen must have decided he had done all he could to fulfill his promise to Thomas A. Scott. In the face of continued temporizing by Roberts, and the active and—in McKeen's view—hostile opposition of the Pennsylvania's Lines West management, Riley's conscience was clear. Because of the absolute importance of his railroad to Terre Haute, the transaction could never be a vengeful act, but it could be and was a declaration of independence.

Greenville, Illinois, in a late-19th-century postcard view taken from atop the railroad's water tower. The town's waterworks is at right. The classic Vandalia-styled depot was built in 1884 to replace an earlier two-story station which had burned. Collection of the Bond County Historical Society, Greenville, Illinois.

For Henry S. Ives, the transaction would be a coup of monumental proportions, *if* he could bring it off. The young financier spent the next few days in a feverish attempt to round up the necessary money. Time was of the essence if he were to steal this march on the mighty Pennsylvania; he needed to close the deal quickly. Meanwhile, Ives continued his negotiations with Robert Garrett for control of the B&O, which required even more in the way of fund-raising.

The pressure on Ives suddenly intensified on May 18, when *The Indianapolis Journal* picked up and published the rumor that Ives was interested in buying the Terre Haute & Indianapolis. The *Terre Haute Evening Gazette* reprinted the story but also scoffed that the Ives syndicate had surely "met with but little encouragement." Nevertheless, Ives had to shift his efforts into high gear, and so telegraphed McKeen on May 19 that he had the money ready. It was a lie. Because of the ongoing B&O drama, it was obvious that the cash for control of the TH&I would have to come from the Cincinnati, Hamilton & Dayton itself. Frantically, Ives next telegraphed Christopher Waite, general manager of the CH&D, insisting he find the necessary cash and adding, "After seeing article in paper did not dare wait any longer for fear of the enemy catching on, so I wired our party that I had all the money ready and asking [sic] him to let me know when he could deliver the stock." Meanwhile, McKeen telegraphed back that he could probably deliver around June 1. It was clear that, pending satisfactory financial arrangements, Riley McKeen had made up his mind.[13]

Even though the Pennsylvania—"the enemy," as far as Ives was concerned—remained unawares, the young financier was having great difficulty in securing the needed funds. Telegrams flew back and forth between New York and Cincinnati, from Ives to his financial people at the CH&D, and to a number of investors now interested in his apparently successful operations. In desperation, Charlie Rockwell was dispatched to Terre Haute later in the week to sound out banker McKeen on providing some of the money himself, hopefully something like $500,000 in the form of a loan. While he made no commitment, Riley must have at least entertained the idea.[14]

At a called board meeting on Monday, May 30, the directors of the Cincinnati, Hamilton & Dayton authorized Henry Ives to purchase 20,000 shares of Terre Haute & Indianapolis stock for $2 million. To pay for it, they also directed Ives to sell their company's stock interest in a leased line, the Dayton & Michigan. Now fortified with the necessary funds, Ives was at last ready to close the deal. Once more, Charlie Rockwell played the role of herald, traveling to Terre Haute to see McKeen on Tuesday and arrange for a meeting with Ives the next day.[15]

Eager now to complete the deal, Ives also traveled to Terre Haute and met with McKeen on Wednesday morning, June 1. He brought with him members of the CH&D's top management, Christopher Waite and William Ramsay, the CH&D's general counsel. The ubiquitous Charlie Rockwell was also in attendance. Once again, John Williams was at McKeen's side. While Ives and McKeen sat down to negotiate in Riley's office suite over the bank, Williams took Ramsay down the hall to his own office, where the two lawyers reviewed the various legal agreements made by the TH&I, in particular the lease of the St. Louis, Vandalia & Terre Haute and the operating contracts with the Pennsylvania. They were called back to Riley's conference room after he and Ives had come to an agreement.[16]

As previously decided, McKeen would sell 11,160 shares of Terre Haute & Indianapolis stock for a total of $1,447,500. In addition, Ives had agreed to purchase the bulk of McKeen's stock in the Terre Haute & Logansport at 50 cents on the dollar, or $25 per share. The 4,446 shares of Logansport stock came to an additional $111,150 and made the entire transaction worth a grand total of $1,558,650. Upon inquiry by Ives, Williams agreed to take the same price for his 1,535 shares of Logansport stock.

In an obvious hurry, Ives merely wanted the two legal counselors to witness an oral summation of the agreement and objected when Williams wanted to write it all down; but Williams insisted that there be a written contract. And so, with Ramsay's help, Riley's lawyer John Williams transformed the terms into a binding legal document to protect his employer and friend.

Since McKeen had agreed to deliver only 8,560 shares of TH&I up front, he had to go into the market to buy 2,600 additional shares to fulfill the agreement. The contract gave him 30 days to do so. At Williams's suggestion, a clause was added for Riley's protection, preventing the Ives party from buying any stock during the period. Once Williams's pencil draft of the contract had been corrected, Ives and McKeen signed it. As an afterthought, Ramsay decided his party should also have a copy, and Waite dictated the agreement over to Rockwell.

To pay for it, Ives had agreed to produce $250,000 cash now and another $639,500 on June 4, when McKeen delivered the first 8,560 shares of TH&I stock and all 4,446 shares of Logansport stock. Riley had agreed to extend credit for the balance, accepting Ives's six month note for $669,150 at 6 percent interest. As collateral, Riley would continue to hold all the stock included in their transaction.

Ominously, before Ives and McKeen had signed the draft, a telegram arrived for McKeen from Jacob McCullough of the Pennsylvania Lines. The newspaper report on the proposed sale had finally reached the Pennsylvania's executives, and McCullough wanted to know if it was true. Riley's response, carefully worded and approved by both his party and Ives's, was thoroughly deceptive and misleading. Though the agreement was about to be signed, the actual transaction technically would not be completed for several days, so Riley telegraphed McCullough that "no trade had yet been consummated." And then, signing the agreement, the actual deed was done.

Before the meeting concluded, Ramsay took John Williams aside and told him that, before any changes were made in the TH&I board, he wanted the old board to pass a resolution directing the president of the company to sell the 8,840 shares of TH&I stock held in the treasury. Williams abruptly refused and protested indignantly. Such an action was improper, and he would not consent to such a resolution by the old board. Ramsay retreated, and after handshakes all around, the Ives party returned to Cincinnati in an exultant mood. Arrangements had been made to meet again for the formal transfer of control that Saturday, June 4.

If Riley McKeen had any further thoughts or misgivings in the matter, it was too late now. He was honor-bound as a businessman to go through with the deal. Over the next few days, he had to round up some additional stock. He really only controlled directly 7,587 shares of TH&I: 6,000 shares in his own name, with an additional 1,526 shares owned by the bank and 41 shares owned by his sister Ella. The remaining 973 shares needed by Saturday came from other relatives and friends who left their stock in Riley's care and who only wanted to sell if he did.[17]

The presence of Ives's CH&D business car on a siding at the Terre Haute depot was not overlooked by the Terre Haute newspapers, which had a field day handling the rumors. The Wednesday *Evening Gazette* headlined the front page with a story noting Ives's arrival the previous night and reprinted parts of a *Cincinnati Enquirer* story that insisted the sale was a fact. The *Gazette* editors doubted bravely, echoing the general hope of Terre Hauteans that the story could not be true, and solemnly pronouncing it a calamity if it proved to be otherwise. As disingenuous with the public as he had been with McCullough, McKeen had been quoted earlier in the day as denying he had sold the company for the amount rumored, whereupon he refused further comment.[18]

The rumors intensified on Thursday. The *Gazette* printed an Indianapolis dispatch that quoted Ives and Waite the previous night denying that they had closed the deal but admitting that negotiations were continuing. By Friday morning, however, all doubt had evaporated. Headlines bannered "The Vandalia Sale," and the papers were bulging with as much detail as could be had unofficially. The transfer was announced for the next day. There were dispatches and reprinted stories from newspapers in Cincinnati, Indianapolis, and Chicago. Putting the best face on what was generally viewed as bad news, the editors tried to explain McKeen's reasons for selling to Ives and the CH&D, with plenty of emphasis on Riley's rumored disenchantment with the Pennsylvania people. Of course, it was no mere rumor.[19]

The Cincinnati, Hamilton & Dayton contingent returned to Terre Haute on Friday night. With Ives this time were CH&D General Manager Christopher C. Waite; General Counsel William Ramsay; Corporate Secretary-Treasurer Frederick H. Short; and CH&D Director William Proctor of Cincinnati. On Saturday morning, June 4, 1887, the CH&D party met with McKeen and Williams in Riley's office at the bank to perform the official transfer. The drafts for cash were paid to McKeen and Ives's note for the balance signed and given. McKeen signed over the first 8,560 shares of TH&I to Ives as trustee, plus the Logansport stock, then transferred one share each to Ives, Waite, Ramsay, and Short, plus the absent George H. Stayner and Christopher Meyer, to qualify them as company directors.[20]

Once more William Ramsay approached John Williams and renewed his request for a resolution by the old board directing the sale of the TH&I treasury stock. Again Williams objected. This time, however, Ramsay persisted, and the infuriated Williams responded in some heat. He would not ask any director of the company to do something he himself would not do; and he, Williams said grimly, would never vote for any such resolution. It was becoming apparent that, even if Riley McKeen had no problem with the proceedings, his friend and counsel John Williams did.[21]

The two parties were now joined by the old board members: besides McKeen and Williams, Riley's brother-in-law Frank Crawford; McKeen's friend and former partner Deloss Minshall; and the secretary of the company, George Farrington, were present. Two additional directors were absent: Josephus Collett and Henry Ross.

The board meeting was called to order with Riley in the chair. John Williams quickly introduced the resolution instituting a new company bylaw empowering the board to elect replacement directors to fill vacancies. Then McKeen as president reported on and received approval for a lease contract he had made with the Evansville & Indianapolis Railroad for joint use of the TH&I's Brazil to Saline City branch. Then, after taking a breath, the board moved on to the minuet of reorganization.[22]

McKeen presented the written resignation of Henry Ross as director, which was accepted. To replace him, Frederick H. Short of the CH&D was nominated and elected. Williams immediately followed with his own resignation, but Short interrupted the process by motioning that the president be authorized to sell the company's 8,840 shares of treasury stock to Henry S. Ives at a price of $62.50 per share.

The resolution took the old board members by complete surprise and filled them with some consternation. Minshall quickly petitioned for a delay in the proceedings and, in some agitation, dragged John Williams across the room for a quick consultation. Why such a resolution, he wanted to know, and would he be personally responsible if he voted for it? What was going on here? In disgust, Williams suggested Minshall consult Ramsay instead and called the CH&D lawyer over to them. Minshall repeated his question, and Ramsay tried to sooth him with assurances that no such responsibility would be his if he voted for the resolution. If the resolution were passed by the new board, he blandly observed, it would look too much like they were selling the stock to themselves. Reluctantly, Minshall returned to the table, and the resolution was passed.[23]

The dreary transfer of power continued. Ramsay replaced John Williams as director, Waite replaced Frank Crawford, Minshall was succeeded by Ives, and George Farrington was replaced by the absent Christopher Meyer, a wealthy but naïve young German who was one of Henry Ives's most faithful financial backers.

To complete the reorganization, Farrington and John W. Cruft resigned their positions as secretary and treasurer, respectively, and Frederick H. Short assumed both jobs. A new position of vice president and general manager was created, and Christopher Waite was elected to it. And, finally, the positions of assistant secretary and assistant treasurer were created for Farrington and Cruft, new titles for what would essentially be the same responsibilities.

Now it was Riley's turn, and, perhaps with a trace of sadness, he resigned the presidency in favor of Ives. Ramsay took time for a brief eulogy, and then Henry Ives took the chair. The new order had begun. In a final bit of business, almost as an afterthought just prior to adjournment, Short moved that Henry Ives & Company be appointed as fiscal agents for the Terre Haute & Indianapolis. And in that one stroke, the company's future was forever altered and its fate sealed.

The Saturday newspapers trumpeted the formal transfer of ownership. There were but few details left to add, the biggest news having been delivered the day before. In fact, over the next few days the mood of the papers, and probably the city at large, was one of mute resignation, the coverage of Ives and the new CH&D ownership terse and restrained. Riley McKeen remained largely out of sight and mind and would spend a great deal of the summer ahead out of town, presumably most of it on vacation. The only drama left to savor was the ongoing negotiations between Ives and Garrett for the B&O and the speculation over just what the Pennsylvania would now do.[24]

There were already rumblings from over the horizon. Rumors cropped up almost immediately that the Pennsylvania people would, like a cuckolded suitor, strike back at their earliest opportunity. From an Indianapolis paper came the not-so-fantastic story that the Pennsylvania would withdraw all St. Louis traffic from the Vandalia Line, an assertion which was promptly denied by James McCrea, general manager of the Pan Handle. Ives's partner George H. Stayner, meanwhile, was quoted from Baltimore—where he was conferring with Robert Garrett—as smugly saying that the B&O had gotten the best of the Pennsylvania through the TH&I deal. And Garrett was impressed enough by Ives's triumph to postpone his trip to Europe and grant yet another extension on the young man's B&O stock option.[25]

The speculation over the Pennsylvania's response was warranted. While its top officials tried to maintain a calm and disarming lack of concern publicly, inside the company seethed with outrage, especially the maligned Lines West organization. McKeen had betrayed them with Judas-like audacity. Now they would rise up and smite this new interloper.

The company Henry Ives had bought was in a prosperous condition. The Terre Haute & Indianapolis was conservatively capitalized, with slightly less than $2 million in stock and $1.9 million in issued bonds (out of a total of $2.2 million authorized). It owned almost $1 million in securities, or at least had owned that amount.

A Pittsburgh Mogul type (2-6-0) bears down on the photographer with a long freight train. Collection of the Vigo County Historical Society, Terre Haute.

The TH&I treasury stock, which the new board had just sold to Ives, had accounted for about two-thirds of the total securities owned, the rest being mainly stock and bonds of the St. Louis, Vandalia & Terre Haute. Most impressive of all, the company maintained a cash surplus of almost $1 million. Together, these assets were a treasure chest and a temptation young Henry Ives would find impossible to resist.[26]

It didn't hurt that 1887 was shaping up to be one of the best years on record. Freight tonnage rose 16.6 percent on the TH&I and 21.5 percent on the St. Louis, Vandalia & Terre Haute. Even the Logansport road reported a 7 percent gain. Most of the increase was accounted for by through business, with tonnage in that category up a whopping 30.7 percent on the TH&I and an even bigger 34 percent on the leased Vandalia road.[27]

It was not just the TH&I which benefited. The country's business was active, spurred not a little by explosive growth in the railroad network. The year 1887 would see the greatest expansion of railroad mileage yet recorded, heating up the demand for steel rails and building material. Coupled with greatly increased expenditures for new equipment and betterments to existing rail lines, railroad spending pumped up industrial activity to maximum, simultaneously creating a heavy flow of railroad traffic. In the latter half of the 19th century, the U.S. economy rose and fell on the strength of the nation's rail carriers.[28]

Under this heavy tide of traffic, over-capacity practically vanished, and rates were almost universally maintained. The Pennsylvania profited mightily as a result, its through tonnage having increased 12.2 percent on Lines West and nearly 17 percent on the parent line east of Pittsburgh.[29]

On the TH&I, the traffic relationship with the Pennsylvania Lines continued as usual. But there were other changes. Under CH&D supervision, the TH&I terminated its traffic agreement with the Cincinnati, Indianapolis, St. Louis & Chicago Railroad, abruptly ending a relationship that dated back to the Indianapolis & Cincinnati loan in the early 1860s. Denied its traditional outlet to St. Louis, Ingalls's Big Four turned to the Bee Line–owned Indianapolis & St. Louis, a partnership which would quickly blossom into a merger with the Vanderbilt interests, creating the Cleveland, Cincinnati, Chicago & St. Louis in 1889. The traffic thus lost to the TH&I was more than made up by greatly increased interchange business with the CH&D lines at Indianapolis. There were new through-car passenger trains between St. Louis and Cincinnati and, under CH&D auspices, talk of through passenger service from St. Louis to Detroit, operated jointly with the Wabash via Logansport.[30]

To the general public, it looked like the TH&I sale had turned out to be a good thing; but inside, at the heart of the company, the view was much different. With the appointment of his banking firm as the company's fiscal agent, Henry Ives had immediate access to the TH&I's considerable wealth, and he did not waste any time in putting it to his own use. The 8,840 shares of TH&I treasury stock sold to him by the board were transferred to New York, a draft from Ives's firm for $552,500 taking its place in the company coffers. Likewise, the cash on hand of almost $1.5 million was transferred to Ives's bank. Unfortunately, no one was paying any attention.[31]

Riley McKeen quickly settled into his most enjoyable role: Terre Haute's friendly banker. Never one much enamored of traveling, for business or pleasure, McKeen now had even more time to spend at home, entertaining friends and family. He had remarried in September 1883, just two years after Ann Crawford McKeen's untimely death. It was a comfortable match with Sarah Dowling, the beautiful widow of a close friend. Sarah's late husband Thomas had been the proprietor of one of Terre Haute's daily newspapers and had been an active Methodist churchman with Riley. In fact, given their friendship and positions, it is entirely likely that the two families were well acquainted and that Ann and Sarah had been equally friendly. The new McKeens exhibited a quaintly Victorian domesticity as they left town on their honeymoon tour in Riley's private railroad car, for they were also accompanied by Sarah's daughter Lizzie and Ann's youngest, Edith.[32]

McKeen's bank occupies an important corner at Sixth and Wabash in downtown Terre Haute. The building was constructed in 1875 by Riley and his friend and partner Deloss Minshall. This 1880s view also shows the adjoining block and the street railway horsecar with its Rose Polytechnic Institute advertisement. Community Archives, Vigo County Public Library, Terre Haute.

Now that McKeen was merely a company director, he was largely divorced from the railroad and took time off in July for a long fishing trip. He completed the acquisition of the last 2,600 shares necessary to fulfill his contract with Ives, making the transfer on June 13. Other than a brief and perfunctory board meeting in Terre Haute on June 25, called in haste by General Manager Waite to grant endorsement authority to the assistant treasurer, McKeen had no contact with the TH&I organization. He had no knowledge of the flight of cash and securities, except for its logical transfer from his to another trustee bank. And he was unaware of the storm brewing in Pittsburgh.[33]

7

THE CRASH

The Pennsylvania's Lines West organization moved with stealth and speed. The first order of business was to mount an offensive against the Terre Haute & Indianapolis, and to that end, the 1879 plan to break the Vandalia lease was dusted off, updated, and set in motion.

Within days of the June 4 TH&I sale to Ives, George B. Roberts was in Pittsburgh to consult with his Lines West executive corps. They all headed west together on Tuesday, June 7: Roberts, Jacob McCullough, General Manager James McCrea, and the Lines West general counsel, Joshua Twing Brooks. Wednesday was spent in conference with their hired counsel in Indianapolis, Judge Lyman Trumbull of Trumbull, Robbins & Trumbull and John M. Butler of Butler, McDonald & Mason. Judge Trumbull had the complaint ready by the end of the month.[1]

The first salvo was fired on Wednesday, July 6, 1887, when the Pennsylvania-controlled St. Louis, Vandalia & Terre Haute filed suit for vacation of its lease to the Terre Haute & Indianapolis. On Thursday, July 7, a deputy U.S. Marshall appeared at the TH&I offices in East St. Louis, Illinois. There a subpoena was served on a bewildered company cashier, F. W. Bland, requiring the TH&I to make an appearance at the U.S. Circuit Court for the District of Southern Illinois at Springfield.[2]

The Pennsylvania Lines's complaint was multi-faceted and maintained that the lease of the Vandalia to the Terre Haute & Indianapolis was nothing short of illegal. By the terms of the Illinois law in force at the time—in 1868, when the lease was executed—all Vandalia company stockholders who were Illinois residents had to personally approve any lease in writing. The Pennsylvania's lawyers now produced a list of 58 such stockholders who had sworn they had not approved the lease in question, rendering it void. The suit also contended that the TH&I was without power under its charter to accept the lease. Finally, it complained that the TH&I had withheld profits due the Vandalia company according to the agreement—which, in fact, it had, because the conflict with the Pan Handle over the Indiana Central's unfulfilled commitment was ongoing. Therefore, the Pennsylvania's lawyers asked the court to invalidate the lease, force the TH&I to surrender the Vandalia, and order an accounting of what was really owed to whom under the terms of the contract.[3]

But that was not all. Pennsylvania money had built the St. Louis, Vandalia & Terre Haute. The Pennsylvania and its subsidiaries owned most of its stock. It was theirs, and they wanted it back. So their first motion in the case was for the appointment of a receiver, in order to get the railroad out of the TH&I's hands immediately.[4]

The Cincinnati, Hamilton & Dayton forces swung right into action. Receivership of the Vandalia would amputate their new acquisition at the knees. Responsibility for the defense rested with CH&D General Counsel William Ramsay and a hired lawyer, former Ohio Governor George Hoadley; but they knew enough to call in their brightest legal light, TH&I Counsel John G. Williams.

Whatever his feelings might have been concerning Ives and the CH&D's steward-ship of the Terre Haute & Indianapolis, John Williams was not about to abandon the Terre Haute road now. Rushing back from a visit down south, Williams accepted leadership of the company's team of lawyers and started gathering legal bullets.[5]

The proceedings began in Springfield, Illinois, on July 14 with hearings on the appointment of a receiver before Circuit Judge Walter Quinton Gresham, the same judge who had opposed the TH&I's striking workers a decade earlier and a fellow Indiana Republican and political acquaintance of Riley McKeen. Argument contin-ued the following day, then the court recessed so Gresham could deliberate. The Pennsylvania forces contended that receivership was necessary to protect their prop-erty; but the defense had an easy time demonstrating the obvious solvency of the TH&I and, therefore, the complete lack of danger to the Vandalia road. Thus im-pressed, Judge Gresham denied the motion for a receiver on Friday, July 16, and set the date for opening arguments in the suit in October. The TH&I had cleared its first hurdle. Now the question was: Would Henry Ives clear his?[6]

For Henry S. Ives, capture of the Terre Haute & Indianapolis would prove to be the high-water mark of his meteoric financial career, yet it had been intended only as a sideshow. The real goal was acquisition of the Baltimore & Ohio, for which the young financier had risked all. Only with the B&O safely in hand could Ives have considered the rest of his program a success.

Robert Garrett had been momentarily impressed by Ives's audacious moves in snatching the Vandalia Line from under the Pennsylvania's nose. In his paranoia, Garrett blamed the hated Pennsylvania for many of his troubles. But he was lucid enough to see that Ives did not have the wherewithal to exercise the option on his B&O shares.

Ives labored mightily to raise the needed funds. He had come up with $2 million in earnest money by hypothecating assets from the CH&D's treasury and illegally issuing CH&D stock, but Garrett wanted nearly $16 million for his B&O shares, far more than Ives could possibly raise on his own. So, while Garrett continued to extend the deadline, Ives went to see Jay Gould. Hoping that Gould would want the B&O's telegraph subsidiary for his own Western Union, Ives tried to entice him with an offer to sell it for $3.5 million. But the wily Gould knew a pigeon when he saw one. Convinced Ives could never deliver on the deal, Gould showed him the door.[7]

Desperate to keep the B&O deal alive, Ives decided to raid the Terre Haute & Indianapolis treasury and called the company's New York directors together for a board meeting on July 1. He needed their technical approval to sell the remaining $300,000 in unissued TH&I mortgage bonds, which, under McKeen, had been held in reserve to refund maturing obligations. The other directors present—Christopher Waite, Frederick Short, and Christopher Meyer—willingly complied, unaware that Ives had already disposed of the securities the previous day. While they were at it, Ives asked for authority to sell the company's other securities as well, namely the

$100,000 in St. Louis, Vandalia & Terre Haute bonds and $50,000 worth of American Bottom, Lime, Marble & Coal Company bonds, effectively cleaning out the TH&I cupboard. But this was too much for CH&D's conscientious General Manager Christopher Waite to accept, and he voted no in protest.[8]

Time was running out for Ives, even as the Pennsylvania opened fire on the TH&I. Simultaneously with its move to break the Vandalia lease, the Pennsylvania's top management began to tighten the noose on Henry Ives & Company. Mysterious pressure soon was applied to Ives's lenders, and further credit became impossible to get. After circulating rumors on the street that Ives's deal with Garrett was dead, the bears launched a July 13 raid on Cincinnati, Hamilton & Dayton stock, the majority of whose shares were in Ives's name but pledged as collateral on loans placed all over town. Scraping additional security together by hypothecating every asset he could lay his hands on—including the TH&I's treasury stock—Ives managed to weather the storm, but his financial situation was in critical condition.[9]

Garrett knocked the shaky props out from under Henry Ives barely one week later. In a letter dated July 20, printed in a Philadelphia newspaper, Garrett declared the negotiations at an absolute end and dealt Ives a death blow by announcing the reason why: The young man could not come up with the cash. Garrett managed to cripple him further by refusing to return the $2 million down payment. The fatally wounded Ives syndicate countered with a suit to regain its money, but it was too late. Garrett sailed off to Europe, and Ives headed for bankruptcy.[10]

All the attention in the press had finally awakened the innocents, particularly the Cincinnati, Hamilton & Dayton's minority stockholders. With rumors and innuendo flying around concerning Ives's financial condition, not to mention his questionable methods, some CH&D shareholders now became alarmed.[11]

The Cincinnati, Hamilton & Dayton Railroad was as highly regarded in its home town of Cincinnati as the Terre Haute & Indianapolis was in Terre Haute. It was the object of much civic and commercial pride, a crown jewel and a pillar of financial strength. The idea that it had been raped and pillaged as some now suggested was worrisome, to say the least, particularly for those who had not disposed of its stock.

By the end of July, enough disaffected stockholders had come out of the woodwork to begin putting together an opposition faction. The movement to oust Henry Ives and his partner, CH&D President George Stayner, began in earnest on August 1. With a called shareholders meeting scheduled for Saturday, August 6, the minority stockholders met the day before and appointed to represent them a committee consisting of three local Cincinnati businessmen: Julius Dexter, Thomas J. Emery, and Gazzam Gano. When Ives and Stayner called the company meeting to order early Saturday afternoon, they faced an angry contingent insistent on answers to some pretty brutal questions. Overwhelmed by the hostility and unwilling to come clean, Ives stalled by maintaining that the books were still in New York, quite unfortunately beyond his reach. But if they were here, he assured them, wishing that he could allay their fears, he could easily demonstrate just how satisfactory his administration had been.[12]

Unfortunately for Ives, the minority stockholders were not about to be put off so easily. They had seen how the market had battered their stock and had heard the rumors of Ives's imminent collapse. Now they were thoroughly alarmed. It was decided that the committee of Dexter, Emery, and Gano would accompany Ives back to New York so that the books could be examined and the CH&D's condition properly assessed. Without taking any further action, the meeting was then adjourned.

Pretty as a picture: TH&I No. 121 with crew in an unidentified location sometime during the 1880s. The clean-lined, cap-stacked American type was turned out by the Pittsburgh Locomotive Works in 1884. The TH&I—and successor Vandalia Railroad—favored the Pittsburgh builder and the Schenectady Locomotive Works. Both would become components of the American Locomotive Company (Alco). Collection of the Vigo County Historical Society, Terre Haute.

Before the CH&D meeting early that Saturday morning, the CH&D executive committee had sent an urgent telegram to Riley McKeen, summoning him to Cincinnati. Whether the local management of the railroad was now making common cause with the minority stockholders or simply acting at their request, it was deemed crucial to have McKeen participate in the inquisition. After all, if Ives had gutted the CH&D, he probably had gutted the Vandalia Line, too.[13]

In a scene worthy of high drama, McKeen called on John Williams to accompany him, and together they hurried to the depot, where a special train awaited. Leaving

Terre Haute at 10:47, the train raced across Indiana, the tracks cleared of all other trains. They made it to Indianapolis in 83 minutes, making more than a mile a minute at one point between Greencastle and the capital city. It was one of the fastest runs ever over the TH&I. After a pause to change engines, the special left Indianapolis at ten past noon, running the 98 miles to Hamilton, Ohio, in 121 minutes. In another 29 minutes they were in Cincinnati, having covered the entire 196 miles from Terre Haute in 3 hours and 53 minutes, a new record.[14]

McKeen and Williams arrived just as the CH&D stockholders meeting was ending. Huddling with the leaders of the opposition, it was quickly decided that they would also go to New York with Dexter, Emery, and Gano, leaving that very evening. If it were true that Ives & Company was about to collapse, McKeen and Williams would be there to protect the TH&I's interests.

At 11 o'clock, Monday morning, August 8, Riley and John Williams attended a hastily called Terre Haute & Indianapolis board meeting chaired by Ives in New York City. At that meeting Williams, as general counsel, was appointed to represent the company at any meeting of creditors of Ives & Company, but only to report back without taking any action. Waite and McKeen tried to amend the motion so Williams might have some actual authority but were outvoted. And with that, the meeting was adjourned so that the real fireworks could begin.[15]

Moving to the New York offices of Legal Counsel George Hoadley, Henry Ives now confronted his opposition. Present were the Cincinnati, Hamilton & Dayton stockholders committee of Dexter, Emery, and Gano; the CH&D's Christopher Waite representing management; Riley McKeen and John Williams representing the TH&I; and Irving Evans of Boston, one of Ives's creditors. For five hours they grilled Ives, asking what had happened to the CH&D's assets: Where was the cash reported in the company's annual report of March 31 and the proceeds of the stock issue? Ives temporized lamely, unable and unwilling to account for it all. He would need time to get the figures together for them, so the meeting was adjourned until 9 that evening.[16]

Meanwhile, on the stock exchange, CH&D stock was pounded by the bears. It had closed as high as 120 the previous week; now it sank to 40. With all his stock pledged for loans, Ives's position was precarious, and the unnamed forces gunning for him pulled the trigger. Late in the afternoon, counsel for one of Ives's biggest creditors, William Fellowes Morgan & Company, called to inform the young financier that his $2 million loan was being called and the collateral securities sold. As word quickly spread, other creditors joined the assault. Kessler & Company called an $800,000 loan. A "certain National Bank president," as the newspapers put it, called another large loan at the end of the day. An unnamed Ives & Company creditor was quoted as saying: "It had been decided to push the matter to the end, no matter what the effect to Ives might be." The effect was devastating.[17]

The CH&D group reassembled at 9 that evening as planned but was forced to wait on Ives. When he finally showed up an hour later, he announced he was too tired to worry over figures that night and that they might as well all go home. Perhaps, he said cheerily, he would have a statement tomorrow. And inviting them to return the next day at noon, he bade the infuriated group goodnight.

The angry Midwesterners were joined by Christopher Meyer on Tuesday. Realizing now that he had been duped, Meyer was anxious to save his huge investment. When Ives finally materialized well past 1 o'clock, he was met with determined opposition which would settle for no less than his and Stayner's resignations from CH&D management. They wanted the books, and the company, back. Even Meyer threatened criminal action if Ives did not comply.[18]

Ives and Stayner soon called a CH&D board meeting and resigned, replaced by A. S. Winslow as president and Christopher Meyer as vice president. Winslow was vice president of the First National Bank of Cincinnati and the brother of James Winslow of Winslow, Lanier & Company—soon to be named the CH&D's fiscal agents. He was also one of the former CH&D stockholders who had previously sold out to Ives.[19]

After the CH&D board meeting was adjourned, a TH&I board meeting followed at 4:45, during which Ives resigned the presidency and one of his associates resigned from the directorate. Riley McKeen was promptly re-elected president of the Terre Haute & Indianapolis, and John Williams was restored to the board as a director. Afterward, Ives met with his creditors. CH&D stock which had brought no more than 40 at noon was back up to 100 at the bell.[20]

It was all but over. On Wednesday, August 10, the CH&D stockholders committee met at the Drexel-Morgan building to hear an accounting of Ives's stewardship of their road, which the *Cincinnati Enquirer* observed "was not half as bad as had been represented." And then the creditors descended upon Ives & Company. Shortly before the final bell on Thursday, August 11, the stock exchange was treated to an announcement that Henry Ives & Company had suspended operations, and for the first time ever, a failure was greeted with ringing cheers.[21]

It would take weeks to untangle the mess. Ives's affairs were a labyrinth of larceny and hypothecation. In the meantime, the people who had sold him control to begin with now tried to take it back. The Cincinnatians again held the reins of the CH&D, and McKeen had a grip on the TH&I. But despite the sanguine predictions being repeated in the papers, Ives's administration of both roads would soon prove to be costly.

In the aftermath of Ives, McKeen tried to regain some degree of control, and, although he was no longer a significant stockholder in the Terre Haute & Indianapolis, the CH&D people seemed willing to let him have a free hand. To that end, at a meeting at the CH&D headquarters in Cincinnati on August 22, the TH&I board accepted Frederick H. Short's resignation as secretary-treasurer and re-appointed George Farrington and John W. Cruft to their former, once again separate posts. At the same time, Christopher Waite resigned as general manager, and his duties devolved on McKeen as president. Ives, Stayner, and Meyer were absent from the proceedings, but Waite and A. S. Winslow were present as directors, and the votes were unanimous.[22]

It quickly became clear that Ives had indeed gutted the treasury. Stripped of all of its securities and most of its cash, the TH&I was seriously injured. Worse still, with Ives and company diverting every available penny, the company had accumulated a substantial floating debt—bills unpaid—and that debt would grow with its cupboard bare. The ultimate remedy would be unpleasant. For the moment, however, McKeen concentrated on trying to salvage as much as he could from the wreck of

Darlington, Indiana, on the Logansport road at the turn of the last century.
Collection of Wesley Tribbett, Darlington, Indiana.

Ives & Company, grimly realizing how little the Terre Haute & Indianapolis could expect as an unsecured creditor.[23]

As bad as the TH&I's financial condition now was, Ives's worst legacy at the moment was of a legal nature. The forced cancellation of its lease of the St. Louis, Vandalia & Terre Haute could prove fatal to the Terre Haute & Indianapolis. Coal traffic had steadily eroded over the past three years—not precipitously, but the trend was clear. With competition from within the industry by other producing districts and carriers and from without by a competing energy source, natural gas, the TH&I's coal earnings were in definite decline. That left the company increasingly dependent upon the through freight and passenger traffic only made possible by its lease of the Vandalia company and traffic agreements with the Pennsylvania Lines. If the Pennsylvania forces were successful in breaking the lease, the game would be over. The TH&I might be able to survive as a local line, but it certainly would cease to be Terre Haute's financial mainstay with its large shops and yards and general offices.[24]

The Pennsylvania was bound and determined, not only to proceed with the suit, but to win it decisively. It mattered not that Ives now was eliminated. It seemed likely that the CH&D would proceed with the purchase that Ives had arranged. And even if not, the Pennsylvania people had had enough of foreign control of their St. Louis, Vandalia & Terre Haute, especially of that by William Riley McKeen.

It was a serious and dangerous challenge, one that the Pennsylvania was publicly confident of winning. With the added approval of the national business press, the Pennsylvania's position often appeared characterized as Goliath to the TH&I's David, without the sober realization of what that analogy might imply.

Another view of Darlington showing the depot, team track, and mill.
Collection of Wesley Tribbett, Darlington, Indiana.

If the TH&I had a champion in the upcoming battle, it was courtly and capable John G. Williams. As lead lawyer on the TH&I legal team, Williams crafted a brilliant defense. Hearing of this case in equity began in Springfield, Illinois, before Judges Gresham and Allen on October, 18, 1887. As mentioned previously, the Pennsylvania, acting through its St. Louis, Vandalia & Terre Haute subsidiary, contended that, under the law binding at the time, neither it nor the TH&I had the authority to make a lease; that there was money due under the terms of the contract; and that whether the lease were valid or not, there should be an accounting under the agreement.[25]

Williams dismantled the Pennsylvania's case with precision. Filing what is called a demurrer, the defendant answered each point advanced by the Vandalia company. First, the TH&I defense suggested that the case had no equity. The law in force at the time of the lease had been preceded and followed by other laws that tended to grant the proper authority to the two corporations. Second, the TH&I argued, even if the lease were invalid, the Vandalia company had waited 17 long years to seek relief, meanwhile leaving the agreement in force and its property in the defendant's hands. Third, ejecting the TH&I from the Vandalia's property was a *legal* action, not a question of equity. And, almost sardonically, in its last point the TH&I defense threw up its hands in bewilderment over the complaint's completely contradictory nature—that first it claimed the lease contract invalid and in the next breath demanded the TH&I be held to account under its terms.[26]

It was a masterful performance and a strong defense of the TH&I's position, but it would be after the first of the year before the judges made their ruling in the case. In the meantime, another legal battle engulfed McKeen personally.

Even though Riley was once again president of the Terre Haute & Indianapolis, he no longer legally controlled the company. It was true that he held the 11,160 shares bought by Ives as collateral for the note still outstanding, but the shares were now registered to Ives as "trustee." As the management of the Cincinnati, Hamilton & Dayton would be quick to point out, Ives was "trustee" for them. But Ives's note for the remaining $669,150 plus interest—coming to a total of more than $700,000—was still in Riley's hands and unpaid.

The CH&D people seemed intent on completing the transaction. Ives may have been a scoundrel, but his purchase of the Vandalia Line was a good idea, and the CH&D took steps to follow through. To do so, Julius Dexter, the CH&D's new president, kept after McKeen about the note. Despite the fact that Riley and John Williams had sat Dexter down and carefully explained every detail of the deal back in August during the last few hours of Ives's control, Dexter seemed unclear about what was now required. He happened to meet Williams in New York over Thanksgiving weekend on November 24 and 25 and made a point of asking exactly when the note came due. When Williams, who was in town to see Ives, explained that it was a six-month note that came due on December 4, Dexter became concerned. What he would like to do, he told Williams, was pay $100,000 in 90 days and the balance on as easy terms as McKeen would grant. Since Williams would not comment one way or the other, Dexter insisted he wire Riley immediately with his proposal and ask for an extension of time. McKeen's answer has not been preserved, but judging from subsequent events, was probably a polite "no."[27]

Dexter telegraphed McKeen personally several times more as the due date drew nearer and finally sent one of the CH&D's legal retainers, Lawrence Maxwell, to see McKeen on Saturday, December 3, 1887. Having asked to see the contract, Maxwell studied it for a moment then pointed out that Ives had no authority from the CH&D to buy the Terre Haute & Logansport stock. That made the amount he had agreed to pay erroneous. Maxwell then smoothly proposed that Riley accept $226,500 instead as payment in full and hand over just the 11,160 shares of TH&I stock. McKeen, who had a keen wit and was probably amused by this effrontery, told Maxwell that it was out of the question. The amount necessary to fulfill the contract was plainly indicated on the note. *That* was what McKeen would take before he released the stock. Maxwell rose in a huff and threatened trouble if Riley did not change his mind. But McKeen refused.[28]

Having seen how completely Ives had stripped the TH&I treasury, McKeen knew why the CH&D people were suddenly trying to adjust the note. They were in no position to pay the approximately $700,000 due, even if they had already expended nearly $900,000 on the deal. But Riley stood firm. It was apparent that he had now changed his mind about selling the TH&I. Therefore, he actually preferred that the CH&D default on the note.

Somehow, Terre Haute had gotten wind of the impending deadline; the newspapers announced that the note Ives had given McKeen was now due and the three-day grace period would be up on Wednesday, December 7. The city seemed to hold its collective breath.[29]

On Wednesday, the last day before default, Julius Dexter and Lawrence Maxwell made one last pilgrimage to McKeen's door. Once more they offered $226,500 as payment in full and demanded the withheld stock; and one last time, McKeen refused.[30]

The next day, the *Terre Haute Evening Gazette* led its front page story with an emphasized "Hurrah," noting that it was "the earnest wish of everyone in Terre Haute" that the railroad remain in McKeen's hands. However gratifying such public elation might have been, McKeen knew the battle had only just begun. That morning the CH&D had filed suit in federal court seeking to enjoin McKeen from selling the collateral stock and to force him to either accept the $226,500 as payment in full or return the $889,500 already paid him by Ives. Long before the day was out, Judge Walter Q. Gresham granted the temporary injunction.[31]

Ironically enough, the very same TH&I train which carried the U.S. Marshall from Indianapolis to serve Gresham's injunction papers on McKeen also bore a mysterious visitor. After registering under a false name at the Terre Haute House, young Henry S. Ives met quietly with McKeen and Williams somewhere away from the bank. When later questioned by reporters who had recognized Ives, Riley would not explain the surreptitious visit. It is likely that Ives had come to offer his cooperation in McKeen's impending fight with the CH&D. As the "trustee" listed in the sales contract, Ives retained the right to vote the stock, and McKeen would require his proxy or his support to exercise control.[32]

If Ives did not already have enough of a reason to favor McKeen over the CH&D, Julius Dexter soon gave him another. On Tuesday, December 13, Ives was arrested in New York City on a charge of grand larceny preferred by Dexter. Hauled off to police court, the young man was threatened with jail but was promptly bailed out by his sister. At his arraignment two days later, Dexter testified that Ives had stolen a $100,000 CH&D draft intended as partial payment for the TH&I stock purchase, but the judge found the evidence unconvincing and dismissed the case. As he left the courthouse, the jaunty Ives promised to sue Dexter for malicious prosecution. It was a narrow escape from jail for the "young Napoleon," and it would not happen again.[33]

While McKeen's attorneys—General Benjamin Harrison, soon to run for president, and John M. Butler, who was also helping the Vandalia try to break the TH&I's lease—put together his defense, Riley proceeded with the business of running the Terre Haute & Indianapolis. The rapidly approaching new year would bring with it the annual stockholders meeting and the election of the directorate. McKeen wanted to have the board re-formed the way it had been before the debacle. Regardless of the CH&D suit, with Ives's proxy, McKeen could name the board he wanted. Aware of that fact and now recognizing that Riley had no desire to relinquish the TH&I, the

CH&D changed its tactics, filing a new suit against McKeen on New Year's Eve night. This time the CH&D's Indiana solicitor, Charles W. Fairbanks, went to the Indianapolis home of Judge William Woods seeking to enjoin either McKeen or Ives from voting the TH&I shares held as collateral. Probably annoyed at having his holiday evening interrupted, Woods told Fairbanks to see him in chambers on Monday and ordered him off his steps.[34]

This is Coatesville, Indiana, at the turn of the last century; and it looks like there are several passengers for the next train. The depot building is typical of the TH&I's early small-town station design. Courtesy of the Coatesville Public Library, Coatesville, Indiana.

First thing Monday morning, January 2, 1888, Woods had a temporary injunction notice wired to McKeen, postponing the stockholders meeting scheduled for 10 A.M. The judge then proceeded to entertain the motion by Fairbanks and Ramsay on behalf of the CH&D. By noon Judge Woods had heard enough, and he was not at all impressed with the CH&D argument. Title to the stock in question was legally with Ives but in equity with McKeen. At 12:20 the temporary injunction was dissolved, and the annual stockholders meeting in Terre Haute was back on schedule.[35]

A dozen or so gathered in McKeen's conference room at the bank and were called to order promptly at 2 o'clock by Deloss Minshall in the chair. Riley presented his proxy for the 11,160 shares, and the CH&D's Lawrence Maxwell, who was there with Dexter, immediately objected, entering a formal protest in the minutes. Henry Ives, who was also in attendance, had no objection at all. As the balloting proceeded, McKeen, Minshall, Josephus Collett, Henry Ross, George Farrington, John Williams, and Henry S. Ives were all elected directors of the company. Except for Ives, who would not attend another board meeting after this day, the board was purged of its Cincinnati, Hamilton & Dayton influence and refilled with Riley's friends and associates. Maxwell and Dexter rose and protested one more time, but it was too late. McKeen had taken back the chair and the company.[36]

On that same day, January 2, 1888, McKeen's attorneys filed his answer to the charges contained in the CH&D's first suit, begun back on December 8. The CH&D filed its exceptions to McKeen's answer on February 6 but dismissed the suit on February 17. By then, however, McKeen's relationship with the CH&D would turn ugly.[37]

All of Terre Haute celebrated McKeen's victory over the CH&D as if it were their own. The railroad's employees were especially joyous. It had become a tradition to hoist the TH&I flag atop the depot when there was news of good omen for the Terre Haute road, and it was flying tall and proud long before daylight on Tuesday morning.[38]

More good news came on Wednesday, January 11, 1888. On that date, Judge Gresham rendered his decision in the Vandalia lease-breaking case. The Pennsylvania's lawyers had only modified one of the charges in their complaint, despite the rapier-like sharpness of the TH&I's point-by-point answer. Gresham, while acknowledging that the lease might have indeed been invalid originally, observed that the 17-year delay to seek relief suggested inexcusable negligence by the Vandalia company. It had waited far too long. Therefore, he had no choice but to sustain the TH&I's demurrer and dismiss the case. The Terre Haute & Indianapolis had beaten the mighty Pennsylvania.[39]

The jubilation, if there was any, was short-lived. As expected, the Pennsylvania's lawyers quickly announced that they would appeal the case all the way to the U.S. Supreme Court, if necessary. They had no intention of leaving their Vandalia in McKeen's care.[40]

They would have to for the time being. When the CH&D dismissed its first suit against McKeen on February 17, 1888, that action eliminated the original injunction restraining McKeen from disposing of the 11,160 shares of TH&I stock he continued to hold as security for Ives's note. With the note now long past due and in default, Riley was at last free to sell the collateral. Accordingly, McKeen scheduled a special private sale for March 8, 1888, and advertised the fact in newspapers in New York, Indianapolis, and Terre Haute. He also personally notified the Cincinnati, Hamilton & Dayton and Henry Ives on February 27. On the advertised day, McKeen sold the stock to himself for $750,000. Immediately contacting Dexter and the CH&D with the results, Riley informed them of the surplus existing over and above the $709,000 amount of the note with interest and advised them that it was being held for whoever could properly claim it. And with that, Riley McKeen had again become the controlling owner of the Terre Haute & Indianapolis and Terre Haute & Logansport railroads.[41]

The Cincinnati, Hamilton & Dayton was not the least bit interested in collecting the residue of McKeen's stock sale. On February 17, after it had dismissed its first suit, the CH&D filed its third and final action against McKeen in federal court. What the CH&D wanted now was to invalidate the whole deal, cancel the defaulted note, and have the original $889,500 they had paid through Ives returned to them. It was an absolute impossibility, as far as McKeen was concerned.[42]

The CH&D's case rested on familiar ground: a plea of *ultra vires,* the contention by the complaining corporation that it had been completely without the necessary legal authority to do what it had done, thereby washing its hands of its own actions. This improbable legal oasis became a frequent gathering place as the common law heritage of a predominantly agrarian nation slowly and painfully accommodated itself to the realities of corporate industrialism. Much the same argument was being used in the Pennsylvania's attempt to break the Vandalia lease, and it, like the CH&D case to come, would go a long way in helping to define the oasis as a mirage.

In its new complaint, the CH&D maintained that it had no authority to purchase the stock of another railroad. This astonishing assertion conveniently ignored the fact that the company owned and controlled a number of other lines, including the Cincinnati, Hamilton & Indianapolis, which connected its own railroad to the TH&I. In spite of this argument, the CH&D also insisted that Henry Ives had purchased the TH&I's stock as the former's agent and trustee, making it CH&D property. McKeen, the CH&D charged, knew and understood that the CH&D had no power to make such a purchase and that Ives was acting for the CH&D and using CH&D money. The CH&D also accused McKeen of being Ives's accomplice in making a secret deal to sell the TH&I's treasury stock, for which, it was alleged, McKeen was to receive a large sum of money under the table from Ives; further, the CH&D claimed that the sales contract McKeen had made with Ives was only designed to conceal their fraudulent activities.[43]

This last charge of fraud and deception was particularly remarkable, considering how many CH&D people had been involved in the negotiations from the beginning and how completely the CH&D had assumed control of the entire Vandalia Line system following the transfer proceedings of June 4, 1887. In answer to the other parts of the complaint, it was maintained that McKeen could easily have speculated that the CH&D was somehow involved in the transaction; but Riley's defense would continually emphasize Ives's actions as a financier and his ongoing stock market activities—particularly the attempt to buy the B&O—as leading McKeen to believe it was really Ives and his friends who were buying his TH&I stock.

McKeen and his legal team of John M. Butler and John B. Elam were much more concerned about the implications of the CH&D's claims of fraud and collusion. This was a flagrant assault on McKeen's sterling reputation, and it was wholly unjustified. Fortunately, it did not take much effort to prove the charge utterly without foundation.

Riley's lawyers filed his answer to the CH&D's bill of complaint on February 28, 1888. On April 2 the CH&D filed exceptions to McKeen's answer, which the court overruled on April 27. The CH&D replied on May 1; and on May 8, the Judge

MAXINKUCKEE EXCURSIONS.

On Sunday, June 15th inst., and on each
Sunday thereafter during the summer,
the Vandalia line will run its LAKE
SPECIAL, which was so popular last
season, leaving Terre Haute at 5 a. m.,
arriving at Lake Maxinkuckee at 10:45
a. m.; leaving the lake at 6 p. m. and ar-
rive at Terre Haute at 11:45 p. m. Fare
for the round trip only $3. The lake
special is just the train for those wishing
to spend the day at Garland Dells (the
Shades of Death), as it passes Waveland
at 6:00 a. m., returning leaves Waveland
at 10:22 p m. Fare, Terre Haute to
Garland Dells and return, only $1 50,
which includes transfer from Waveland
to the Dells and return.

Terre Haute to Lake Maxinkuckee and
return $3; Terre Haute to Garland Dells
and return $1.50. These tickets are
good only on the lake special on the day
sold.   Geo. F. Farrington,
                  General Agent.

The excursion business was a TH&I staple. In the days before air conditioning, Marmont
on scenic Lake Maxinkuckee was a popular destination for families looking to escape
their hot city homes. This advertisement for the 1890 summer season promised a full day
on the beach, but required the excursionist to be at the depot bright and early at 5 A.M.
For those disinclined to enjoy the pleasures of the lake an alternate destination was offered
with the bloodcurdling name of The Shades of Death. Marmont became Culver by the
end of the decade, but remained a popular resort well into the 20th century.

Of interest is the Vandalia line herald which tops the ad. Most likely, it was an invention
of the advertising department of the *Terre Haute Evening Express* as it did not appear
elsewhere, and, as far as the author can determine, was never used on locomotives or
cars. Curiously, the *Express* was partially owned by Riley McKeen at the time.

referred the entire case to William P. Fishback, the master in chancery. When the master's report was finally issued at the end of September 1890, it contained five large volumes of evidence obtained from months of depositions. Everyone from Ives to Jacob McCullough of the Pennsylvania's Lines West organization was heard from. And the master's recommendation was to find for the defendant. After final hearing in court in mid-April 1891, Judge James Jenkins overruled all but one of the CH&D's exceptions to the master's report and dismissed the case against McKeen on July 23, 1891. The CH&D appealed, but its case was weak, and the verdict was clear.[44]

8

CARETAKER

In the wake of the debacle, McKeen's primary concern was the Terre Haute & Indianapolis itself. Though he maintained a calm and confident front, Riley was far from sanguine about the outcome. The company's situation was critical. Deprived of most of its securities and looted of all its cash, the TH&I was dangerously vulnerable. It was important to move quickly to recover as many of the TH&I's stolen assets as possible. By the time a sense of organizational stability had been regained early in 1888 with McKeen once again firmly in control, the job of corporate restoration was well under way.

With his general counsel, John G. Williams, fully occupied with the continuing Vandalia lease litigation, McKeen personally undertook negotiations with Ives's creditors in an attempt to salvage the TH&I's embezzled assets. Typical of this action was the settlement made with William Fellowes Morgan & Company concerning $100,000 worth of St. Louis, Vandalia & Terre Haute second mortgage bonds Ives had sold in his desperate attempt to stay afloat. The proceeds were never credited to the TH&I, and the bonds had since been hypothecated by Morgan to the firm of Kidder, Peabody & Company, which refused to relinquish them. It took the threat of a suit in the spring of 1888 to get Morgan to settle, and then for only 20 cents on the dollar. Realizing it was probably the best he could do under the circumstances, Riley reluctantly accepted Morgan's paltry offer and got board approval on July 14.[1]

As bad as the misappropriation of the Vandalia securities was, the loss of the Terre Haute & Indianapolis treasury stock was worse. After Ives had purchased the stock on behalf of the Cincinnati, Hamilton & Dayton, the TH&I was left with nothing but a draft on Ives's New York bank for the purchase price. With Ives's firm in bankruptcy, the draft was now worthless. Despite his best efforts to track down the stock, McKeen was only able to recover 2,600 of the original 8,840 shares. The results of his recovery mission had been discouraging so far, prompting McKeen to advise his stockholders that he was unable to determine just how bad the final outcome of the Ives interlude would be.[2]

Significantly, stockholder confidence in McKeen seemed unshaken, in spite of the fact that it had been his selling of control which had made the disaster possible. Riley accommodated the few who had lost faith by purchasing additional small blocks of TH&I stock whenever someone wished to sell. Over the next few years, McKeen gradually increased his personal holdings, and those of his bank, to a total of more than 14,000 shares.

Because the book value of the company had declined precipitously thanks to the loss of more than $2 million in assets, each TH&I share was now worth less and no longer commanded a premium over its par value price. To appease the outside stockholders, it was more important than ever, therefore, to keep the dividends regular and generous. With that goal in mind, the directors declared the normal semi-annual payout of 3 percent on July 14, 1888. And McKeen's board would declare another 3 percent after the fiscal year ended on October 31, even though doing so pushed the company into the red by $12,000, the TH&I's first ever reported deficit.[3]

There is a story behind this picture; unfortunately, no one has it straight, yet. St. Louis, Vandalia & Terre Haute engine No. 142 is decked out in bunting and flags for President Grover Cleveland—that's his picture on the smokebox. The problem occurs in identifying the date and occasion. In a memoir in the April 1962 issue of *Railroad Magazine*, "Carload Andy" Ospring relates the story told him by his father, "Old Dutch Andy," a longtime Vandalia Line engineer, that this is the "Honeymoon Train" of Grover Cleveland, who wed young Frances Folsom in 1886 and supposedly went west to celebrate. But according to all of his biographers, Cleveland and his bride honeymooned in Deer Park, Maryland, where a mob of overzealous reporters earned the president's hostility. Since presidential candidates of the day did not campaign to any real extent, there is only one other plausible possibility. In October 1887 Cleveland, his wife, and a select group from his first cabinet toured the West and South, passing through Indianapolis, and most likely through Terre Haute, where this picture was taken. The two men are identified as engineer Jack Van Cleve and fireman Frank Smith. The gaily decorated 4-4-0 American type is a Pittsburgh Locomotive product of 1883. Collection of the Vigo County Historical Society, Terre Haute.

The year 1888 had not ended all that badly for the TH&I, in spite of the company's financial troubles. Revenues had dropped somewhat from the year before, but then 1887 had been an extraordinarily good business year for American railroads. Only less favorable rates and increased expenses had spoiled an otherwise acceptable company report. Part of those expenses were due to the cost of building a new iron and steel drawbridge over the Wabash River; increased train and engine weights had made the old 1870 structure obsolete.[4]

Perhaps the biggest disappointment for McKeen and his fellow railroad executives across the country was the failure of the new Interstate Commerce Commission to halt the demoralization of rates. The creation of the commission in 1887 had encouraged many within the industry to hope for at least some rate stabilization; but the ICC was toothless and ineffectual, and the incidence of competitive rate wars continued practically unabated.[5]

McKeen's Vandalia Line was itself locked into continuing combat and plunged into a brief but costly war involving passenger rates to and from St. Louis. Hostilities began in mid-September 1888, with sharp competition between the TH&I and the Bee Line on local fares from St. Louis. Before it ended, the war had spread to affect all passenger rates between St. Louis and Cincinnati, Cleveland, Columbus, and Pittsburgh. It was not the first time the combatants had been so engaged, and it would not be the last, either.[6]

As he entered the new year of 1889, McKeen must have reflected with bitter irony that he found himself even more occupied with railroad business than ever before. By now he had hoped to be free of the cares of the TH&I's presidency, able to devote full attention to the bank and his growing interest in politics. Instead, between the time-consuming negotiations to recover lost assets, the increasingly involved requirements of litigation, and the ongoing executive demands of the TH&I, Riley found himself exasperatingly busy. Even so, he found the time to help get his friend and former counsel Benjamin Harrison elected president, and he stayed active in Republican Party circles. But it could not go on like this forever. Riley was approaching his 60th birthday and was growing tired.

McKeen still wanted to unload the Terre Haute & Indianapolis as soon as he was able to restore the railroad to financial health. However, he now realized there was only one possible buyer, who, for the moment at least, was no longer interested in buying. In fact, the Pennsylvania was not even willing to discuss purchasing the TH&I until its litigation to break the Vandalia lease was fully exhausted. Although the lower court had ruled against them, and in favor of McKeen's company, the Pennsylvania's officers fully expected to win on appeal. By now they must have known that there was really no other reasonable option than to buy the TH&I. But they also knew that once shorn of the leased Vandalia, McKeen's road would be in no position to bargain, and the Pennsylvania could then dictate its own terms. So McKeen simply had to wait for the court to have its say.

In the meantime, putting the TH&I back on its feet was proving to be a challenge. Although the company managed to end the year 1889 with a net profit, earnings continued to be squeezed by low and unstable rates. A six-month strike by Clay County coal miners cost the TH&I dearly, resulting in a 45.6 percent drop in coal tonnage and a 36 percent decrease in local freight revenue. Fortunately, grain traffic was up over 63 percent on the TH&I and increased more than 50 percent on the St. Louis, Vandalia & Terre Haute, helping to offset the loss in local traffic with increased through tonnage.[7]

Little further progress was made on asset recovery early in the year. Hampered by the increasingly doubtful condition of Ives's affairs, McKeen's efforts to negotiate the return of additional securities had reached a virtual standstill.

Henry Ives, along with his partner George Staynor, had finally been arrested and thrown in jail at the end of January 1889, and the pair remained there to face charges brought by the CH&D. Ives would eventually be brought to justice in September in a trial which would last three weeks and end in a hung jury, ten for conviction and only two for acquittal. The young financier would not go free until March 1890, but by then he would face a sentence of a different kind, having begun to display the early symptoms of the tuberculosis, which would take his life in but four years more.[8]

By the end of 1889, McKeen had to face some difficult facts. No matter how hard he had tried to avoid it, the Terre Haute & Indianapolis would have to swallow its loss in some fashion. The only questions remaining were: How could the situation be put to rest, and at what cost?

Again, Riley turned to his trusted lieutenant John G. Williams, who was dispatched to Cincinnati to negotiate with the officers of the Cincinnati, Hamilton & Dayton. On December 14 Williams finally had an agreement by which the remaining claims against Ives's bankrupt concern were sold to the CH&D for $262,500. A somber TH&I board listened as Williams explained the deal at the January 6, 1890, meeting. Although the TH&I was swapping claims totaling over $2 million in face value for what seemed like a pittance, it was the best that could be expected. The agreement also cleared title to the 2,600 shares of TH&I treasury stock which had been claimed by both companies and recovered by McKeen for the TH&I. It also returned, as part of the CH&D's payment, an additional 1,000 TH&I treasury shares which the CH&D had recovered.[9]

Acceptance of Williams's negotiated settlement with the CH&D meant that the TH&I would finally have to adjust its general accounts, and this was a bitter pill to swallow. Until the settlement was signed, the books had forlornly continued to carry as deferred assets the claims against Ives & Company and the cash transferred to the CH&D's treasurer, in the vain hope that they would someday be returned. Now they would have to be taken off the books and their value written off. It would be a red flag waved at the company's outside stockholders. A way had to be found to cushion the blow, to somehow offset such a drastic write-down. Once again, with John Williams's help, McKeen would find a solution.

Ever since he had reassumed the presidency of the Terre Haute & Indianapolis in August 1887, McKeen had also filled the position of general manager that had been created for Christopher Waite. Now Riley wanted to lighten his load by sharing the responsibilities, and the perfect candidate was available. John G. Williams, who had been elected a vice president in January 1888, was quite willing to assume the position; and accordingly, the board approved his appointment as the new vice president and general manager. It was the first time McKeen had ever had an executive officer serving beside him at that rank, and it indicated just how much Riley wished to let go.

The print was labeled: "Vandalia Line, between Terre Haute and Indianapolis." Given the terrain, it is likely Reelsville, Indiana, in the early 1890s. If so, the train is the eastbound afternoon accommodation. Collection of the Vigo County Historical Society, Terre Haute.

McKeen was not the only one to value Williams highly. The Pennsylvania's Lines West officer corps also had high regard for Riley's new general manager, having faced him in court. Williams quickly put the Pennsylvania's respect and his newly acquired executive authority to work. By the spring of 1890, with McKeen's blessing, Williams was negotiating an agreement which would benefit both parties.

The time had come to put an end to the longstanding conflict over the proper division of the profits and losses under the TH&I's lease of the Vandalia. McKeen's company could no longer afford the controversy, and the Pennsylvania was most anxious to get the Vandalia company's finances back to normal and finally begin fulfilling the sinking fund requirements of the first mortgage.

Working with Joshua Brooks, Jacob McCullough, and Thomas Messler of Lines West, Williams finally worked out an arrangement acceptable to both sides by early May. While it would be a costly settlement for the TH&I, it would finally bring an end to the feud.

It should be recalled that in February 1868, when the joint parties had agreed to build the St. Louis, Vandalia & Terre Haute and the TH&I had agreed to operate the new line by lease, a separate operating agreement had been made to divide any profits and share all losses incurred by the new Vandalia company under the lease.

This division was made by the amount of the $1 million in second mortgage convertible bonds purchased by each of the joint parties. By this calculation, McKeen's TH&I had assumed a two-tenths share, the Indiana Central a three-tenths share, and the Pan Handle a five-tenths share. When the Pan Handle had leased the Indiana Central in 1869, it took over that company's share and wound up with eight-tenths of the Vandalia company's profits or losses. Unfortunately, the St. Louis, Vandalia & Terre Haute began generating losses in 1873 and continued to run at a deficit through 1884, causing a growing friction between the Pan Handle and TH&I managements. Then the Pan Handle repudiated the Indiana Central lease in 1875 and refused to cover any more than its original five-tenths share of the Vandalia's losses. The Indiana Central had gone bankrupt, and its obligations had been legally extinguished with its reorganization, leaving its three-tenths share unpaid. McKeen's Terre Haute & Indianapolis, unwilling to assume all of the resulting deficiency, began accruing the shortfall and, pending a resolution, refused to pay any further lease-generated net income to the St. Louis, Vandalia & Terre Haute or any share of the profits made since 1884 to the Pan Handle. The resulting standoff had poisoned relations between the Pennsylvania's Lines West organization, which staffed both the Pan Handle and the Vandalia company, and McKeen's TH&I ever since. It had also provided part of the legal justification for Lines West's attempt to break the lease, which was still pending on appeal to the U.S. Supreme Court.[10]

Admitting that an accounting and settlement was now desired by both sides, regardless of the ongoing litigation, the new agreement carefully tabulated who owed what to whom. It was determined that the Terre Haute & Indianapolis owed the St. Louis, Vandalia & Terre Haute $944,822.30 in withheld net income, including interest. The TH&I also owed the Pan Handle $133,350.47 in Vandalia road profits, with interest. And the TH&I was owed $402,019.28 for the Indiana Central's share of the Vandalia's losses from 1875 to 1884, again including interest.[11]

In an amended operating contract dated May 8, 1890, John Williams got his Lines West counterparts to agree to a new division of responsibility under the lease operation, the very same split which McKeen had suggested back in 1876. The Pennsylvania Lines grudgingly accepted five-sevenths, and the TH&I increased its share to two-sevenths. On this basis the Pan Handle and TH&I also divided the longstanding Indiana Central deficiency, and McKeen's company swallowed an additional $114,863 of the losses. Since the agreement called for the Pan Handle to pay what it owed the TH&I directly to the Vandalia company instead, McKeen's company was left with a bill for $657,666 to the Vandalia, plus the $133,350 it still owed the Pan Handle.[12]

Unfortunately, the money the TH&I had set aside for the purpose had been looted by Ives during his brief control of the company. Thus, the agreement allowed McKeen's company to pay the Vandalia debt with a series of promissory notes which would fall due in monthly installments over a two-year period. The Pan Handle agreed to accept a combination of cash and notes for what it was owed.

The TH&I and Pan Handle formally signed their contract on July 8. Williams then personally presented the new agreement to the Vandalia company's board for ratification at a meeting in Terre Haute on August 4. Curiously, none of the Lines West directors was present; only the Illinois directors and McKeen.[13]

Judging from the parallel electric interurban line, this picture of a westbound Vandalia Line passenger train near Pecksburg, Indiana, was made sometime around 1900. Presumably named for TH&I founding director and one-time president Edwin J. Peck, Pecksburg cannot be found on a map today. It was a town site once located in Hendricks County between Clayton and Coatesville which never grew beyond a handful of houses and gradually disappeared by the end of the 1930s. Guilford Township Historical Collection; Plainfield Public Library, Plainfield, Indiana.

Regardless of how it was to be paid, Riley still had to come up with a total of $791,016 that the TH&I simply did not have. It was an enormous burden for a company already staggering from the financial blow of Ives's administration. With its cupboard bare, and carrying the additional weight of a substantial floating debt, the TH&I would have to scrimp and save any way it could to cover its obligations. Since he had to keep his dividends going to soothe outside stockholders, McKeen was forced to resort to a time-honored management device: postponing all but the most urgent maintenance expenses in hope they could be made up later. It would prove ultimately to be the company's undoing.[14]

For the time being, however, Riley had found the means to help rebalance his general account. The settlement with the St. Louis, Vandalia & Terre Haute had allowed that company to begin paying the cumulative dividends currently in arrears on its preferred stock. McKeen was then able to revalue the 3,260 Vandalia preferred shares still held by the TH&I, boosting their listed worth from 25 percent of par to 125 percent and adding $326,000 in stated value to the books. With a modest increase in the value of the 5,000 shares of Vandalia common it held—prompted by an exceedingly optimistic view of the future prospect of dividends—the TH&I put an additional $55,000 in its general account. While fully acceptable in practice, it was merely an accounting maneuver, and a questionable one at that. Furthermore, it did nothing to repair the serious loss of financial strength the company had suffered.[15]

The crew is ringing the bell as a trim Schenectady-built 4-4-0 American type drifts by the photographer with a turn-of-the-last-century Vandalia Line passenger train. Collection of the Vigo County Historical Society, Terre Haute.

The balance sheet inflation only disguised the fact that the TH&I had gone from wealthy to impoverished without a change of clothes. Yet, in spite of its tenuous financial condition, the Terre Haute & Indianapolis had already embarked on a startling program of expansion.

Perhaps McKeen had by now stopped worrying about his company's long-term viability, assuming that, as soon as the litigation had been decided, he would be able to dispose of the TH&I once and for all. It was clear that Riley had practically withdrawn from day-to-day operations, leaving the railroad in General Manager John Williams's hands. Curiously, McKeen also seemed to allow his friends on the board more latitude. With his blessing, the railroad now took three steps that were intended to strengthen its role as Terre Haute's instrument of commercial advancement but that would, in fact, weaken the company significantly. It was as if everyone concerned were intent on extracting as much civic benefit as possible from the TH&I before finally turning it over to the Pennsylvania Lines.

The first project was undertaken in the spring of 1889, even before McKeen had finished stabilizing the company and the settlement had been reached with Lines West. The proposal appears to have been brought to McKeen by his fellow TH&I board member and business associate Josephus Collett. Collett, who had promoted the Evansville, Terre Haute & Chicago from Terre Haute to Danville, Illinois, in the 1870s, had gone on to build a number of other railroads as a contractor. These roads were scattered throughout the Midwest and West, from Ohio to Nevada; and unlike the ETH&C, most were originally constructed as narrow gauge lines. McKeen probably invested in several, and he served as a mortgage trustee for at least one.[16]

At a meeting called by McKeen on May 27, 1889, Collett introduced the board to Joseph E. Young and U. W. Weston, who represented the Indiana & Lake Michigan Railway. Young, a railroad contractor from Chicago who had a long career in railroad promotion and construction, had gotten his start as a young civil engineer on the staff of the Ft. Wayne & Chicago, a predecessor of the Pennsylvania's Pittsburgh to Chicago line. He later promoted an Indiana Central predecessor, the Chicago & Great Eastern, and constructed that line's entrance into Chicago. In the 1870s Young's firm built the Chicago, Danville & Vincennes, which, after reorganization as the Chicago & Eastern Illinois, then absorbed Collett's Evansville, Terre Haute & Chicago. Now, at 58, in the twilight of his long and prosperous career, Young had taken up the contract to build the Indiana & Lake Michigan, a short piece of railroad projected from South Bend, Indiana, to St. Joseph, Michigan.[17]

Like a friendly salesman, Joseph Young pitched his latest project to McKeen and the TH&I board. As the contractor, he needed money to build the St. Joe road. Might the TH&I be interested in the little line as an extension of the leased Terre Haute & Logansport? All Young wanted was the use of some engines and cars during construction, plus the TH&I's endorsement on the I&LM's $480,000 in mortgage bonds, the trustee for which was none other than Josephus Collett. In return, Young would transfer all of the I&LM's stock to the TH&I, in effect building McKeen's road 40 miles of new railroad to operate. The TH&I board, in its inexplicably expansionist mood, enthusiastically agreed to the deal. Within a month McKeen negotiated the final contract and a lease and received the board's formal ratification.[18]

Perhaps McKeen and his board had been persuaded that the Indiana & Lake Michigan project was a virtually cost-free commitment, since it required no initial cash investment. If so, they were sorely misled, for expenses were quick to materialize.

Construction began almost as soon as the ink on the contract was dry. Completion had been promised by the first of December, but the work lagged. When Young finally turned the Indiana & Lake Michigan over to the TH&I on January 1, 1890, it was far from finished. Although tracklaying had been completed, the road was still totally unballasted and devoid of station facilities, both along the line and at its terminus in St. Joseph. For better or worse, McKeen decided to accept the line as it was and have the TH&I complete the job. It turned out to be for worse.[19]

On April 1, 1890, work resumed by TH&I forces to stabilize soft and narrow embankments, finish building bridges, and ballast the track; but an unusually late thaw and then heavy and prolonged spring rains held up the job and added to the expense. The TH&I was not able to open the new line for business until August 4.

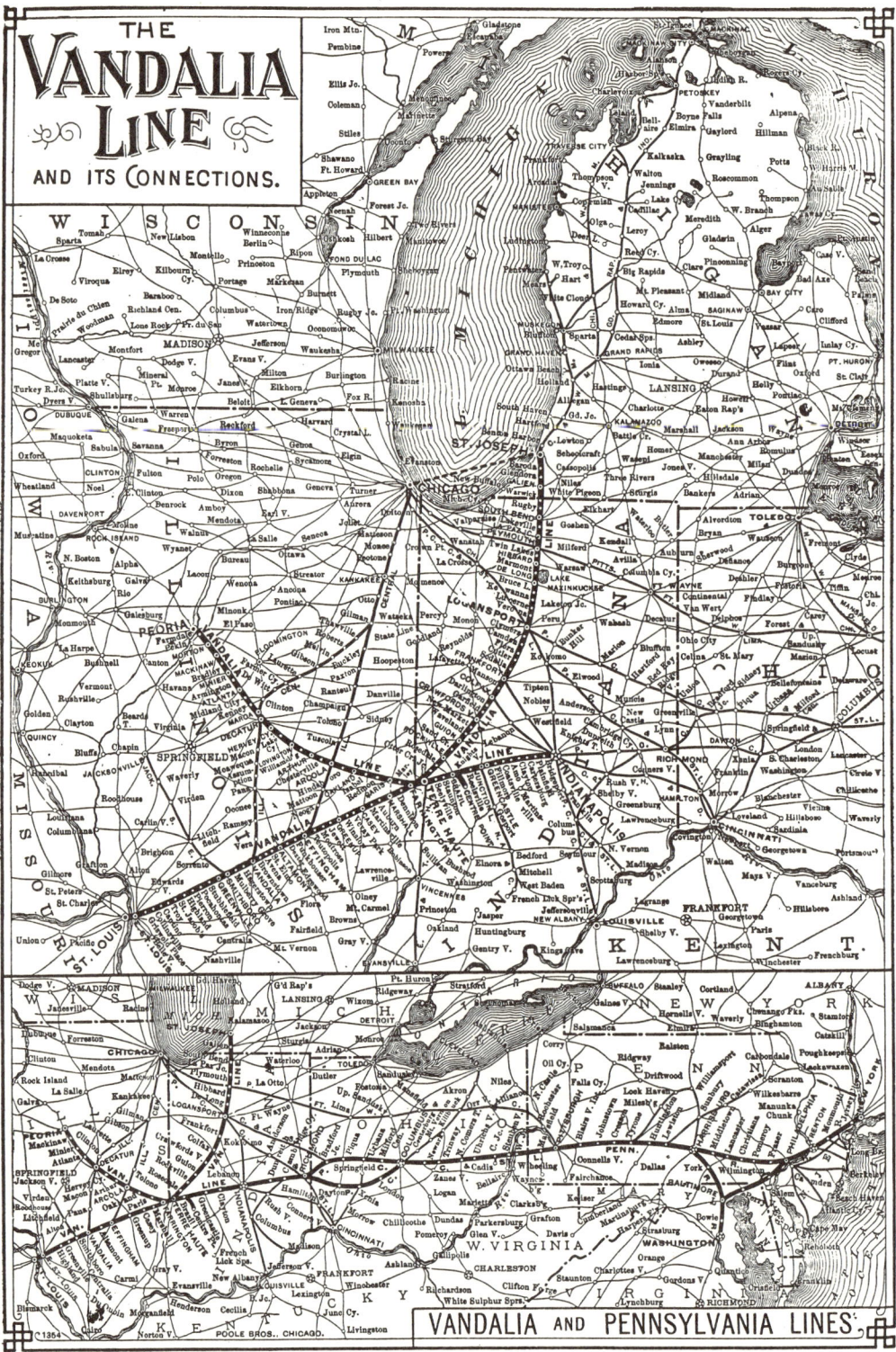

McKeen's Vandalia line on the eve of its sale to the Pennsylvania.
Map from *Traveler's Official Guide,* June 1893.

The Indiana & Lake Michigan proved to be an instant and continuous drain on the TH&I's already stressed bottom line, running at an annual deficit that started out at more than $16,000 in 1890 and gradually escalated to better than $25,000 by 1895. Apparently encouraged by the prospects of substantial freight and passenger interchange at St. Joseph with both the Chicago & West Michigan Railroad and Lake Michigan steamer lines, McKeen had hoped the extension would increase the traffic of the Terre Haute & Logansport, which itself had continued to run a yearly deficit. But the I&LM had too many terminal deficiencies in St. Joseph to generate much business there, and the line had been located through sparsely settled agricultural territory.[20]

At the time the I&LM was finally put into operation, right-of-way had still not been secured through St. Joseph to the property that had been purchased for a warehouse and dock facility. The new line opened so late in the navigation season that the lack of a dock was more of a theoretical problem, but the TH&I was also handicapped by a roundabout connection with the Chicago & West Michigan. Both problems remained unsolved through 1891 and helped increase the deficit. Not until mid-May 1892 was track finally extended to a new deepwater terminal on the St. Joseph River. Yet its location and limited size made the new dock and warehouse facility less than adequate. Carloads of lumber, a prime traffic commodity, could not be handled easily; nor could coal be transshipped to tugs and steamers, a significant blow. At least TH&I passenger trains were able to use the Chicago & West Michigan depot in St. Joseph beginning in 1892, taking advantage of an improved connection with the C&WM.[21]

In an effort to increase business on the leased Logansport and St. Joe lines, McKeen had the TH&I enter into a partnership with Michigan Congressman Frank Wheeler for a new steamboat line on Lake Michigan, the St. Joseph & Lake Michigan Transportation Company. Wheeler provided two of the boats as his share of the investment, and the TH&I, acting through the I&LM, provided the necessary working capital. Two additional steamers were leased from the Delta Transportation Company. Service was provided during the 1892 season with a double daily line of boats between St. Joseph and Chicago and a daily line to Milwaukee.[22]

The hope had been for a sizeable passenger traffic to Chicago and increased freight business by way of Milwaukee. Unfortunately for McKeen and the TH&I, business was, to quote John Williams several years later, "extremely unprofitable." The summer excursion season was cut short by bad weather, low lake transportation rates made it impossible to secure any seaboard freight business, and rate agreements with railroad lines west of Milwaukee were not finalized until so late in the season that little freight traffic was generated. The fact that the boat line was not a carferry and all freight required physical transfer made it a costly interchange to begin with, leaving little margin for success. The TH&I was forced to throw in the towel after only one miserably expensive year. Problems lingered even after the Lake Michigan line was ended because the business depression that began in 1893 made disposal of the boats difficult. It was a sorry episode, even more ill-advised than the investment in the Indiana & Lake Michigan road itself.[23]

For the Terre Haute & Indianapolis, 1892 was notable for more than just a misguided foray into steamboating, for late in the year, an additional 175 miles of railroad was grafted onto the Vandalia Line system. It was the culmination of McKeen's personal, decade-long campaign to acquire the line to Peoria. But the genesis of the story begins much earlier.

Chauncey Rose had campaigned for a railroad from Terre Haute to Decatur, Illinois, before the Civil War. In fact, the TH&I's founding father was among those who in 1861 chartered the line eventually built as the Paris & Decatur. Construction would not begin until 1870, when the most influential stockholders, who lived in Paris, Illinois, about 18 miles northwest of Terre Haute, convinced adopted Terre Hautean Robert G. Hervey to take over as general contractor. The Canadian-born Hervey had led a checkered business career and was not an experienced railroad builder, but he did have connections with British financial interests which could and did provide the capital necessary to finish the Paris & Decatur. As contractor, Hervey wound up with the bulk of the line's stock.[24]

Rear-end crew members of this Terre Haute & Peoria freight train pose with the station agent at an unidentified location (likely Arcola, Illinois). Collection of the Vigo County Historical Society, Terre Haute.

Shortly after the Paris & Decatur was opened, late in 1872, Hervey agreed to take over construction of a second railroad which had been organized in 1869 to build between Decatur and Peoria. This line, the Peoria, Atlanta & Decatur, had been promoted by the same contractors who built the eastern half of the Toledo, Peoria &

Warsaw. In fact, the TP&W offered to lease the unbuilt PA&D in April 1872. But by the end of the year, the contractors' almost complete lack of progress had caused great dissatisfaction in the road's on-line communities, many of which had bonded themselves to subscribe to the PA&D's stock. Hervey assumed the role of a white knight and took control of the Peoria line.[25]

From its opening, the Paris & Decatur had operated trains into Terre Haute by way of trackage rights over the Indianapolis & St. Louis, but in October 1873, Hervey chartered the Paris & Terre Haute to build southeast from Paris to a point on the Vandalia just west of Terre Haute. This new line was finished just over one year later, and trains began running into Terre Haute using trackage rights over McKeen's Vandalia Line. At the same time, the line into Peoria was also completed. In October 1874 Hervey merged his three roads into one by having the Peoria, Atlanta & Decatur buy the Paris & Decatur and Paris & Terre Haute. The PA&D was then renamed the Illinois Midland.[26]

The new railroad operated a 175-mile line between Terre Haute and Peoria, but it was a weak and seriously flawed creation. Besides being poorly and lightly built, the Illinois Midland did not own a foot of main track in any of its three most important terminal cities. It got no closer to Terre Haute than seven miles west, just over the state line; it entered and left Decatur over the tracks of the Illinois Central, from two miles south to 15 miles north of the city; and its entry into Peoria was over a ten-mile stretch of the Toledo, Peoria & Warsaw. Although the lack of terminal facilities was a significant deterrent to developing a healthy amount of on-line business, the most serious handicap was the constant and sizeable expense of using other companies' tracks.

Hervey had intended to remedy at least part of the trackage problem, but he never got the chance. With the depression of the 1870s in full swing before the Illinois Midland was completed, the road would have been in desperate straits even without its manifold shortcomings. To forestall nervous creditors, Hervey tried to petition the Midland into receivership in the local state court system, and a receiver was appointed in September 1875. But the bondholders, particularly the English contingent represented by the London banking houses of Grant Brothers and Waring Brothers, quickly intervened; and in December 1876, a mortgage foreclosure suit, which soon overtook and superseded the state court action, was filed in federal court.[27]

The Illinois Midland's list of creditors was lengthy and often competing, which introduced a large and ever-growing number of interested parties. Down that list was the Terre Haute & Indianapolis Railroad, whose claim of more than $30,000 for unpaid track rental, terminal services, and interline freight charges was eventually sold to the Warings.[28]

At first, the litigation barely progressed as competing interests jockeyed with each other for priority. The court's actions produced little more than a series of succeeding receivers, eventually four in number over ten years' time, each of whom issued receiver's certificates to cover the deficits generated by the continuing operation of the Illinois Midland. As the four groups of bondholders—each one representing a different mortgage on the Midland or one of its three component parts—fought over the estate, the receivers' debt piled up.

The litigation finally reached its climax in the early 1880s, by which time the bondholders had largely closed ranks behind the leadership of Waring Brothers and the New York banking house of Simon Borg & Company. The major holdup now was their rather vociferous protest against all those receivers' certificates that had been issued, whose holders naturally demanded priority ahead of the mortgages. Such a position was anathema to the bondholders, especially the foreign bondholders, and they complained bitterly to the court when it turned a sympathetic ear to some of the certificate holders.[29]

Riley McKeen was more than just an interested spectator, thanks to the TH&I's claim, but he became more deeply involved as the litigation dragged on. The third of the four receivers appointed, a Belgian émigré named Louis Genis, opened a running loan account with McKeen & Company after he was placed in charge of the Midland in December 1878. The balance eventually reached more than $30,000 and was still outstanding when Genis was replaced as receiver in April 1882. Just one month earlier, when the Midland's survival was in doubt, McKeen had offered to have his TH&I run the bankrupt road for the court, in place of a receiver. The judge, while seemingly intrigued by the idea, ultimately rejected it in favor of a new receiver.[30]

Train time is near in this early-20th-century scene at Arthur, Illinois, on the Terre Haute & Peoria. The station agent is on the platform with his customers, and the express crew is at the ready. Collection of Noel Dicks, Arthur, Illinois.

In a late 1890s view at Arthur, Illinois, the freight crew is busy, and the station agent presides. Collection of Noel Dicks, Arthur, Illinois.

By the time the court entered its foreclosure decree in the spring of 1885, both McKeen & Company's and the TH&I's claims had been sold and assigned to Waring Brothers, but Riley's interest in the property had been kindled. Along with Josephus Collett and David J. Mackey, a railroad promoter from Evansville, Indiana, McKeen was in attendance at the Midland's foreclosure sale on September 30, 1886, in Springfield, Illinois. There the court's commissioner sold the entire property to a representative of Simon Borg & Company, which had organized the bondholders' purchasing committee.[31]

Over the next six weeks, McKeen, Collett, and Mackey joined forces with the two principals of the Indianapolis banking firm of S. A. Fletcher Company, Stoughton J. Fletcher and Francis M. Churchman, and the five put together a competing bid. McKeen's group appealed the sale at the confirmation hearing on November 17. Then, having apparently optioned or purchased Waring Brothers' bondholdings, they offered their own bid on November 24. It was inexplicably lower than what the Borg faction had offered, and it was made even less enticing after Borg & Company added a sweetener. Justice Harlan quickly confirmed the latter offer on November 30 and left Riley and his associates empty-handed.[32]

In January 1887 Borg & Company organized a new company, the Terre Haute & Peoria, to take over the Midland. Even so, McKeen's interest in the property remained, and it only ended when Ives bought his controlling ownership of the TH&I later that spring.[33]

Riley had been far too busy to think about the Peoria line in the aftermath of the Ives debacle. Only after some semblance of stability had been restored by 1890 and he had unloaded the TH&I's day-to-day management on John Williams's shoulders did McKeen have time to consider the pokey little TH&P. By then, however, there was a complication.

When the Borg interests had organized the Terre Haute & Peoria to take ownership of the Illinois Midland property, they had prudently scaled back the funded debt of the new company, issuing less than half as many new bonds as there had been old. Since the Midland property had been bought mostly with depreciated old bonds picked up at a fraction of their face value, the bondholders group could afford to be conservative. The more than $3.7 million in par value TH&P common and preferred stocks that was also issued to the bondholders group was their means of escape. With its own investment safely secured by a mortgage lien, Borg & Company turned over the operation of the property to a hearty band of entrepreneurs led by a man who would become something of a nemesis and political rival for Riley McKeen, a very successful young railroad lawyer named Charles Warren Fairbanks.[34] Fairbanks's railroad career had begun in 1874, when an uncle had arranged a legal retainer for him with the Indianapolis, Bloomington & Western. The IB&W job brought Fairbanks to Indianapolis and eventually gained him a reputation as a highly competent corporate lawyer. It was also where he earned the confidence and trust of Austin Corbin, the New York banker who reorganized the IB&W in 1879, relying in part on Fairbanks's legal skills. As a member of Corbin's circle, Fairbanks was able to participate in a number of additional railroad reorganizations, and the young lawyer's fortune grew in tandem with his reputation. The opportunity to take over the Terre Haute & Peoria likely came through Alfred Sully, one of Corbin's closest associates, who had participated with Simon Borg & Company on the Illinois Midland bondholders' purchasing committee.[35]

Fairbanks's tiny band of investors did not have to pay very much for the TH&P stock, but, on the other hand, they did not get much in the way of a railroad, either. The Terre Haute & Peoria started life in 1887 with the same shortcomings that had handicapped the old Illinois Midland. The only improvement was lowered expectations: The TH&P started each working day with greatly reduced interest charges thanks to the scaled-back debt load. Fortunately, the bondholders had thought to leave the new company with a little working capital, setting aside about $475,000 worth of the new bonds to be used to improve the old road. Fairbanks's general manager, Daniel H. Conklin, who had also been the Midland's last receiver, put the cash realized from the bonds to good use, purchasing a number of newer locomotives and enough new steel rail to relay the entire main line. It was only light 56-pound section, but it was replacing old iron rails, some of even lighter weight.[36]

Of course, none of the TH&P's new steel rail was laid in any of its three big on-line cities. The company still labored under the disadvantages, and expense, of large amounts of leased trackage rights. While not a deficit operation, the TH&P was no moneymaker either. Moreover, once the proceeds from the bonds were gone, there

Charles Warren Fairbanks.
Fairbanks Collection,
Indiana Historical Society,
C6525.

was no real surplus being earned to pay for further improvements. Saddled with meager receipts and high operating expenses, the railroad quickly began to deteriorate. Fairbanks, realizing just how limited the TH&P's prospects were, was ready to entertain offers.

One such possibility materialized in 1890, when the Cincinnati, Hamilton & Dayton seemed interested in a lease. Given the fact that Fairbanks also served as the CH&D's Indiana solicitor, the idea may have first come from him. It was rumored that the CH&D was also looking at the Indianapolis, Decatur & Western, a line it would have needed to reach the TH&P, and which it would actually later acquire; but the Cincinnati company was still suffering from the effects of its own encounter with Henry Ives and did not have the wherewithal to pull off such a deal. By mid-August the CH&D's president announced the end of all negotiations. That left McKeen's TH&I.[37]

Riley McKeen was not unacquainted with Charles Fairbanks. In fact, he was all too well acquainted with the brittle and coldly reserved young lawyer. In his capacity as solicitor for the Cincinnati, Hamilton & Dayton, Fairbanks helped put together and prosecute the action against McKeen to recover the TH&I stock Ives had purchased. It had been a particularly nasty litigation. The plaintiff's baldly mendacious attempt to blacken the defendant's good name still rankled deeply, and there is some evidence to suggest that Riley held Fairbanks at least partially responsible for the needlessly cruel attack. As a rule, the genial, kind, and loyal McKeen did not easily dislike very many people; but in Charles Fairbanks he would find an exception.[38]

As much as he might want the Terre Haute & Peoria for his Vandalia Line system, McKeen seemed loathe to deal with Fairbanks personally. On Saturday, June 27, 1891, Fairbanks took TH&I General Manager John Williams and Riley's son Benjamin, a TH&I operating official, on an inspection tour over the Peoria road. Although the party left Terre Haute in McKeen's own private car, Riley was conspicuously absent. Williams admitted to a newspaper reporter present that negotiations were under way but far from complete.[39]

Instead of talking to the TH&P's stockholders, McKeen negotiated with the bondholders, who continued to be represented by Simon Borg & Company. The TH&I board was apprised of the pending deal on May 9, 1892, and the directors authorized Riley to both buy and lease the Peoria road. Fairbanks and his fellow owner-directors were so anxious to dispose of their property that they actually ratified the unfinished lease contract in June 1892. The next few months were spent ironing out

It's a turn-of-the-last-century winter day as the Peoria Division accommodation navigates the Illinois prairie outside Arthur. Ten-wheel locomotives (4-6-0) were a practical necessity on the Terre Haute & Peoria due to the road's light bridges and spindly 56-pound rail. Collection of Noel Dicks, Arthur, Illinois.

the details, including the amount and price of the TH&P stock the TH&I was to buy, and a commitment to increase the Peoria road's mortgage debt. McKeen knew that the TH&P would require substantial improvement, and he wanted an adequate amount of bonds available to reimburse the TH&I.[40]

As it turned out, McKeen was able to purchase control of the Terre Haute & Peoria for only $100,000, a figure which probably still gave Fairbanks and his associates a tidy profit. For its money the TH&I received 70 percent of the Peoria road's common shares and 30 percent of its preferred, an investment with a total face value of almost $1.9 million. On October 1 the TH&I also leased the Peoria road for a term of 99 years and agreed to endorse the TH&P's bonds, including $700,000 in new bonds called for in the lease contract. All in all, it was a good deal for the bondholders and the remaining outside stockholders, whose securities were now guaranteed continued dividends. It was not quite the same for McKeen's Vandalia Line, which added 175 miles of additional railroad to its operating system.[41]

In spite of the low price, the Terre Haute & Peoria was no bargain. John Williams quickly discovered that the property had gone considerably downhill since his inspection trip 16 months earlier. The roadbed was still almost completely unballasted

and deteriorating. The track, although recently relaid with lightweight steel, was only partially spiked, and the splicebars were light and either broken or missing bolts. After a careful inspection, the TH&I's engineering forces determined that a substantial proportion of the Peoria road's ties needed to be replaced without delay and that a number of bridges required immediate strengthening or rebuilding. And the expenses ballooned. As the general manager would report to his president the following year, "so many unexpected things had to be done for the sake of safety, if nothing else, that the large operating loss, upon careful investigation, seems to have been unavoidable." In its first full year of operation, the TH&P cost McKeen's road more than $102,000 and helped push the Terre Haute & Indianapolis into only its second reported deficit.[42]

The embarrassment did not end there. Peoria line grades were so bad west of Decatur, and the engines acquired along with the TH&P so light and feeble, that eastbound trains of as little as 15 loaded cars required doubling, or stopping for multiple trips up hills, in as many three to four places between Farmdale and Maroa, north of Decatur. The Vandalia Line transportation department decided to remedy the situation by purchasing four new heavy freight locomotives. But the new power was found to be too heavy for the track and bridges and had to be swapped temporarily with lighter TH&I engines off the main line. Repairs and improvements to the road were rushed—adding to the expense—so that the new engines could be used as intended.[43]

Whatever McKeen had seen in the Terre Haute & Peoria seemed to elude the ledger book. The largest traffic item in 1893 was grain, which comprised almost half the tonnage. When added together with flour and other milled products, hay, fruit and vegetables, and livestock, the TH&P's agricultural products business was 57 percent of total tonnage. Bituminous coal, the second largest item, represented only 14 percent of tonnage carried. At the low rates such traffic commanded, the TH&P only reported a paltry $2,400 per mile in gross earnings. And, it should be noted, since the TH&I's accounts ended on October 31, only three months of the depression were included in these results.[44]

In comparison, the leased Terre Haute & Logansport, which was also a deficit operation for the TH&I, outperformed the Peoria line significantly, grossing $4,000 per mile. Similar in length, the Logansport road's total tonnage was nearly twice that of the Peoria's. The Logansport's traffic in 1893 was dominated by bituminous coal at 33 percent of tonnage and lumber at 17 percent. Almost all of the latter commodity originated in Michigan and had shown a whopping 513 percent increase over the previous year, thanks to operation of the Indiana & Lake Michigan extension. In contrast, agricultural traffic represented only 17 percent of the Logansport's total tonnage.[45]

Things did not get much better in 1894. The depression of the 1890s dragged down the general level of business, and the Terre Haute & Peoria continued to run at a substantial loss to the TH&I. Even with expenses brought under control, the Peoria road cost McKeen's company almost $110,000. It is difficult to characterize Riley's dogged enthusiasm for the road as anything more than poor judgement.[46]

Peoria was an important gateway, and McKeen may have entertained the notion of an increased amount of east-west business from that point. The Cincinnati,

There must be something important happening in this circa 1910 shot of the Arthur, Illinois, depot. A double-headed set of locomotives seems like overkill for the four-car train; and there is a larger crowd than usual waiting to board on the platform. This is quite possibly a work train, taking a group of local Arthur men farther up the line to help clear the railroad of drifted snow. Arthur's station was a "Union Depot," jointly maintained by the Vandalia Line and the Chicago & Eastern Illinois, whose tracks occupy the far side of the building and cross the Van where the locomotives sit. Collection of Noel Dicks, Arthur, Illinois.

Hamilton & Dayton was similarly mesmerized, for at the time it was briefly pursuing a lease of the Peoria road, it was also rumored to be dickering for control of Russell Sage's Iowa Central. But the Terre Haute & Peoria was completely unsuitable for any amount of through traffic and had enough trouble handling its modest local business.[47]

Distribution of TH&I coal probably figured heavily in McKeen's plans for the Peoria route. Like the Logansport road purchase, acquisition of the Peoria line meant the theoretical extension of the marketing and delivery territory of Brazil and Terre Haute mines. Unfortunately, the two industrial centers on the TH&P, Decatur and

Peoria, were already well supplied: Decatur from the mining district just to its north; Peoria from mines in its immediate vicinity. As a result, the Peoria road's coal traffic figures would show virtually no growth at all.

The Terre Haute & Peoria was simply a bad investment. Its operation by the TH&I merely preserved another railroad line that happened to serve McKeen's home city. The fact that it was a poorly built and unprofitable piece of track was secondary to its status as an arm of Terre Haute commerce, and therein lay the real justification for its purchase.

Similar reasoning motivated the building of Terre Haute's grand new Union Depot, the third and final addition to the TH&I's burden. The company's officers and directors had contemplated building a new terminal as far back as 1872. The current Terre Haute station had been in use since 1861, a converted brick hotel that suffered from its makeshift design. But the biggest problem with the old depot was its location, at Tenth and Chestnut streets, two blocks south of the TH&I's east-west main line. Since the station tracks were at a right angle to the railroad, all trains passing through Terre Haute required a backup move either to enter or leave the depot,

This late 1880s picture of an Evansville & Terre Haute crew perched on boxcars also shows the old Terre Haute Union Depot at Tenth and Chestnut streets to the immediate left. Also just barely visible on the hazy horizon to the right of the Vandalia Line roundhouse is the extensive TH&I shops complex. Community Archives, Vigo County Public Library, Terre Haute.

Moving about 100 yards east, the photographer captures a better view of the old Terre Haute Union Depot in the late 1880s. Also visible is the big TH&I roundhouse. A horsecar occupies Chestnut Street in front of the old station. The hip-roofed addition to the rear of the old building is the attached Ohmer's Hotel, which catered to the business traveler. Community Archives, Vigo County Public Library, Terre Haute.

a significant operating headache. The addition of the Chicago & Eastern Illinois, Evansville & Terre Haute, and Evansville & Indianapolis railroads as tenants only overloaded an already inadequate facility.[48]

Once McKeen reassumed control of the railroad after the Ives affair, the problem of what to do about the old Union Depot returned to consideration. As both the controlling owner of the station's proprietor and the city's leading businessman, Riley must have come under increasing pressure to do something about this civic shortcoming. After all, did not Terre Haute, Queen City of the Wabash Valley, deserve a more appropriate railway station, especially since it was the headquarters of the magnificent and expanding Vandalia Line? In an era of increasingly ostentatious urban development, the answer was obviously "yes." Yet, because of the tenuously uncertain financial condition of his railroad, McKeen had to proceed with caution.

Pride seems to have precluded approaching his tenants for help in shouldering the cost, although he may have broached the subject with the Evansville & Terre Haute, with which he had financial dealings. At some point, perhaps at the city government's suggestion, the Big Four, which had recently absorbed the Bee Line, was also considered as a participant. But in the end it was McKeen's TH&I which valiantly and proudly assumed sole responsibility. Riley and John Williams would both reap the attending civic gratitude, but at a heavy cost to the railroad.[49]

McKeen seems to have made up his mind by 1890, for plans were invited. Sometime during the first half of the year, Samuel H. Hannaford & Sons of Cincinnati was chosen as the architect and general contractor. By summer Hannaford had a basic design worked out, which, after revision, was accepted by McKeen and his general manager on Wednesday, August 6. But the financial pressure on the TH&I had been increased by the terms of the Vandalia rent settlement, and McKeen postponed his new station plans. Not until after the first of the new year was anything more done.[50]

At the newly re-elected board's first meeting, on January 5, 1891, Riley polled the directors individually for what was termed "an informal expression as to the advisability of building a new Union Depot." The expressions were unanimously positive. Encouraged, Riley let the contract to Hannaford shortly thereafter, and excavation for the new station began early that spring.[51]

It was to be a grand and beautiful station in the proper location, where the north-south Chicago & Eastern Illinois and Evansville & Terre Haute tracks crossed the east-west TH&I. The building itself sat in the southwest quadrant of the crossing, constructed of red stone and pressed brick. Italianate in design, the structure was dominated by a 200-foot cone-capped tower, which formed the interior corner of the almost triangular headhouse. Attached to the station, and sheltering each set of station tracks, were two soaring steel-framed train sheds with slate roofs: The one on the north-south axis was 400 feet long; the other over the east-west Vandalia Line tracks, 700 feet long. Separate brick outbuildings for the handling of mail and express flanked the headhouse and completed the arrangements.[52]

Impressive to see from the circular asphalt drive it fronted, between Ninth and Sycamore, the new Union Depot was even more grand inside. Originally, the ground floor concourse and rotunda were to be finished in marble, but the growing costliness of the construction dictated economy. Instead, the first floor was finished in quartered oak, and the two upper office floors received hard oiled pine. Illumination was by electric light, with power supplied by a separate plant installed by Westinghouse.[53]

A spacious lady's salon was included, as was a particularly handsome barber shop. But the most distinctive interior feature was the grand new restaurant opened by Ohmer's, a Dayton, Ohio, railroad restaurant chain. Entry was through elegant plate-glass doors. The restaurant was filled with stylish wooden tables and green potted plants and also contained a large, circular cherry-wood lunch counter with revolving stools. The gustatory delights which emanated from the basement kitchen via dumbwaiters were intended to be the city's finest. On the depot's opening day, the dining room waitresses all wore striking white gowns to mark the occasion.[54]

Terre Haute was not in any discernibly festive mood when its glorious new Union Depot finally opened on August 15, 1893, perhaps in part because it was eight months late. The previous summer, construction had been on schedule for a planned opening in December 1892, but problems with some of the interior details and possible conflict over the cost overruns halted construction for several months. For whatever reason, there was no celebration.[55]

McKeen and his board had contracted for a new station originally priced at $200,000, which was a considerable sum for its day. But the final cost turned out to

Above: The new Terre Haute Union Depot, shortly after its opening in 1893. The landscaped depot park which will occupy the grassy open space in front of the building has not yet been constructed. Note the train sheds that flank the head house. Collection of the Vigo County Historical Society, Terre Haute.

Below: This 1897 view shows the train sheds and station tracks of the new Terre Haute Union Depot. The Vandalia Line locomotive at left has its pops lifted, indicating a full head of steam, while another engine occupies the Chicago & Eastern Illinois tracks to the right of the crossing. Collection of the Vigo County Historical Society, Terre Haute.

be 35 percent higher, or $270,000, certainly a luxurious indulgence for a road in the TH&I's straits. Where the money was to come from had been occupying quite a bit of McKeen's time.[56]

By the end of 1890, after the expensive settlement with the Pan Handle and St. Louis, Vandalia & Terre Haute had placed additional short-term financing requirements on the TH&I, the floating debt the company was carrying became uncomfortable. Riley had raised the company's total mortgage debt limit by $600,000 in 1885, to $2.2 million, but had only used half of the increase. During his brief control, Ives had disposed of the remaining $300,000 in unused bonds for his own purposes, and the proceeds were never recovered after Ives's bank collapsed. With the entire $2.2 million now outstanding, there was nothing left in reserve.[57]

Since a mortgage-bond refinancing would soon be necessary for the remaining 7 percent bonds of 1873, which would come due in April 1893, and with the financial stresses imposed in the wake of the Ives' debacle, McKeen elected to raise the debt limit. Accordingly, a mortgage debt increase was approved by the stockholders in January 1889. But the company managed to scrape by and was able to reduce its debt by economizing, so nothing more was done about a new mortgage. Presumably because the company had failed to act within two years, the new $3 million debt limit was re-presented and passed again in January 1891. By this time, however, thanks to its recent spending binge, the TH&I really needed the money.[58]

The ancient 1860s-era Terre Haute Union Depot building pictured just prior to its destruction in the fall of 1924. The old building had survived for many years as a railroad office facility. Built in the 1850s as a hotel, it was converted to a station in 1861 by the TH&I. The new Union Depot of 1893 is visible in the distance. Collection of the Vigo County Historical Society, Terre Haute.

Early in 1892 McKeen began negotiations with Blair & Company, a New York investment bank. At first it was intended to extend the old 1873 first mortgage at a reduced rate of interest, but after various legal problems surfaced, the railroad and Blair decided on a brand new 5 percent bond issue. Along with the previously issued 5 percent consolidated mortgage bonds, the new first mortgage would raise the TH&I's total outstanding bonded debt to $2.5 million, a relatively modest $300,000 increase, and leave a comfortable cushion under the debt limit. The contract was finalized and approved by the board in August 1892.[59]

Technically, McKeen had already spent the new capital. A sum of $100,000 was used to help finish paying off the notes given to the St. Louis, Vandalia & Terre Haute in the settlement over back lease rental, freeing the TH&I from this obligation by the end of the year. Another $100,000 went to cover the cost of the Terre Haute & Peoria stock McKeen had agreed to buy that fall. And the last $100,000 was used as down payment on 1,000 badly needed new freight cars.[60]

The TH&I's Spartan economic measures, necessitated by the loss of assets during the Ives regime and the expensive Vandalia rental settlement, had left the railroad chronically short of equipment. It was a situation McKeen could no longer ignore. So, along with the new mortgage bond issue, Riley also worked out a car trust agreement with Blair & Company. While not exactly a new way to pay for equipment purchases—the Pennsylvania had made use of car trust contracts for years—this particular form of financing had not yet become common. It was essentially a conditional sales agreement between the lender, builder, and user, and the resulting costs went on the ledger as ordinary operating expenses rather than being capitalized as long-term debt. With his short-term focus and a driving need to clean up his balance sheet, the car trust arrangement must have appealed strongly to McKeen.[61]

The trust agreement, approved by the TH&I board in August 1892, covered the purchase of 700 new boxcars, 150 flatcars, 100 furniture cars, and 50 refrigerator cars. The order was placed with hometown Terre Haute Car and Manufacturing Company. Once construction commenced in September, deliveries began at approximately 100 cars per week. Costs were typical for the period, running from $330 per flatcar to $580 for each furniture car.[62]

The new cars were apportioned between the TH&I proper, the Vandalia, and the Logansport. Costs were divided in the same formula, 41.5 percent each to the TH&I and the Vandalia company and 17 percent to the Logansport road. New equipment for the Terre Haute & Peoria had been provided for in the TH&I's lease of that company, covered by the new Peoria line mortgage.

The new arrangements with Blair allowed McKeen to announce an actual reduction in interest charges in his 1892 report to stockholders. With the retirement and replacement of the old 7 percent bonds with the new 5 percent issue, the TH&I's annual interest bill dropped from $142,000 to $125,000, and that looked impressive on the balance sheet. The new car trust added almost $70,000 per year in extra car maintenance expense over the next six years but did not affect the general ledger accounts.[63]

As 1892 came to a close, things were actually beginning to look a little brighter for the Terre Haute & Indianapolis. McKeen had brought the lingering problems of the Ives interlude to what appeared to be a satisfactory resolution. He had dazzled most observers, if not his outside stockholders, with an expanded system. A new showpiece of a Union Depot was on its way to completion in Terre Haute. And he had put long-term financing in place to mop up most of the floating debt and cover the costs of the expansion.

Also, 1892 marked the end of the Pennsylvania's long fight to strip the TH&I of the St. Louis, Vandalia & Terre Haute. In May, on the ruling of the U.S. Supreme Court, McKeen and the TH&I won. The validity of the lease was sustained, largely because it had remained in force for 17 years before anyone thought to protest it. Now that they had finally exhausted all appeals, the Pennsylvania's executives had to face defeat. They also had no other alternative left but to buy McKeen's stock in the TH&I.[64]

Significantly, negotiations were handled by the Lines West management; this time, for the most part, George Roberts stayed out of the discussions until the end. While it is not clear when the bargaining began, progress was fairly swift, and an actual agreement was reached by early August 1893.

For Riley McKeen, it was long past time to let go of the property he had faithfully served since the Civil War and controlled absolutely for 20 years. He was 63, a millionaire, and tired of the responsibility that the 650-mile Vandalia Line system imposed.

This time the Pennsylvania did not demand a thorough inspection and careful appraisal of the property, nor did its officers quibble over petty details. If they paled at the extent and condition of McKeen's TH&I, the Pennsylvania's men did not show it. There was no balking over the Logansport road lease either, for the Lines West executives had actually found a good use for what Roberts had once considered an expensive white elephant.

Back in 1871, during its aggressive period of midwestern expansion, the Pennsylvania had leased the Jeffersonville, Madison & Indianapolis Railroad. Although built as a north-south artery, the new acquisition was used as an extension to Louisville from the east, by way of Cambridge City and Columbus, Indiana, mainly because the JM&I's main stem from Louisville to Indianapolis lacked a Pennsylvania-controlled outlet to the north. This deficiency was partially corrected in 1882, when Lines West worked out a trackage rights arrangement over the Wabash-leased Indianapolis, Peru & Chicago line from Indianapolis to Kokomo, on the former Indiana Central. At last the JM&I could compete for north-south freight business and Chicago-bound passenger traffic. But the Wabash's IP&C line had serious operating drawbacks which the Pennsylvania Lines found restrictive. Therefore, although it renewed the trackage rights agreement in 1888 with IP&C successor Lake Erie & Western, Lines West did so for only a ten-year period, fully intending to develop a better alternative.[65]

The most likely solution to the problem, and the one eventually undertaken, first surfaced late in 1889. On December 18, at one of their regular semi-annual conferences held to discuss the operation of the St. Louis, Vandalia & Terre Haute, McKeen and Lines West Vice President Jacob McCullough broached the possibility of using Riley's Logansport road as part of a new line between Indianapolis and Logansport. Even though the proposal was vague at first, Riley must have thought McCullough sufficiently interested to have the TH&I pay for a route survey in the summer of

The bridge over Mill Creek, just east of Amo, Indiana, has collapsed, taking a Vandalia Line engine and train with it. Guilford Township Historical Collection, Plainfield Public Library, Plainfield, Indiana.

1890. The proposed route was from the western edge of Indianapolis on the TH&I to Frankfort on the Logansport road, a 38-mile line by way of Lebanon. While nothing further was done at the time, the plan was attractive enough to Lines West to make acquisition of the Logansport road a non-issue. Indeed, the Pennsylvania would build an entirely new railroad over the same route some 25 years later and end the trackage rights to Kokomo.[66]

The agreement between William Riley McKeen and the Pennsylvania Company was signed on August 18, 1893; and it gave Riley everything he had originally asked for back in 1885. The Pennsylvania Company agreed to buy the 14,000 shares of Terre Haute & Indianapolis stock McKeen owned at his long-maintained price of $75 per share.[67]

The $1,050,000 price tag was to be paid for with a combination of cash and, fittingly enough, brand new 4½ percent consolidated mortgage bonds of the Pan Handle, a specified portion of which could later be exchanged for more cash at McKeen's option. Since the bonds-for-cash exchange option extended to January 1, 1895, the transaction would not technically be completed until after that date. To protect Riley, one of the provisions of the agreement was that he would remain

VANDALIA LINE.

TERRE HAUTE AND INDIANAPOLIS RAILROAD COMPANY.

LESSEE
ST. LOUIS VANDALIA & TERRE HAUTE R.R.

OPERATING
TERRE HAUTE & LOGANSPORT R.R., INDIANA & LAKE MICHIGAN RY.
and TERRE HAUTE & PEORIA R.R.

W. R. McKEEN, President, Terre Haute, Ind.
JOHN G. WILLIAMS, Vice-President and Gen. Manager, Terre Haute, Ind.
T. J. GOLDEN, Att'y in State of Illinois, Marshall, Ill.
JOS. HILL, Asst. Gen. Manager, St. Louis, Mo.
GEO. E. FARRINGTON, Secretary and Gen. Agt., Terre Haute, Ind.

B. THOMPSON, Treasurer, Terre Haute, Ind.
W. S. RONEY, Auditor, "
E. A. FORD, Gen. Passenger Agt., St. Louis, Mo.
J. M. CHESBROUGH, Asst. Gen. Passenger Agt., St. Louis, Mo.
H. W. HIBBARD, Gen. Freight Agent, "
E. R. DARLOW, Asst. Superintendent, "

N. K. ELLIOTT, Supt. Transp., Terre Haute, Ind.
G. H. PRESCOTT, Supt. Motive Power and Machinery, Terre Haute, Ind.
F. C. CRAWFORD, Paymaster, "
CHAS. R. PEDDLE, Purchasing Agent, "
R. R. BENTLEY, Gen. Baggage Agt., Pittsburg, Pa.
H. G. SLEIGHT, Car Accountant, Terre Haute, Ind.

OFFICIAL LOCAL TIME-TABLES.—MAY, 1893.

ST. LOUIS TO INDIANAPOLIS.

Mls	Central time.	20	8	2	10	12	6	18
	[LEAVE]	A.M.	A.M.	A.M.	P.M.	P.M.	P.M.	P.M
	St. Louis¹ +Union Depot δ	*8 10	*8 40	†11 25	*5 30	*8 00	*9 00	*9 10
0	Main Street...	...	...	11 30	5 35	...	...	...
2	East St. Louis+...δ	8 25	8 53	11 40	5 45	8 15	9 15	9 25
9	Griswold Place...	...	9 00	11 53	6 02	...	...	...
13	Collinsville...δ	...	9 18	12 01	6 16	...	...	9 47
15	Cantine...	...	9 21	12 04	6 20	...	...	...
19	Formosa...	...	...	12 12	6 33	...	...	...
23	Troy+...δ	...	9 32	12 15	6 45	8 51	...	...
27	St. Jacob's...δ	...	9 44	12 26	6 56	9 00	...	...
32	Highland +...δ	...	9 55	12 35	7 06	9 10	...	10 18
37	Pierron...δ	...	10 03	12 43	7 15	...	...	...
41	Pocahontas...δ	...	10 11	12 51	7 25	...	...	...
47	Stubblefield...	...	...	...	7 35	...	...	...
51	Greenville³+...δ	...	9 35	10 30	1 03	7 47	9 43	10 36 10 56
55	Smithboro²+...δ	...	...	10 38	1 16	7 55	9 50	10 43 11 04
59	Mulberry Grove...δ	...	...	10 48	1 23	8 04	...	...
65	Hagerstown...	...	...	10 57	1 33	8 16	...	...
69	Vandalia³+...δ	...	10 00	11 04	1 40	8 24	10 12	11 08 11 34
77	Brownstown...δ	...	...	11 18	1 63	8 39	...	...
								P.M.
79	Avena...	...	...	11 21	...	8 43	...	11 27
83	St. Elmo...	...	...	11 30	2 03	8 49	...	...
88	Altamont⁴+...δ	...	10 25	11 40	2 13	9 02	10 42	11 44
92	Dexter...	...	...	11 47	...	9 10	...	...
96	Funkhouser...	...	...	11 54	...	9 18	...	14
100	Effingham³+...δ arr.	...	10 43	12 05	2 33	9 25	11 10	12 05
100	Effingham... lve.	...	10 46	12 10	2 38	P.M.	11 18 12 10	7 00
104	Teutopolis...δ	...	...	12 17	2 46	...	11 25	...	7 09
110	Montrose...δ	...	...	12 27	2 56	...	...	...	7 20
114	Woodbury...	...	...	12 34	...	...	...	...	7 30
118	Jewett...	...	...	12 39	3 12	...	...	...	7 38
122	Greenup Crossing⁶+δ	...	...	12 48	3 22	...	11 52 12 46	7 50
129	Vevay Park...	...	...	1 00	...	...	...	...	8 02
132	Casey +...	...	...	1 07	3 44	...	12 07	1 02	8 10
139	Martinsville+...	...	...	1 18	3 55	...	...	...	8 24
150	Marshall+...	...	12 03	1 40	4 17	...	12 34	1 30	8 43
151	Marshall Crossing⁷...	...	...	...	4 21	...	...	...	8 50
157	Dennison...	...	...	1 54	4 33	4	...	...	9 03
168	Terre Haute⁸ δ arr.	...	12 42	2 20	5 00	A.M.	1 10	2 10	9 30
168	Terre Haute +... lve.	...	12 47	2 35	5 05	†7 15	1 20	2 20	A.M.
173	Glenn...	...	...	2 46	5 16	7 26	...	...
175	Seelyville...δ	...	...	2 51	5 21	7 31	...	...
179	Staunton...	...	...	3 00	5 30	7 40	...	...
181	Newburg...	...	...	3 04	5 33	7 44	...	...
183	Brazil+...	...	1 15	3 10	5 40	7 51	1 47	2 55
185	Knightsville...	...	...	3 17	5 46	7 57	...	...
186	Harmony...	...	...	3 19	5 48	7 59	...	...
190	Eagles...	...	...	3 26	5 56	8 12	...	...
193	Reelsville...	...	...	3 31	6 00	8 18	...	...
196	Hamricks...	...	...	3 38	6 06	8 19	...	...
200	Junction³+...δ	...	1 41	3 44	6 12	8 26	2 16	3 26
201	Greencastle+...δ	...	1 49	3 52	6 20	8 34	2 24	3 36
208	Fillmore...	...	...	4 05	6 31	8 45	...	...
212	Coatsville...δ	...	...	4 14	6 39	8 54	...	...
215	Amo...	...	...	4 20	6 44	9 00	...	...
217	Pecksburg...	...	...	4 25	6 49	9 05	...	...
220	Clayton...	...	...	4 32	6 56	9 12	...	...
222	Belleville...	...	...	4 36	6 58	9 15	...	...
223	Cartersburg...	...	...	4 40	7 01	9 19	...	...
226	Plainfield...	...	...	4 47	7 08	9 26	...	...
231	Bridgeport...	...	...	4 57	7 18	9 36	...	...
234	Ben Davis...	...	...	5 03	7 26	9 42	...	...
240	Indianapolis¹⁸+...δ	...	2 50	5 20	7 45	10 00	3 30	4 50
	[ARRIVE]	P.M.	P.M.	P.M.	A.M.	A.M.	A.M.	A.M.

INDIANAPOLIS TO ST. LOUIS.

Mls	Central time.	5	21	1	7	3	13
	[LEAVE]	A.M.	A.M.	P.M.	P.M.	P.M.	P.M.
0	Indianapolis¹⁸+...δ	†7 30	*1150	*1 00	*1100	*4 00	
6	Ben Davis...	7 48	...	...	...	4 16	
9	Bridgeport...δ	7 54	...	...	...	4 22	
14	Plainfield...δ	8 04	...	1 36	...	4 32	
17	Cartersburg...δ	8 11	...	...	...	4 40	
19	Belleville...δ	8 14	...	...	...	4 44	
20	Clayton...δ	8 17	...	...	...	4 47	
23	Pecksburg...	8 24	...	...	...	4 54	
25	Amo...δ	8 28	...	...	...	5 00	
28	Coatsville...δ	8 34	...	...	...	5 07	
32	Fillmore...δ	8 45	...	...	...	5 16	
39	Greencastle ▾...δ	8 56	12 53	2 10	12 12	5 28	
40	Junction³+...δ	9 01	12 58	2 15	12 17	5 34	
44	Hamricks...	9 07	...	...	...	5 40	
47	Reelsville...δ	9 14	...	...	...	5 46	
51	Eagles...	9 19	...	...	...	5 54	
54	Harmony...	9 26	...	...	...	6 00	
55	Knightsville...δ	9 28	...	...	...	6 03	
57	Brazil+...	9 34	1 32	2 40	12 48	6 09	
59	Newburg...	9 37	...	...	...	6 14	
61	Staunton...δ	9 40	...	...	...	6 18	
65	Seelyville...δ	9 48	...	...	...	6 28	
67	Glenn...	9 52	...	...	...	6 32	
72	Terre Haute⁸ δ arr	10 05	2 05	3 05	1 20	6 45	P.M.
72	Terre Haute+... lve.	10 11	2 20	3 10	1 35	P.M.	*4 05
83	Deanison...	10 38	...	...	...	...	4 34
90	Marshall Crossing⁷... δ	10 52	...	...	...	...	4 48
91	Marshall+...δ	10 56	2 52	3 39	2 18	...	4 53
101	Martinsville...	11 20	...	...	...	...	5 15
108	Casey +...δ	11 36	3 18	4 04	2 50	...	5 27
111	Vevay Park...	11 48	...	...	...	...	5 34
118	Greenup Crossing⁶+δ	12 01	3 32	4 17	3 07	...	5 47
122	Jewett...	12 10	...	...	...	...	5 55
126	Woodbury...	12 16	...	...	...	...	6 01
133	Montrose...δ	12 27	...	...	...	...	6 09
136	Teutopolis...δ	12 37	4 00	...	9	...	6 18
140	Effingham³+... δ arr.	10 10	4 10	4 48	3 45	A.M.	6 25
140	Effingham...δ arr.	1 10	4 15	4 51	3 49	*4 00	P.M.
144	Funkhouser...	1 18	...	...	...	4 06	
148	Dexter...	1 26	...	...	...	4 12	
152	Altamont⁴+...δ	1 34	4 35	5 08	4 12	4 20	
158	St. Elmo...δ	1 44	4 44	...	...	4 31	
162	Avena...	1 56	4 52	...	...	4 39	17
164	Brownstown...δ	2 02	...	...	...	4 42	A.M.
171	Vandalia³+...δ	2 18	5 08	5 34	4 48	4 59	*5 36
175	Hagerstown...	2 26	...	...	...	5 06	
181	Mulberry Grove...δ	2 38	...	...	...	5 18	
185	Smithboro²+...δ	2 46	5 31	5 54	5 10	5 25	6 00
189	Greenville³+...δ	2 57	5 40	6 02	5 20	5 35	6 09
194	Stubblefield...	3 06	...	...	...	5 41	
199	Pocahontas...δ	3 18	...	...	...	5 51	
203	Pierron...δ	3 27	...	...	...	5 59	
208	Highland +...δ	3 38	6 12	...	...	6 10	6 44
213	St. Jacobs +...δ	3 48	...	...	...	6 20	6 54
219	Troy +...δ	4 01	...	...	...	6 31	
221	Formosa...	4 05	...	...	...	6 35	
225	Cantine...	4 13	...	...	...	6 42	
227	Collinsville...δ	4 19	...	...	...	6 46	7 22
231	Griswold Place...δ	4 28	...	...	...	6 56	
238	East St. Louis +...δ arr.	4 45	7 05	7 15	6 45	7 15	7 45
	Main Street...	...	...	...	...	6 55	7 50
240	St. Louis¹+...δ	5 00	7 20	7 30	7 00	7 30	8 00
	[ARRIVE]	P.M.	P.M.	P.M.	P.M.	A.M.	A.M.

N.B.—Trains marked * run daily; † daily, except Sunday. + Coupon stations; δ Telegraph stations.

PARLOR AND SLEEPING CAR ARRANGEMENTS.

Train No. 20—Solid Vestibuled train St. Louis to New York without change. Also Parlor Car for Indianapolis and Cincinnati without change. All meals served in dining cars.

Train No. 8—Has Free Reclining Chair Cars from St. Louis to Chicago.

Train No. 12—Has Through Pullman Sleeper to Cincinnati.

Train No. 6—Has Pullman Sleeper for Indianapolis, in which passengers can remain until breakfast time. Also Pullman Vestibuled Sleeping Cars to Philadelphia, New York, Baltimore and Washington without change.

Train No. 18—Solid Train to Chicago, has Vestibuled Pullman Compartment and Sleeping Cars, Free Reclining Chair Car Combination Coach and Smoker.

Train No. 1—Has Parlor Car from Cincinnati, via C. H. & D. Also Free-Reclining Chair Car from Chicago to St. Louis.

Train No. 21—Solid Vestibuled train New York to St. Louis, via Penna. Lines and Indianapolis. Dinner served in Dining Car.

Train No. 7—Has Pullman Vestibuled Sleeping Car for St. Louis, which is placed at Indianapolis Depot so that passengers can retire after 9 00 p.m. Also Pullman Combination Sleeping and Chair Car from Indianapolis to Evansville, via Terre Haute and E. & T. H. R.R., arriving Evansville 8 30 a.m.

Martinville St. Jacobs and Collinsville are flag stations for No. 1 on Sundays.

One Stop-over ticket issued, good for fifteen days, upon regular unlimited first-class, local, or coupon ticket, reading one way.

For other through line arrangements of Vandalia Line, see condensed time-tables of "The Pennsylvania Lines West of Pittsburgh," on preceding pages.
For Time-Tables of Terre Haute and St. Joseph, and Terre Haute and Peoria lines, see next page.

VANDALIA LINE.

OFFICIAL LOCAL TIME-TABLES.—MAY, 1893.

TERRE HAUTE AND ST JOSEPH LINE.

64	52	Mls	STATIONS.	Mls	51	53
P. M.	A.M.		(Central time.)		A.M.	P.M.
+4 00	+6 20	0	lv.+.Terre Haute*.δar.	223	11 45	7 30
4 11	6 31	5	....Ellsworth......	218	11 34	7 19
4 15	6 35	δ	...Otter Creek Jn...δ	217	11 30	7 15
4 31	6 49	13	....Rosedale......	210	11 15	7 03
4 37	6 54	16	....Jessup's.....δ	207	11 10	6 56
4 44	7 00	18	....Catlin......	204	11 04	6 51
4 57	7 10	23	+....Rockville....δ	200	10 53	6 40
5 05	7 18	27	...Sand Creek...δ	195	10 44	6 31
5 12	7 26	31	....Judson.....δ	192	10 37	6 24
5 18	7 31	33	....Guion 11......	190	10 31	6 18
5 39	7 41	38	....Waveland....δ	185	10 20	6 07
5 36	7 48	41	...Brown's Valley..	182	10 13	6 00
5 48	7 57	46	...New Market...δ	177	10 02	5 48
5 51	8 02	48	....North Union...	175	9 58	5 43
6 00	8 12	53	arr.Crawfordsville.Jn 13.lve.	170	9 48	5 35
6 15	8 12	53	lve.Crawfdsville.Jn..δ arr.	170	9 48	5 23
6 19	8 16	53	+.Crawfordsville.δ	170	9 44	5 20
6 28	8 26	58	....Garfield......	165	9 34	5 08
6 35	8 32	61	...Darlington...δ	162	9 28	5 01
6 45	8 42	65	....Bowers......	158	9 19	4 52

P. M.	A.M.		LEAVE] [ARRIVE		A.M.	P. M.
5 15	7 10		....Indianapolis....		10 45	6 15
6 55	8 50	69	+....Colfax 13.....δ	154	9 10	4 44
7 06	9 00	74	....Manson......	149	9 00	4 33
7 16	9 11	79	+ .Frankfort 14...δ	144	8 50	4 22
7 27	9 20	84	....Kilmore......	139	8 39	4 12
7 34	9 26	87	....Moran......	136	8 34	4 06
7 38	9 30	88	....Sedalia......	134	8 30	4 02
7 49	9 38	93	....Cutler......	130	8 21	3 51
7 58	9 46	97	...Bringhurst...	126	8 14	3 41
8 02	9 48	98	.....Flora.....δ	125	8 09	3 36
8 11	9 58	102	....Camden.....δ	121	8 01	3 25
8 18	10 06	106	....Woodville...	117	7 53	3 16
8 25	10 14	110	....Clymer's....δ	113	7 46	3 05
8 40	10 30	116	ar.+Logansport 18 lv.	106	7 34	2 50
8 45	10 35	116	lve.Logansport.arr.	106	7 30	2 40
8 55	10 46	121	....Verona......	102	7 22	2 32
9 02	10 54	125	....Lucerne......	98	7 14	2 25
9 14	11 05	130	...Grass Creek....	92	7 04	2 14
9 23	11 16	135	....Kewanna.....δ	88	6 56	2 04
9 29	11 24	139	...Bruce Lake....	84	6 51	1 56
9 39	11 34	144	...De Long 16...δ	79	6 43	1 46
9 50	11 45	149	Marmont(LakeMaxinkuckee)	74	6 34	1 36
9 50	11 45	149	Marmont(LakeMaxinkuckee)	74	6 19	1 15
9 57	12 13	152	....Hibbard 17...δ	71	6 14	1 07
10 02	12 17	155	....Twin Lakes....	68	6 09	1 01
10 10	12 25	160	+....Plymouth 18...δ	63	6 08	12 50
10 18	12 37	165	......Harris......	58	5 52	12 37
10 23	12 43	168	...La Paz Jun. 19...δ	55	5 46	12 28
10 31	12 51	173	....Lakeville......	50	5 39	12 18
10 55	1 15	183	arr.+South Bend 20 lve.	40	+5 20	11 55
P. M.	1 15	183	lve..South Bend δ arr.	40	A.M.	11 55
	1 23	186	....Oliver's......	37		11 40
	1 36	192	....Rugby......	31		11 28
	1 46	197	....Warwick.....	26		11 19
	1 55	201	....Gallen 21...δ	22		11 10
	2 10	207	...Glendora......	15		10 57
	2 18	212	....Baroda......	11		10 50
	2 28	216	....Derby.....δ	7		10 42
	2 35	219	...Vineland......	4		10 34
	2 45	223	+...St. Joseph...δ	0		+10 25
P. M.			ARRIVE] [LEAVE			A.M.

PASSENGER AND FREIGHT AGENTS.

Passenger.

W. F. Brunner, District Passenger Agent, Indianapolis, Ind.
Geo. E. Rockwell, City Passenger Agent, "
J. W. Campbell, Traveling Passenger Agent, "
Geo. E. Farrington, Gen. Agent, Terre Haute, Ind.
Chas. M. Wheeler, Traveling Passenger Agent, "
Jas. R. Barnett, City Passenger & Ticket Agent, "
Chas. E. Owen, Traveling Passenger Agt., Kansas City, Mo.
Arch. I. Eaton, Traveling Passenger Agent, Wichita, Kan.
Chas. C. Curtice, Traveling Passenger Agt., Ft. Worth, Tex.
Geo. T Hull, Traveling Passenger Agent, Denver, Col.
W. D. Wetherell, Special Passenger Agent, St. Louis, Mo.
Fred L. Davis, City Passenger Agent, "

Freight.

Geo. E. Farrington, General Agent, Terre Haute, Ind.
W. H. Coleman, Commercial Agent, South Bend, Ind.
A. D. Pendleton, Commercial Agent, Indianapolis, Ind.
R. H. Thomson, Commercial Agent, Pittsburg, Pa.
F. S. Holmes, Commercial Agent, Cincinnati, O.
S. B. Humphrey, Commercial Agent, Milwaukee, Wis.
J. E. Gavin, Commercial Agent, Kansas City, Mo.
E. L. MacDonnell, Contracting Fht. Agt., Muskegon, Mich.

*N.B.—Trains marked * run daily; † daily, except Sunday; ‡ Sunday only. + Coupon stations; δ Telegraph stations.*

TERRE HAUTE AND PEORIA LINE.

I. H. Burgoon, Division Superintendent.
J. H. Sessions, Division Freight Agent, Decatur, Ill.
J. C. Milspaugh, Division Passenger Agent, Decatur, Ill.

5	3	1	Mls	STATIONS.	Mls	2	4	6
P. M	A.M			(Central time)		P. M	A.M	
+3 00	+7 05	0		lve.+TerreHaute 8 δarr.	174	7 05	11 05	
3 15	7 20	8		...Farrington...δ	166	6 47	10 46	
3 20	7 25	11		....Ferrell.....	163	6 40	10 40	
3 27	7 32	13		....Marley.....δ	161	6 35	10 35	
3 32	7 37	15		....Nevins.....	159	6 30	10 30	
3 39	7 44	17		....Neeley.....	157	6 25	10 25	
3 50	7 55	22		arr.+Paris 23.δ lve	152	6 15	10 15	
3 55	8 00	22		lve...Paris ...arr	152	6 10	10 10	
4 07	8 10	26		....May's.....δ	148	6 00	10 01	
4 17	8 20	,0		..Redmon..δ	144	5 51	9 52	
4 27	8 30	34		...Borton Juno 14..δ	140	5 41	9 43	
4 29	8 32	35		...Isabel .....δ	138	5 38	9 40	
4 40	8 44	39		+....Oakland 15...δ	135	5 27	9 30	
4 49	8 53	43		.....Dora.....δ	131	5 16	9 20	
4 58	9 00	45		+...Hindsboro..δ	129	5 11	9 15	
5 04	9 08	48		.....Kemp....δ	120	5 00	9 08	
5 10	9 14	51		....Filson.....	123	4 55	9 00	
5 20	9 25	55		arr.+Arcola 28 δ.lve.	119	4 45	8 50	
5 30	9 33	58		...Chesterville..δ	116	4 33	8 35	
5 40	9 43	64		+....Arthur 27...δ	110	4 23	8 25	
5 47	9 50	67		....Fairbanks...	107	4 15	8 15	
5 53	9 56	69		...Williamsburg..δ	105	4 10	8 10	
6 04	10 06	72		+....Lovington 18..δ	102	4 00	8 00	
6 11	10 12	74		....Ul'rich.....	100	3 53	7 53	
6 19	10 19	78		....Lake City...δ	96	3 47	7 47	
6 28	10 28	81		...Prairie Hall...	93	3 38	7 38	
6 37	10 37	85		...Hervey City 19..δ	89	3 30	7 30	
6 42	10 42	87		...Mount Zion...δ	87	3 24	7 24	
6 50	10 50	89		....Turpin.....	85	3 15	7 15	
6 58	10 58	93		...Suffern.....	81	3 06	7 06	
7 00	11 00	93		..Decatur Junction.δ	81	3 05	7 05	
7 03	11 03	95		Decatur(Main St.)δ	79	3 02	7 02	
A. M		95		arr.+Decatur 18.lve.	79	3 00	+7 00	P. M.
+6 30	P. M.	95		lve...Decatur δ.arr.	79	12 45	A.M.	9 00
6 55	11 35	108		....Maroa 31...	66	2 20		8 35
7 09	12 00	113		....Rowell....δ	61	2 08		8 15
7 18	12 13	116		+....Kenney 32...δ	58	2 00		8 05
7 30	12 22	121		+..Midland City 33 δ	53	1 49		7 53
7 37	12 35	124		....Tabor.....	50	1 42		7 40
8 03	12 42	127		+...Waynesville...δ	46	1 36		7 33
8 10	12 50	133		+....Atlanta 34...δ	41	1 22		7 15
8 25	1 05	141		+....Mt. Joy.....	37	1 15		7 04
8 30	1 16	143		+.Armington...δ	33	1 04		6 43
8 45	1 29	148		....Center.....	31	12 56		6 35
8 55	1 34	151		+....Minier 35..δ	26	12 47		6 20
9 10	1 49	156		....Bradley....	22	12 37		6 05
9 25	1 59	159		+..Mackinaw...δ	18	12 26		5 53
9 37	2 11	164		...Allentown...	15	12 15		5 40
9 52	2 25	169		+....Morton.....δ	10	12 04		5 20
10 05	2 52	174		+....Farmdale 86...δ	5	11 53		5 10
A. M.	3 05			+....Peoria 17...δ	0	+11 40		+4 50
	P. M.			ARRIVE] [LE..VE		A.M.		P. M.

CENTRE POINT DIVISION.

44	42	Mls	STATIONS.	Mls	43	45
P.M.	A.M.		LEAVE] [ARRIVE		A.M.	P.M.
+4 00	+6 00	0	......Brazil......		7 45	5 50
4 08	6 10	2	...Knightsville..δ		7 33	5 40
4 26	6 45	6	...Asherville...δ		7 17	5 12
4 34	6 50	8	...Stearleys....		7 11	5 06
4 45	7 00	10	...Centre Point..δ		+7 05	+5 00
P.M.	A.M.		ARRIVE] [LEAVE		A.M.	P.M.

CONNECTIONS.

[1] With railroads diverging. [2] With Jacksonville South-eastern R.R. [2½] With Jacksonville South eastern R.R. [3] With Illinois Central R.R. [4] With Wabash R.R.; Ohio & Miss. Ry. [5] With Ill. Cent.; Wabash, and Ind. & Ill. So. R.Rs. [6] With Peoria, Dec. & Evansv. Ry. [7] With Big Four Route. [8] With Terre Haute & St. Joseph, and Terre Haute & Peoria Divs.; Evansville & Terre Haute R.R.; Evansville & Indianapolis R.R.; Chicago & Eastern Illinois R.R. [9] With Monon Route. [10] With Pennsylvania Lines; Big 4; Lake Erie & Western and Cincinnati, Hamilton & Dayton R.Rs. [11] With Indianapolis, Dayton & Western Ry. [12] With Peoria Division Big 4 and Monon Route. [13] With Big 4. [14] With Lake Erie & Western Ry.; Clover Leaf R.R. and Monon Route. [15] With Pennsylvania Lines and Wabash R.R. [16] With Chicago & Erie Ry. [17] With Nickel Plate. [18] With Pennsylvania Lines and Lake Erie & Western R.R. [19] With Baltimore & Ohio R.R. [20] With Chicago & Grand Trunk; Michigan Central R.R., and Lake Shore & Michigan Southern Ry. [21] With Michigan Central R.R. [22] With Chicago & West Michigan Ry., and Vandalia Line steamers. [23] With Big 4. [24] With Chicago & Ohio River R.R. [25] With Clover Leaf Route. [26] With Illinois Central R.R. [27] With Chicago & Eastern Illinois R R. [28] With Wabash R.R. [29] With Peoria, Decatur & Evansville Ry. [30] With Wabash R.R.; Indianapolis, Decatur & Western Ry.; Peoria, Decatur & Evausville Ry., and Illinois Central R.R. [31] With Illinois Central R.R. [32] With Illinois Central R.R. [33] With Illinois Central R.R. [34] With Chicago & Alton R.R. [35] With Chicago & Alton R.R. [36] With Toledo, Peoria & Western Ry. [37] With Chicago, Burlington & Quincy; Chicago, Rock Island & Pacific; Big Four Route; Iowa Central; Jacksonville South-eastern Line; Lake Erie & Western; Peoria & Pekin Union; Peoria, Decatur & Evansville; Rock Island & Peoria, and Toledo, Peoria & Western R.Rs.

Left and right: Schedule Pages from the *Traveler's Official Guide,* June 1893.

president of the company and nominally in control until the terms of contract were completely fulfilled. However, the Pennsylvania men, interested in keeping outside stockholders undisturbed until a stronger position could be secured, insisted on keeping McKeen head of the company through the end of 1895.[68]

Crew members of Vandalia Line shifter No. 221 pose proudly with their steed circa 1908. The print carries a numbered key which we happily translate for posterity: (*left to right*) engineer John Zink, fireman Dan Segars, brakeman R. V. Pryor, conductor W. T. Ball, and brakeman George Wills. The engine was built for the TH&I by Schenectady in 1903 and was formerly No. 3. From the private collection of Lynn Pentelow, Plymouth, Indiana.

Another important provision in the sales agreement provided for transferring ownership of the Logansport road. Sometime before the end of 1893, McKeen was to have the TH&I itself buy the 8,000 shares of Terre Haute & Logansport he owned for $200,000. It was, at $25 per share, the same price he had gotten from Ives in 1887 and very likely the same price he had quoted to Roberts in 1885. The actual sale and transfer was handled at the last board meeting of the year, on December 30.[69]

The TH&I stock sale agreement was signed by McKeen and James McCrea, first vice president of Lines West. George Roberts presented the contract for Pennsylvania Company board approval on September 12, and the parent Pennsylvania Railroad board also approved the deal soon afterward. It was finally done. The Pennsylvania had control of the railroad to St. Louis at last.

There is some irony in the fact that the agreement was signed only three days after the new Union Depot opened in Terre Haute. Almost at the same time McKeen's fellow townsmen got their first look at the wonders of the grand new station, the company that had made it possible was passing forever from local control. But Terre Haute would not get this sobering piece of news for months.

As he had done when he originally bought the stock from Chauncey Rose 21 years earlier, McKeen remained silent about the transaction until forced to comment; there was no official announcement. Only after the new board was elected on January 1, 1894, did Terre Hauteans at large find out that the railroad in which they had invested so much pride—and, for many, blood, sweat, and tears as employees—had finally passed into the hands of the mighty and distant Pennsylvania system.[70]

Three of the TH&I's directors were now Pennsylvania men, James McCrea, John E. Davidson, and Joshua Twing Brooks, replacing Riley's friend Harry Ross, his brother-in-law Frank Crawford, and TH&I Corporate Secretary George Farrington. Though the public would not know it, by the terms of the sales contract, Riley himself was one of the Pennsylvania's designated representatives on the TH&I board, giving them a theoretical majority of four.

McKeen assured reporters that there would be no change in the list of officials and that he would remain president. But Riley also made it clear that the TH&I was to belong to the Pennsylvania and that he had always meant that it should. "It is," he said, "a part of the Pennsylvania system."[71]

With the TH&I being Terre Haute's largest employer, there was much concern over the loss of local control. The railroad's extensive shops complex to the east of downtown had a very large payroll. Including train service workers based locally, the railroad employed an army of men, estimated by some to total as many as 1,000 to 1,200. Riley addressed the concern right away, indicating that the shops would remain in Terre Haute for a long time to come. But regardless of the assurances, the city of nearly 40,000 remained on edge for days.

Despite McKeen's continued presence and his position as president of the company, the three Pennsylvania men took control from the beginning. At the first directors meeting, following the annual stockholder gathering that had elected them, McCrea, Brooks, and Davidson, the first, second, and fourth vice presidents of Lines West, reorganized the board. McKeen was re-elected chief executive, and John Williams was re-elected vice president and general manager. The old company bylaws governing the conduct of business were summarily repealed, and new bylaws similar to those in force on other Lines West properties were installed.[72]

At long last, the TH&I's operating organization was restructured to conform to Pennsylvania practice. The Vandalia Line system was divided into three operating divisions, Mainline, Michigan, and Peoria, each with a separate superintendent. Perhaps recognizing a future top executive when it saw one, the Lines West contingent placed Riley's son Benjamin in charge of the new Peoria Division, a thankless job which could have only honed the young man's abilities.[73]

The Pennsylvania could not have picked a worse time to make its purchase. While 1892 had been a good year for its own system of roads and 1893 started out well for it and the TH&I, the financial depression that was in full swing by summer had a dramatic effect on railroad traffic and earnings for both lines.

151. C. & 150. 149.

T. H. & I. R R.

1

OFF.

TOOL HO.

2
DRY HO.

HOSE
HO.

HEAT'G
BLRS.

COACH PAINTING

D.H.

CAR

4" W. PIPE.

50

LUMBER

AN

6" W. PIPE

TRANSFER TABLE.

CAR REPAIR SHOP.

12'

1 IRON SHED.

T. H. & I. R. R. CA

72'

1 IRON & STEEL STORAGE.

BAGGAGE RM.

TRIANSHED

ALL IRON EXCEPT WOOD ROOF BOARDS COVERED WITH SLATE.
20' TO EAVES.

HEAVY REPAIRS.

M.

1 COACH & CABINET S.

1
U.S. EXPR.

1 LUMBER SHED.

FENCE

OFF. 1ST
UPHOLST'G
2D

STORE
RM.

LUMBER
1 SHED.

7 CABOOSE SHOP

1
AM. EXPR.

CARPENTER SHOP

PLANING & SAWING

BENCH WORK

D.H.

1 BOLT RM.

ENG.

CONVEYOR

TWO NIGHT WATCHMEN AND CLOCK, 17 STATIONS.-
HEAT STEAM IN PAINT SHOP AND OIL CAN HO.
STOVES IN OTHER BUILDINGS.- FUEL COAL.-
LIGHTS LARD OIL LAMPS AND TORCHES; GAS IN ROUND HO.-

CORE
SHED.

ENG.
60 H.P.

WINDOWS

MACHINE SHOP.

BLKSM. SHOP.

EARTH FLOOR

1 COAL RM.

SMALL
1 OIL HO.

BRASS
FOUNDRY.

COPPER & TIN SHOP 2D

PATTERN LOFT 2D

IRON HO.

HOSE CART 300'2½"HOSE

PATTERN SHOP 2D

PUMP
REPAIR
SHOP.

1 OFF.

MACHINE SHOP

H.R.C. POSTS

R. CH.
12" HAV. RK.

20'

46

D.H.

2

WINDOWS

IRON
1 HO.

D.H.

2½"HYD.

CH. 36"

ENG.
60 H.P. 1

ERECTING SHOP

RAISED 6'

RAISED 6'

D.H.

SHED
DRINC
W. TANK

2
T. H. & I. MACHINERY DEPT.
OFF'S 2d

BOILER SHOP

1 PIPE SHED.

1

WINDOWS

HALL B. ONLY.

HEAT'G
BLR.

D.H.

AIR BRAKE
REPAIR SHOP

OIL CAN HO.
COMM'N FLOOR.

1

E ROUND HO.

WINDOWS ALL AROUND.

Scale of Feet.

50 40 30 20 10 0   50   100

35

148   147.

T. H. & I. YARD.

COACH REPAIR SHOP   COACH HO.

40

SILVERING RM.

COAL SHED.

IR YARD.

MATERIALS

SHOPS

COAL TIPPLE

TRANSFER TRACKS.

VANDALIA SIDE TRACK.

ROAD

N. 12TH ST.

8" W. PIPE

D.H.

TERRE HAUTE BRONZE & BRASS FOUNDRY
J. SCHNEIDER & SON.
FOUNDRY
MACHINE SHOP.
ONEIL & STEPHEN
HEAT STOVES:- FUEL COAL.
LIGHTS KEROSENE LAMPS.
No Fire App's.

ROSE'S SUB OF ACRES.

L.

61.
62.
63.
64.
65.

SYCAMORE

D.H.

This Sanborn Fire Insurance Map from 1896 amply illustrates the size and extent of the TH&I shops in downtown Terre Haute, just east of the new Union Depot. © 1896, The Sanborn Map Co., Sanborn Library LLC, All Rights Reserved.

The country was in the throes of a political debate over a bimetal currency, and the congressionally mandated coinage of silver had precipitated a crisis in the nation's money supply. With the outflow of gold threatening to drain the treasury, the United States government appeared headed for bankruptcy. Of course, it was not really that simple, nor was the money crisis alone responsible for the dangerous weakness of the stock market. Nevertheless, with the crash of the gigantic National Cordage Trust early in May, a full-fledged financial panic was set in motion. National Cordage had been preceded into bankruptcy by the overextended Philadelphia & Reading earlier in the year, and by year's end it would be joined by the Erie, the Northern Pacific, and the Atchison, Topeka & Santa Fe.[74]

Snow seems to have been a constant enemy of the Vandalia Line. In this 1910-era scene, a pair of double-headed locomotives struggles into town, led by Mogul No. 532, a 1906 Schenectady graduate. The unidentified interlocking tower appears to be the one erected in 1904 at Effingham, Illinois. Collection of the Vigo County Historical Society, Terre Haute.

After experiencing several years of traffic growth, the Pennsylvania had undertaken a number of expensive improvement programs to expand its capacity. On the heels of the crash, as the effects of the depression quickly materialized, the company immediately postponed or cancelled all expansion projects. Just as quickly, stringent economies were instituted all over the huge Pennsylvania system, including the Lines West of Pittsburgh.[75]

The Terre Haute & Indianapolis had been enjoying what was turning out to be an excellent year prior to the panic, but the downturn was so dramatic in the company's final fiscal quarter that 1893 results seemed only modestly improved over the previous year. Had its leased-line losses not bled it dry, McKeen's road might have shown a nice profit. Instead, led by the staggering $102,000 loss imposed by the newly acquired Terre Haute & Peoria, all four leased lines devoured net earnings. The TH&I shuddered, went ahead and paid out its second semi-annual dividend, and posted an overall $93,000 deficit for the year. This was the state of affairs as the Pennsylvania took over control of the Terre Haute & Indianapolis, and things did not get much better in 1894.[76]

We are looking eastward at St. Elmo, Illinois, early in the last century. In the distance is the interlocking tower constructed in 1895 to protect the crossing with what would become the Chicago & Eastern Illinois. Collection of the St. Elmo Public Library, St. Elmo, Illinois.

It became evident early in 1894 that the business depression would not be a short-lived interruption. Traffic and income deteriorated steadily. Although Peoria road losses were brought under control, the TH&I's other leased lines all reported greatly increased deficits. As a result, total leased line losses jumped to over $193,000 in 1894.[77]

After imposing their standard operating and reporting structure, the Pennsylvania's men left McKeen and Williams with great latitude in the administration of the TH&I, as had been previously agreed. The first semi-annual dividend was declared in late spring as usual, draining another $60,000 from the company's coffers. But as the depression—and operating results—worsened, McCrea and his Pennsylvania Lines associates began tightening the reins. A miners' strike in the summer helped decimate local traffic and earnings, and the nationwide American Railway Union strike, led by hometown Terre Haute hero Eugene Debs, also affected operations. In the face of continued bad news, the Pennsylvania's men forced the issue; dividends had to cease until they were earned. Omitting the second semi-annual payout held the TH&I's overall deficit to $50,000 for the year 1894. Had they paid the full 6 percent as in years previous, however, the TH&I's losses would have widened to more than $110,000. Clearly, McKeen's road was seriously ill, and the Lines West contingent knew it.[78]

The Pennsylvania's concern was evident as the year 1895 began. Although McKeen was re-elected president of the TH&I, he was reduced to a mere figurehead. McCrea, Brooks, and Davidson took virtual operating control at the January board meeting, organizing Pennsylvania-style executive and finance committees to manage the company. Despite his position, Riley was not appointed to either committee; John Williams, the only non-Pennsylvania member on both, chaired the executive committee. Regardless, practically all decisions were now made by committee, usually meeting at Lines West headquarters in Pittsburgh.[79]

Sadly, 1895 began in tragedy. The new year was barely four weeks old when the TH&I ended its 42-year record of never having killed a passenger. Early on the bitterly cold Monday afternoon of January 28, the railroad's premier train derailed on the curve just east of the depot at Coatesville, Indiana. Number 20, a "solid vestibuled Limited" eastbound from St. Louis to New York, was running late and, at about 30 miles per hour, running slow when the engine and mail cars rounded the curve and entered the downward grade. A broken rail sent the last four cars tumbling down the embankment, a parlor car, diner, sleeper, and Riley McKeen's personal business car carrying his brother Sam, his friend and former partner Deloss Minshall, and Minshall's son Charles. Miraculously, of the three, only the elder Minshall was injured, and he not seriously. But two passengers eventually died from injuries sustained in the wreck, and 50 were injured. Had he not been detained by last-minute business, Riley himself would have been aboard.[80]

The Coatesville disaster cost the Terre Haute & Indianapolis over $65,000, nearly three-quarters of which represented personal injury claims. More costly from a Terre Haute point of view was the end of the TH&I's long-celebrated passenger safety record.[81]

Fortunately, business appeared to be rebounding somewhat. Having found the Terre Haute & Indianapolis in a seriously undermaintained condition, the company's new Lines West management increased expenses to compensate. New 85-pounds-per-yard rail, made the mainline standard the previous year, was ordered in quantity to replace older, lighter rail. But the inflated expenses hurt, and leased line losses hit $210,000 by year's end. The results were grim: Even without paying any dividend at all, the TH&I reported a $52,000 deficit.[82]

The annual report to the stockholders tried to put the best face on things. It would be McKeen's last such report as president; the Pennsylvania Lines could hold him no longer. Terre Haute newspapers carried the eulogies at the end of the year, commemorating McKeen's 28-year stewardship of the Terre Haute & Indianapolis. The city openly mourned the fact that Riley and his faithful lieutenant, John G. Williams, were finally stepping down.[83]

The infamous wreck at Coatesville, Indiana, on January 28, 1895. Forty-two years of exemplary passenger safety came to an end when two passengers died from injuries sustained in the derailment of eastbound No. 20. In this scene, probably taken a day later, the tracks have been cleared, leaving two of the four derailed cars—probably the parlor and dining cars—visible on the ground. Guilford Township Historical Collection; Plainfield Public Library, Plainfield, Indiana.

It was the end of an era that had begun when Chauncey Rose secured the charter of the company in 1847. The railroad, and the men who built it, had kept the faith and made Terre Haute into the thriving little city it had become. It was not surprising, therefore, that so many overlooked the TH&I's grave condition, perhaps even including McKeen himself. Considering its modest size and resources, the Terre Haute & Indianapolis had been hugely successful, a partner of the great Pennsylvania system, not a mere pawn.

As he stepped down, McKeen seemed unaffected by the change. His last message to stockholders was brief to the point of being terse, reflecting his practical divorce from daily management of the railroad. He seemed comfortable with what he had accomplished and had no reservations about the property he was now turning over to the Pennsylvania. There is no evidence that Riley McKeen ever worried about his legacy. The job he had first accepted in 1867 was finally finished. The 73-mile-long shortline railroad he had built into a substantial 650-mile midwestern system would go on, an integral part of the mighty Pennsylvania. Riley could now return to being just Terre Haute's leading banker, his first love.

One of the Vandalia Line's trim and speedy Schenectady-built American-types wheels the afternoon express to St. Louis through Coatesville, Indiana, circa 1905. The tail end of the train is rounding the curve, just beyond which is the site of the 1895 Coatesville wreck that ended the TH&I's record of never having killed a passenger. Courtesy of the Coatesville Public Library, Coatesville, Indiana.

POSTLUDE

No one could have known then that the Terre Haute & Indianapolis had only nine more years of life. Not Riley McKeen, and certainly never Terre Haute. The new Pennsylvania ownership was well aware of the company's dangerous weakness and must have entertained thoughts of its ultimate demise through some kind of consolidation; but no one could have foreseen how long and arduous the struggle to get there would be.

The Pennsylvania had a secure grip. One of the last transactions Riley had handled as president was the sale of the TH&I's remaining 3,600 shares of treasury stock to the Pennsylvania Company at par, which gave Lines West 45 percent control of the company. But the transfer was not mere corporate housecleaning; the TH&I badly needed the cash to help pay its bills. It was a sad fact that did not augur well for the future, and it made actual stock control mean a lot less.[1]

McKeen was succeeded as president of the TH&I by James McCrea, first vice president of the Pennsylvania Lines West of Pittsburgh. McCrea had attained the top Lines West job in 1891 upon the death of Jacob N. McCullough and would become, in 1906, the only Pennsylvania Railroad president who had spent most of his career west of Pittsburgh. Gruff, demanding, and as tough as nails, McCrea immediately addressed the TH&I's fatal illness.[2]

Although the Pennsylvania's representatives had reluctantly approved the TH&I's 1895 annual report, McCrea and his colleagues were uncomfortable with its content. They had begun taking heat from outside stockholders over the cessation of dividends and were eager to fix blame on the previous management where it belonged. So, on February 20, 1896, McCrea addressed a president's letter to all shareholders, inviting them to form a committee to investigate both the physical and financial condition of the company and to recommend a course of action. To his astonishment and disgust, of the 28 replies he received representing 12,500 TH&I shares—not including Pennsylvania holdings—more than 80 percent either saw no need for an investigating committee or had no interest at all. In resignation, McCrea gave up the idea.[3]

With outside stockholders unwilling to participate, McCrea and his Lines West officers were left on their own. In the months ahead, they would improvise a survival strategy. In the meantime, the TH&I's run-down physical condition required immediate attention.

The executive committee, meeting in Pittsburgh on March 26, approved new General Manager James J. Turner's request for new motive power. Turner presented a

This postcard view of the Staunton, Indiana, depot from the turn of the last century shows eastbound No. 8, a St. Louis–Indianapolis express. The original main line of the TH&I passed through Staunton and Turner, just west of Brazil, but the right-of-way was narrow and filled with curves. At the time of a Vandalia double-tracking project begun between Knightsville and Terre Haute in 1906, it was found necessary to locate an entirely new right-of-way approximately one to two miles north of the original line between Brazil and Seelyville. This air-line cutoff replaced the route through Staunton as the main line in 1908. The old line remained in service for years as a "local main line," for a time even hosting a daily accommodation passenger train; but by the 1940s it was blocked by stored cars. The old line was finally severed by the end of the 1940s, only remaining in operation between Brazil and Staunton to serve a series of strip mines. Amazingly enough, although its use as a spur ended by the early 1970s, the eastern portion of the old line remained in place into the 1990s. Collection of Ken Pickitt, courtesy of the Clay County Historical Society, Brazil, Indiana.

James A. McCrea, in his official presidential portrait of 1907. McCrea had a long Pennsylvania Railroad career and took over as general manager of the Pan Handle in 1882 after the departure of Darius W. Caldwell. Rising quickly, McCrea attained the top position in the Lines West operating organization in 1891, following the death of Jacob N. McCullough. McCrea was chosen to replace Alexander J. Cassatt as the Pennsylvania's president in 1907. Pennsylvania State Archives: (MG-286) Penn Central Railroad Collection.

list of 26 TH&I engines ranging in age from 33 to 24 years, all of which had boilers and cylinders in such bad condition that they were irreparable. With the committee's blessing, the TH&I ordered 22 brand new Mogul-type freight locomotives and two new eight-wheel passenger engines, all from Pittsburgh Locomotive Works. Financing was arranged through the sale of short-term notes, 17 of which were purchased by the Pennsylvania Company. At the same time, the executive committee approved the remodeling of the old Terre Haute shops and the purchase of new tools. Regardless of the TH&I's shaky financial condition, the Pennsylvania men felt the expenditures were an absolute necessity. Come what may, their new acquisition required improvement.[4]

Very early in the morning of July 29, 1896, following a particularly heavy rainstorm on the previous day, Vandalia Line engine No. 125 was running light with a full crew and a track supervisor aboard to inspect the damage. The trestle over Walnut Fork of Sugar Creek north of Crawfordsville on Logansport road gave way beneath them, and the ensuing wreck cost the lives of the fireman, conductor, and brakeman. As usual, a photographer was on hand later to record the disaster, and a large crowd had gathered to inspect. Historical Collection of the Crawfordsville District Public Library, Crawfordsville, Indiana.

Even though Riley McKeen had retired from the presidency, he would remain on the TH&I's board until the company's demise. Ironically, once he stepped down, McKeen was named to the executive and financial committees, replacing John Williams, who had left the TH&I and would soon also leave Terre Haute. Perhaps the Lines West men were just being perverse, because all meetings would be held in Pittsburgh, without McKeen in attendance. In fact, Riley would not attend many of

Left page: Riley's bank, now the McKeen National Bank, circa 1910. The street railway has been electrified, and the bank may now issue paper currency. Alas, this honored institution will not weather the financial storms of the 1920s and 1930s. After being bought up by the First National Bank of Terre Haute in 1928 to form the First-McKeen National Bank, the name will disappear in a 1932 merger with the Terre Haute National Bank & Trust Company that will create the present-day Terre Haute First National Bank.

Perched atop the McKeen National Bank is a statue of Mercury, purchased by McKeen in 1875 to complete the structure. How Riley happened to come by this zinc-plate reproduction of a famous sculpture by Giovanni di Bologna is not known for certain. The original was placed in the garden of the Medici in Florence, Italy, which McKeen almost certainly never visited but where his eldest son Frank supposedly spent some time. While not the only copy of the famous sculpture, McKeen's may have been the most controversial. Local Terre Haute lore has it that, shortly after the scandalously nude sculpture of the winged Mercury was set in place, a contingent of local matrons visited the banker to complain in outraged offense. Riley, it was said, walked outside his new building, squinted for a long interval up at the statue placed high above the third story, and then commented that, if the ladies could see anything at all objectionable from that distance, their eyes were a lot better than his.

McKeen's bank building still stands at Sixth and Wabash, although shorn of its top two floors in a 1950s makeover. Mercury was saved and now resides at the Vigo County Historical Museum. Community Archives, Vigo County Public Library, Terre Haute.

the infrequent board meetings either. Instead, he maintained the presidency of the bank, took his leisure, and dabbled in politics.[5]

McKeen continued to be active in local finance, and his bank, although not the largest such institution in town, remained one of the most important business lenders. At the time of his retirement from the TH&I, McKeen's bank still had outstanding loans to the railroad in the amount of $100,000, money Riley had advanced during the company's money crunch immediately following Ives's brief administration. As was his custom, McKeen would continue to make money available to virtually any Terre Haute businessman who needed it to maintain or expand his local presence.[6]

McKeen's bank was reincorporated as a National Bank in 1905, allowing it to issue federal currency in the form of banknotes. This twenty-dollar bill bears the signatures of Riley and his son, Samuel Crawford McKeen. From the collection of Mr. and Mrs. W. R. McKeen IV.

In addition, McKeen continued to lend his name to important local enterprises. Although he ceased to be as active as in the past, he still served occasionally as a director and officer, mainly fronting for others. One typical involvement was his presidency of the local street railway company after 1899.

In the late 1850s, McKeen had been a founding director of the Terre Haute Street Railway, a modest horsecar line, but had long since disposed of his stock. In 1890 a syndicate led by Russell Harrison, son of President Benjamin Harrison, one of McKeen's close political friends, purchased the Terre Haute line. With the infusion of new money, the Terre Haute Street Railway electrified and greatly expanded its system. In 1894 the renamed Terre Haute Electric Railway created a power distribution subsidiary and won the contract to light the city, thereby bringing it into bitter conflict with the old contract holder, Terre Haute Electric Light & Power, on whose board Riley's brother Sam McKeen served as a director. The contest between the two opposing firms was played out on the battlefield of local politics. When Harrison's company refused to pay some suddenly heavy city tax levies, the Street Railway was placed in receivership.[7]

Upon foreclosure in 1899, the Boston-based electrical engineering firm of Stone & Webster bought and reorganized the utility. McKeen was elected president of the new Terre Haute Electric Company, parent of the Terre Haute Traction & Light Company. The rejuvenated streetcar company quickly developed into a regional interurban railway, acquiring or building lines east to Brazil, south to Sullivan, and northwest to Paris, Illinois. But McKeen's role was entirely passive. In 1907 Terre Haute Electric leased its railroad to the Terre Haute, Indianapolis & Eastern, a huge electric railway system controlled by Hugh McGowan of Indianapolis, Randal Morgan of Philadelphia, and W. Kelsey Schoepf of Cincinnati. Through it all, until illness forced him to resign in 1910, Riley McKeen remained as the titular head of the Terre Haute company.[8]

McKeen's business dealings seemed as successful as ever, but they were not his sole focus. Now that he was at least semi-retired, Riley longed to play a more active role in politics. He had dabbled in it for years and was considered one of the warhorses of the Indiana Republican party; but McKeen was a financial pillar, not a player, an amateur in a new era of political professionals. Much as he had become an anachronism as the local railroad president who still owned his company, McKeen as the amateur politician would be equally dated. Moreover, he would finally be caught on the wrong side of the state party's warring factions.

Riley McKeen had been a Republican from the very beginning. He grew so active in high party councils that he was considered a legitimate gubernatorial candidate in 1880. The challenge began with his support for Benjamin Harrison, an Indianapolis lawyer who had long been on retainer with the TH&I. Like so many of McKeen's friendships, their relations started through business dealings but matured into something closer. By 1881 Harrison could count on McKeen for important political support in his campaign for the U.S. Senate, and Riley had grown influential enough to be able to provide it. From that point on, McKeen was clearly marked as a "Harrison man."[9]

In 1888 Indiana fielded two favorite sons as presidential timber, Harrison of Indianapolis and Federal Judge Walter Quinton Gresham from Corydon, Indiana.

McKeen's last Terre Haute residence, at 221 South Sixth Street. Riley moved here in the 1880s from an earlier home at Seventh and Cherry streets, remaining until his death in 1913. While a tasteful Italianate design, it hardly qualified as a mansion. Community Archives, Vigo County Public Library, Terre Haute.

Both attracted a substantial following, dividing the Indiana Republican party into two uneven but equally vociferous factions. Among those few who cast their lot with the feisty but less popular Gresham was the young corporate lawyer from Indianapolis, Charles Warren Fairbanks.[10]

This factional division gradually widened into a bitter battle for control of the state party apparatus which, by the early 1890s, threatened to destroy the Republicans' electoral muscle. But as long as Harrison remained president, McKeen's wing held the reins of power. Fairbanks, meanwhile, retreated to the background, mending fences and quietly gathering support among strategically placed younger Republicans. Although he wisely supported Harrison for re-election in 1892, Fairbanks kept his own agenda.[11]

For Indiana Republicans 1892 turned out to be a year of disaster. Harrison's defeat by Cleveland in the fall helped sweep the Democrats back into control of the legislature, which guaranteed the selection of a Democrat as U.S. senator the following spring. The Republican caucus made Fairbanks its nominee, an honorarium in view of the predictable outcome, but a strong indication of his growing stature. The vote also made Fairbanks next in line for the senatorial position opening in 1897, assuming the Republicans could regain the legislature.[12]

By 1896 Indiana Republicans had managed to recover their party's health. Although Harrison's followers still entertained hopes for their hero, they were now clearly in the minority. Fairbanks had emerged as the party's most likely leader; and he consolidated his power by marshalling highly effective support for the national party nominee, William McKinley. With this crucial alliance, and a sweeping Republican victory, Fairbanks' selection as the next U.S. senator seemed a foregone conclusion. It was precisely at this juncture that Riley McKeen mounted the political stage.[13]

Although a very effective politician, the cold and ruthlessly ambitious Fairbanks had made quite a few enemies. These political opponents were outspoken and powerful and absolutely committed to stopping Fairbanks at practically any cost. Given McKeen's dislike for the icy Indianapolis lawyer, and his desire for the post, it was not difficult to convince him to run in opposition. Among those who were the most convincing was ardent Harrison man John C. New, a powerful Indianapolis newspaper editor. Since McKeen's youngest son was married to New's daughter, the connection ran deeper than party faction.[14]

Brief as it was, the race for U.S. senator was McKeen's first and last foray as an active politician, and it was something he really wanted. Since senators were "elected" by members of the legislature, the campaigning was done among the party faithful, the kind of glad-handing McKeen excelled at and enjoyed. But he was still an amateur politician, and a novice at that. In the end, despite the desperate potency of his support, McKeen was no match for the shrewd and well-connected Fairbanks. The outcome was decided well before the caucus met on the night of Tuesday, January 12, 1897. With only 11 votes to Fairbanks's 60, Riley accepted defeat with his usual grace.[15]

Already 67 when he lost the nomination, McKeen probably realized that his one and only chance to serve had passed. Though his name would be mentioned as a possible senatorial candidate again in 1899, Riley gently rebuffed the gesture and supported the eventual winner, brash young Albert Beveridge. Instead, McKeen remained an active and generous party stalwart, continued to attend the state and national Republican conventions, and eventually assumed the regular delegate-at-large position traditionally reserved for the party's elder statesmen.[16]

⊷▭◉▭⊶

For the Terre Haute & Indianapolis and its Pennsylvania Lines management, things went from bad to worse in 1896. Following his failed attempt to enlist outside stockholder support, James McCrea was forced to come to grips with the TH&I's critical financial condition. As leased-line losses continued to mount and it became necessary to spend increasingly scarce funds to overcome the TH&I's deferred maintenance, McCrea and his fellow executive committee members were slowly forced to the wall. In view of their situation, it seems remarkable that management chose that moment to unbalance the company's questionably balanced books.

As he would explain to stockholders in the very next annual report, McCrea felt compelled to drastically write-down the TH&I's assets. Viewed through the conservative eyes of a Pennsylvania-trained executive, the general accounts of the TH&I

A southbound Logansport road local crosses the Sugar Creek bridge northeast of Darlington, Indiana, sometime early in the last century. This also must have been a good spot to fish. Collection of Wesley Tribbett, Darlington, Indiana.

were completely misleading, and not just in the inflated valuation of the St. Louis, Vandalia & Terre Haute preferred stock. McKeen had logically charged all advances made to the various leased lines for improvements and continued to carry them on the TH&I's books as deferred assets, assuming they would eventually be repaid. How else was he to justify spending the TH&I's cash, particularly since the company did not have a penny to spare? Unfortunately, by the end of the 1895 fiscal year, these deferred assets totaled more than $671,000.[17]

To McCrea, it seemed utter fantasy to believe that any leased line losing as much money as all of the TH&I's were—and with as little prospect of breaking even, much less earning a profit—would ever be able to repay such a large debt. Therefore, he reasoned, to continue carrying that debt as a collectable asset was completely unjustified and falsely inflated the value of the company. It had been absolutely crucial for McKeen to maintain the TH&I's facade of financial strength; there was no longer any cash surplus to fall back on. With the company now under Pennsylvania control, McCrea felt no such compulsion and chopped the collectable advances to just under $20,000, writing off over $651,000.[18]

While he was at it, McCrea did not overlook the glaring inflation of the TH&I's owned securities. Although he grudgingly left the Vandalia preferred valued at 125 percent of par, the rest of the list went under the knife. The value of the St. Louis, Vandalia & Terre Haute common was cut by half, and the Indiana & Lake Michigan and Terre Haute & Peoria stock investment was reduced to absolute zero. In all, McCrea wiped $250,000 in security values off the books. Added to the write-down of the deferred assets, the TH&I's general account assets were purposely reduced in value by over $901,000. Suddenly, instead of an implied surplus in the company's treasury, the TH&I had a negative net worth of more than $21,000.[19]

St. Louis, Vandalia & Terre Haute No. 196, built by Schenectady Locomotive Works in 1903. Collection of the Vigo County Historical Society, Terre Haute.

Although it could be argued that McCrea and his Pennsylvania Lines colleagues were being arbitrarily harsh, it must be remembered that their focus was long-term. The Terre Haute & Indianapolis and its leased lines were now a part of a much larger entity. As such, the company's finances had to be solid and had to conform to the Pennsylvania's conservative standards. While not viewed as politically correct by McKeen's Terre Haute neighbors, nor financially palatable by some outside stockholders, to Lines West the adjustment was painfully necessary and inevitable. Moreover, it was a mere taste of what was to come.

Once the company's financial condition was accurately assessed, it was clear things could not go on as before. With its value basically reduced to just physical assets, the Terre Haute & Indianapolis was naked and broke. The crushing weight of the company's expensive lease arrangements now came to bear. As economic conditions suddenly turned downward in the summer of 1896, the TH&I was forced to its knees.

Another of McCrea's decisions shortly upon taking command was to try to contain leased-line losses. As they had increased and showed no sign of diminishing, it became clear that the TH&I would be unable to continue covering them. So, early in 1896, the executive committee ordered the company treasurer to start segregating the accounts of the TH&I and its leased lines, in effect keeping all monies separate. Each line's expenses would be paid only with that line's income. No longer would the TH&I automatically advance any shortfall, regardless of its contractual obligations. It was, as McCrea explained later to the stockholders, the same way a receiver would run the company. With semi-annual bond interest bills coming due on every leased line in the system, it was also an inevitable dead end.[20]

The Terre Haute & Logansport bonds came due first. With the Logansport road account over $40,000 short of the necessary funds to cover the required interest payment, the TH&I treasurer was instructed not to make up any deficiency. Since it had guaranteed the Logansport bonds, the TH&I was technically in default after July 1.[21]

In succession, the same was done with the Terre Haute & Peoria and Indiana & Lake Michigan bonds, whose interest coupons fell due on September 1. The St. Louis, Vandalia & Terre Haute second mortgage bonds had interest due on November 1, but these were jointly guaranteed by the Pan Handle, which went ahead and covered the deficiency.

Forewarned by the Logansport road bond default, the bondholders of the Peoria road formed protective committees for each mortgage early in July. After actual default on the Peoria's bonds in September, the two committees joined hands and sued the TH&I on Halloween, Saturday, October 31, 1896. It was neither trick nor treat for McCrea and his Lines West management. The Terre Haute & Indianapolis was plainly insolvent, and the company's managers readily admitted the fact. Offering no objection to the appointment of a receiver, the Pennsylvania men listened passively as Judge William Woods named Volney T. Malott on Friday, the 13th of November.[22]

Watch the snow fly as a pair of Vandalia Line engines blasts its way through a drifted cut on the northwest edge of Atlanta, Illinois. The townspeople who had walked out to help shovel off the track now stand as spectators at left. This remarkable series of photographs dates from the turn of the last century. Collection of the Atlanta Public Library and Museum, Atlanta, Illinois.

Here the engines, working hard, have made it through the cut. Obviously, wind-driven snow on Illinois's wide-open prairie flatlands made for difficult winters, especially on the Terre Haute & Peoria. Collection of the Atlanta Public Library and Museum, Atlanta, Illinois.

The job done for the moment, both engines, coupled back-to-back to make them bi-directional snowplows, rest at Atlanta, Illinois. Engine No. 514, nearest the camera, was an original Terre Haute & Peoria locomotive, built by Rogers in 1887. Collection of the Atlanta Public Library and Museum, Atlanta, Illinois.

The newly appointed receiver was no surprise. Malott, then president of the Indiana National Bank of Indianapolis, had much experience as a railroad executive and receiver and was highly regarded by all parties. What did raise eyebrows was the name of the lawyer who represented the bondholders and who had filed the suit: It was none other than John G. Williams, now a resident of Indianapolis. Williams would also serve as Malott's counsel throughout the receivership.[23]

As if bankruptcy were not enough, the Terre Haute & Indianapolis was soon overtaken by another disaster. Early in 1897 the state of Indiana filed suit to recover the excess profits it maintained the TH&I still owed to the common schools fund. To do so, the state legislature ignored the legal victory won by the company in 1878 and passed a series of acts which gave new life to the claim. Prior to passage of the enabling legislation, McCrea and his fellow officers tried to be cooperative, handing over all financial information requested, assuming that, in view of the previous court case 20 years earlier, the company could not possibly be liable. But the question of whether or not the TH&I still owed the state a large sum of money had taken on legendary status and had become a political issue legislators could not leave alone.[24]

Somewhat stunned by the suit, McCrea's management turned to the most capable lawyer it could think of, and John G. Williams took command of the TH&I's defense. Crafting his usual meticulous case, Williams counterattacked the obvious unconstitutionality of the state's position. Since the state had lost the original suit in 1878, the legislature had been forced to create artificial grounds for this new one. Such an action was in violation of the contract clause of the U.S. Constitution and the due process portion of the Fourteenth Amendment.

The Indiana Superior Court assigned the case to a special master in chancery who found the company not liable. But in October 1900, the judges sitting in the case ignored their master and ruled the other way. In near disbelief the TH&I's Lines West management now found itself owing the state of Indiana $913,905.01. It was like a nightmare come to life. John Williams quickly appealed to the Indiana Supreme Court.[25]

The state's judgement now hung like the sword of Damocles over the Terre Haute & Indianapolis. Suddenly, the railroad's prospects seemed hopeless. While the losses generated by the company's leased lines were real enough, it had been management's hope that bankruptcy would force an adjustment in the TH&I's commitments. The company could probably succeed with more realistic responsibilities, perhaps shedding the Peoria road entirely and scaling back the interest requirements of the Logansport and I&LM. But the added burden of paying a nearly $1 million penalty made the job completely impossible.

The railroad, freed of its leased-line losses, had begun to show a vast improvement under receiver Malott's administration. With the rebounding economy of the late 1890s propelling increased traffic and earnings, the TH&I appeared remarkably healthy by the turn of the century. Receivership, foreclosure, and reorganization of the Terre Haute & Logansport by Lines West in 1898 removed one obstacle. Receivership and foreclosure of the Indiana & Lake Michigan later that same year removed another; only in this case, the Pennsylvania interests left the road to its bondholders. After reorganization as the St. Joseph, South Bend & Southern, the little line was leased to the Michigan Central.[26]

The interlocking tower at Brazil, Indiana, in 1906. This plant, installed by the TH&I circa 1899, protected the crossing with the Indiana Coal Railroad, then part of the Chicago & Eastern Illinois system. Pictured on the tower steps in white shirt and tie is the leverman who operated the interlocking. The TH&I's Brazil depot is visible in the distance. The tower would be taken out of service in 1916, when the Indiana Coal Railroad was liquidated and partially abandoned. Collection of the Clay County Historical Society, Brazil, Indiana.

Everything remains as it was built at Terre Haute Union Depot in the 1920s, with the exception of the flivvers parked on the drive. A severe lightning strike to the tower will eventually lead to the removal of the coned tower roof, probably in the 1930s, and the steel and slate-roofed train sheds will be gone by the end of World War II; but for now, the station is enjoying its heyday. (Contrast this view with the depot in its last days; see Introduction.) Collection of the Vigo County Historical Society, Terre Haute.

In spite of its financial improvement, the state's pending million-dollar judgement kept the TH&I locked up in bankruptcy proceedings. After the Indiana Supreme Court affirmed the superior court judgement in 1902, Williams took the case to the U.S. Supreme Court. It was quite literally the TH&I's last chance. Williams's defense remained the same; there was no other argument than unconstitutionality. To management's great relief, the justices agreed. In a brief but elegant opinion written and delivered by Justice Oliver Wendel Holmes, the state's contrived case against the TH&I was completely demolished, and on May 31, 1904, the judgement was finally overturned.[27]

The relief in Pittsburgh was almost palpable as the Pennsylvania's Lines West organization now put its long-considered plans in motion. As early as the late 1890s, the intention had been to consolidate the various smaller Pennsylvania-controlled lines into a larger, more easily financed and managed entity. Besides the TH&I, the St. Louis, Vandalia & Terre Haute, and the reorganized Terre Haute & Logansport, the Pennsylvania still owned the 118-mile Indianapolis & Vincennes and had acquired a former Wabash-leased line between Logansport and Butler, Indiana, reorganized in 1901 as the Logansport & Toledo. The Pennsylvania's Lines West executives had planned to merge all of them together into a single company just as soon as the TH&I's situation was resolved. In the meantime, Lines West had gone so far as to buy up and hold matured mortgage bond issues of both the Vandalia and Vincennes companies. Now that the TH&I's long ordeal was finally over, McCrea and his associates set a date for the big consolidation.[28]

First, it was necessary to end the TH&I's receivership. With the company's demonstrably restored health and the court's blessing, Malott was discharged on Tuesday, October 25, 1904, then immediately reinstated as Lines West's trustee. The TH&I board also called a special stockholder's meeting on Wednesday, December 14, to ratify the proposed merger agreement.[29]

Meeting in Terre Haute, the ancestral home of the railroad, the stockholders of the Terre Haute & Indianapolis voted to consolidate the company into an all new Vandalia Railroad Company. Over the years the Pennsylvania Company had gradually increased its TH&I stock holdings; and now that it owned more than 28,000 shares, the outcome was a foregone conclusion. Forty-nine other stockholders owning a total of more than 7,000 additional shares concurred, including such disparate individual owners as Henry Huddleston Rogers of Standard Oil and Adrian Iselin & Company, a Wall Street Bank which had gathered up pieces of Ives's shattered empire. Only ten stockholders owning 2,200 shares voted in opposition.[30]

The local veterans of the Spanish-American War are returning home to Frankfort, Indiana, in this 1901 postcard view. Collection of Leroy Good, Frankfort, Indiana.

At the time of its creation in 1905, the consolidated Vandalia Railroad was almost entirely singletrack from end to end. In order to expand its capacity to meet the needs of its increasing traffic load, the company began adding second main track at various locations between Indianapolis and St. Louis. One such project created a doubletrack road between Knightsville, just east of Brazil, and Macksville, just west of Terre Haute. The project required the construction of an all new right-of-way from Brazil to Seelyville and eliminated street crossings at grade by elevating the tracks in downtown Brazil. Shown here is a work train on the new viaduct over Murphy Avenue, Brazil, in 1907. This overpass, as well as the elevated right-of-way, would be removed and leveled after the railroad was abandoned by its latter-day shortline owner in 1992. Collection of the Clay County Historical Society, Brazil, Indiana.

On December 31, 1904, at midnight, the 58-year history of Terre Haute's pioneer railroad came to a quiet end. On January 1, 1905, the new Vandalia Railroad took its place. The new company was overwhelmingly controlled by the Pennsylvania Company and became one of the operating entities within the Pennsylvania Lines West of Pittsburgh. Its status would not last. Just 12 years later, on January 1, 1917, the Vandalia would disappear into an enlarged Pan Handle.[31]

Among the stockholders attending the TH&I's last company meeting on December 14, 1904, was Riley McKeen. He and close friend Herman Hulman were the last of the Terre Haute directors, the old guard. McKeen still owned 76 shares of the TH&I. After the new year, he would have 114 shares of new Vandalia stock, theoretically worth $100 each, a nice profit, indeed.[32]

The new Vandalia Railroad would have a board of directors which included John Williams and Volney Malott, presumably rewards for a receivership well handled. For the first time in 42 years, McKeen's name was absent from the board. In fact, there was not a single director to represent Terre Haute.[33]

Riley McKeen aged gracefully; the word used most often to describe him in his last years was "serene." Now widowed a third and final time, McKeen enjoyed his status as a senior citizen. There were plenty of grandchildren, products of the marriages of his three daughters and four sons. Of the latter, the first and third sons, Frank and Samuel Crawford, worked with him at the bank. Second son Benjamin had left the TH&I in April 1902 to join the Pennsylvania's Lines West organization and would rise to a regional vice presidency with the parent Pennsylvania. Youngest son William Riley, Jr., became the most celebrated of the progeny. Leaving the TH&I for the Union Pacific in the late 1890s, the younger McKeen eventually developed the famous self-propelled railcar that bore his name. The Pennsylvania bought one of his McKeen cars in 1910, but only one.[34]

Riley McKeen in his last years. This portrait was likely taken for C. C. Oakey's Terre Haute historical volumes published in 1908 and looks heavily retouched. Community Archives, Vigo County Public Library, Terre Haute.

An unusual photograph of an engine replica, lettered for the Vandalia Line and numbered 100. The most reliable explanation of this scene is that local hands from the TH&I's Terre Haute shops built this full-scale model of a locomotive, possibly as a make-work project during the difficult depression times of the mid-1890s. The Pennsylvania–Lines West shield is visible on the boiler running board, suggesting that the project had company sanction. The legend "Honest Money" below the cab window smacks of the 1896 presidential campaign waged between the Republicans and Democrats largely on the issue of the free coinage of silver. Curiously, the model appears to be electrically powered: The Pennsylvania Lines shield is illuminated, and a trolley pole is evident on the cab roof. Indeed, the "locomotive" is sitting on the trolley loop in the driveway in front of Terre Haute Union Depot. Perhaps most interesting of all, the copy of this photograph in the archives of Rose-Hulman Institute of Technology indicates that Riley's son, Benjamin McKeen, an operating executive, is pictured here somewhere among his men. Most likely he is the gentleman in the light-colored jacket midway on the cab steps with a dark mustache and bowler hat. Community Archives, Vigo County Public Library, Terre Haute.

Riley's health began to fail after 1909, and illness forced him to withdraw from active business in 1910. Still, the aging banker was a Terre Haute icon. Local newspapers made it a point to commemorate his birthday every October.

The end came early on the morning of Tuesday, February 18, 1913, after a four-day vigil. It was not unexpected, and most of the family had already gathered to say goodbye. The rest of Terre Haute gathered the next day for the same reason, filing quietly through the family residence where Riley's body lay in state. The newspapers were filled with expressions of condolence from the great and small. When the funeral was held at the McKeen home on February 20, the house itself was jammed with family and friends, while a crowd of hundreds stood outside.[35]

The city practically ground to a halt that Thursday afternoon during the funeral. By order of the mayor and city council, most city offices were closed. Businesses closed early so that the proprietors, many of whom had been Riley's friends and clients, could pay their last respects. As a banker, McKeen had always been quick to lend to those in need and rarely refused a legitimate request. He had often been criticized by his more conservative colleagues in the industry as too easy a touch, but one successful Terre Haute merchant spoke for many when he had observed several years earlier, "I think, after all, that Mr. McKeen's way was the best way."[36]

At 2:30 that Thursday afternoon, out in the sprawling Vandalia yards and shop complex on the eastern edge of the city and downtown in Union Depot, workers paused five minutes from their labors. They were honoring the memory of a man many employees still personally remembered with great fondness. For them, William Riley McKeen's name would be forever linked with their proud railroad. He had been its greatest builder and its most effective protector; and through it all, it was quite clear that Riley McKeen had always done things his way.[37]

AFTERWORD AND ACKNOWLEDGMENTS

Any serious student of the Pennsylvania Railroad and its predecessor lines, particularly of those in the territory west of Pittsburgh, must confront an astonishing lack of historiography. Perhaps this is because the Pennsylvania was such a vast and complex organization, and because it attained that status early in its life. It is certainly *not* due to a lack of source material; the Pennsylvania's managers were remarkably thorough in documenting their operations and inclined to save huge quantities of paper records. Thankfully, this corporate trait lasted to the end, leaving us a legacy of carefully preserved minutes, memorandums, and reports. This book would not have been possible without this marvelously rich tapestry of documents.

However, there is a wealth of additional source material which needs acknowledgment—and continued preservation. Contemporary business periodicals like *The American Railroad Journal, The Railroad Gazette, Railway World,* and *The Commercial and Financial Chronicle* are priceless glimpses into the everyday situations and thought processes of the men who built and operated America's largest and most important 19th-century industry. They are also often difficult to find, particularly in hard copy.

Most difficult of all to locate, but absolutely invaluable, are the small caches of private correspondence and personal papers. Unfortunately, men like William Riley McKeen were intensely private people who often shrank from expressing themselves at all, especially on paper. They were even less willing to discuss or explain their business decisions, making historical research more of a sleuthing exercise. While I never did discover any of McKeen's private papers, the small collection of letters written by George B. Roberts to Richard W. Thompson that I discovered in the Thompson collections at the Indiana Historical Society and the Lilly Library at Indiana University were beacons in the dark.

It has been said that writing a biographical work places the author and subject in an unusually intimate relationship. I can readily attest to that sentiment. Carrying pieces of this book around in my head for many years has left me with a certain fondness for the remarkable Mr. McKeen, and I feel I know him rather well. He was at once both typical and atypical of his age: an able businessman with a strong drive for financial success, yet with a genuine sensitivity to and affection for people. No hint of scandal touches his story. He was forever ethical in his affairs, even when making an occasionally questionable decision. Above all, he is an admirable individual, and he appears all the more so against the backdrop of some of his more rapacious peers. I am honored to have made his acquaintance.

A word is in order on the photographs used to illustrate this book. As much as possible, they were selected from within the story's time frame of 1850–1905. Therefore, while I have fudged here and there (notably at the beginning of the last century), a majority of the photographic images were originally made prior to 1905, and many date from the 19th century. Following this policy often meant settling for less-than-crisp-looking pictures. It also meant using a lot of static shots and very few action scenes—the technology of the period left no other alternative.

In any writing project, especially this one, there is a lot of credit to be shared. One person in particular deserves extra-special mention. The fact is, you simply would not be holding this book at all were it not for the faith, encouragement, and remarkable patience of my wife, Sharon Ann (I love you, sweetie).

This project—which took over ten years to complete—was truly a learning experience for me, and I was blessed to have many good teachers and advisors. Mr. Richard S. (Dick) Simons, former president of the Indiana Historical Society and co-author of *Indiana Railroads,* a groundbreaking work which quite literally helped make this volume possible, served as mentor. Professor James Ward of the University of Tennessee at Chattanooga provided early inspiration, guidance, and helpful encouragement.

Technical expertise and assistance flowed freely from a number of sources. Christopher Baer and Marjorie McNinch at the incomparable Hagley Museum and Library introduced me to the wonders of the archival library and set a standard of excellence few others approached. Just as skilled, helpful, and supportive were Mr. David Lewis and Ms. Susan Dehler and their numerous colleagues at the Vigo County Public Library in Terre Haute. I cherish the many, many hours I spent in both facilities and among these fine folks.

Probably to no one's surprise, I have developed a special enthusiasm and appreciation for libraries and the people who staff them. Here at home, Ms. Ann Cardwell, formerly of the Wheaton Public Library, served long and with great forbearance as my Inter-Library Loan reference librarian and always went that extra mile to find and secure exactly what I needed. The staff in the special collections section at the Cunningham Library at Indiana State University in Terre Haute showed me great kindness early on. So did the staff at the Indiana State Library in Indianapolis, a seriously underappreciated institution. I must have spent what could total up to several months' time in the wonderful and mysterious stacks at the University of Illinois Library in Urbana-Champaign, always fruitfully—and I promise not to hold against the staff there the summer Saturday evening they locked me in and left. Among my other favorites, where I have spent significant amounts of time: the Lilly Library at Indiana University in Bloomington; the Library at Northwestern University in Evanston, Illinois; and the Cook County Law Library in Chicago.

One thing to marvel over is the vast number and diversity of people one meets and gets to know in the course of a project like this one. I have continually delighted in the friends I have made: great people like Wiley W. (Bill) Spurgeon of Muncie, Indiana; Professor Victor Bogle of Kokomo; Ms. Virginia Titus of Terre Haute; Mr. Larry Wilson of Terre Haute; and Mr. Michael McCormick of Terre Haute. And a very special word of appreciation and thanks to Mr. and Mrs. William Riley McKeen, IV, of Bedford, Indiana.

Then there are my many picture sources. You should know that most of the photographs in this volume were secured over an exceedingly hectic four-month period in late 1999. (Budding authors take note: I was unaware until very late in the game that the author is solely responsible for illustrating the book, making my own experience that much more intense.) Suffice to say, were it not for a legion of exceedingly helpful individuals and institutions, this book would have been greatly handicapped.

As might be expected, a significant number of prints came from Terre Haute, and I am deeply indebted to Ms. Susan Dehler of the Vigo County Public Library and Ms. Barbara Carney of the Vigo County Historical Society for their never-ending aid, enthusiasm, and counsel. Furthermore, I want to thank all who provided other illustrations. From the Illinois contingent, they are (in no particular order): Kevin Keaggy (Bond County Historical Society), Greenville; Pat Huck, Troy; Charles Barenfanger, Vandalia; Dorothy Ring (Casey Township Library) and Harold Livingston, Casey; Ms. Terry Gillespie (St. Elmo Public Library), St. Elmo; Noel Dicks, Arthur; and Lucille Peck (Atlanta Public Library and Museum), Atlanta. From Indiana: Ms. Candice M. McKing, North Vernon; JoAnn Pall (Brazil Public Library), Brazil; Mary Moore (Clay County Historical Society), Brazil; Ken Pickitt, Brazil; Cheryl Steinborn (Coatesville Public Library), Coatesville; Susan Sutton (Indiana Historical Society), Indianapolis; Mr. and Mrs. Wesley Tribbett, Darlington; Leroy Goode, Frankfort; Helen Crowe (Frankfort Public Library), Frankfort; Mr. Lynn Pentelow, Plymouth; the delightful Judy Spencer and Mary Johnson (Crawfordsville District Public Library), Crawfordsville; Gloria Reed (*Culver Citizen*), Culver; Phyllis Walters (Plainfield Public library), Plainfield; and John Robson (Rose-Hulman Institute of Technology), Terre Haute.

The risk one runs in trying to name all the people to whom you owe so much is that you might inadvertently leave someone out. I certainly pray I have not. But just in case: Thank you to all.

Richard Wallis
Wheaton, Ill.

NOTES

Abbreviations Used in the Notes

In order to keep the documentation as brief and compact as possible, citations appear in shortened form after the first instance. In addition, frequently used sources are abbreviated as follows:

Appellee Brief: *Brief in Behalf of the Appellee, The Cincinnati, Hamilton & Dayton Railroad Company* v. *William R. McKeen,* U.S. Circuit Court of Appeals, January 7, 1892

ARJ: American Railroad Journal

B&K, *Cent. Hist.*: George H. Burgess and Miles C. Kennedy, *Centennial History of the Pennsylvania Railroad Company* (Philadelphia, 1949)

C&C, *Const. Hist.*: Coverdale and Colpitts, *The Pennsylvania Railroad Company: Corporate, Financial and Construction History of Lines Owned and Operated to December 31, 1945,* 4 vols. (Philadelphia, 1947)

CFC: The Commercial and Financial Chronicle

Church, *Corp. Hist.*: Samuel Hardin Church, *Corporate History of the Pennsylvania Lines West of Pittsburgh,* 15 vols. plus index (Baltimore, 1898–1927)

Master's Report: *Report of the Master in Chancery, The Cincinnati, Hamilton & Dayton Railroad Company* v. *William R. McKeen* (U.S. Circuit Court for the District of Indiana), September 30, 1890

Messler Report: *Report of Thomas D. Messler to the Finance Committee, The Pennsylvania Company,* March 17, 1885 (in Pennsylvania Railroad Board File, number 17; Hagley Museum and Library, Wilmington, Del.)

Oakey, *Vigo Co.*: C. C. Oakey, *Greater Terre Haute and Vigo County,* 2 vols. (Chicago, 1908)

PC&StL-Bd Min: Minutes of the Board of Directors, The Pittsburg, Cincinnati & St. Louis Railway Company (Hagley Museum and Library, Wilmington, Del.)

Penna Co-Bd Min: Minutes of the Board of Directors of The Pennsylvania Company (Hagley Museum and Library, Wilmington, Del.)

PRR-BF: Board Files of the Pennsylvania Railroad Company, with number (Hagley Museum and Library, Wilmington, Del.)

RR Gaz.: The Railroad Gazette (using full volume numbers)

RWT/IHSL: Richard W. Thompson Letter Collection, William Henry Smith Library, Indiana Historical Society, Indianapolis

RWT/Lilly: Richard W. Thompson Letter Collection, Lilly Library, Indiana University, Bloomington

Ry Age: The Railway Age and Northwestern Railroader

StLV&TH-Bd Min: Minutes of the Board of Directors, St. Louis, Vandalia & Terre Haute Railroad Company (Hagley Museum and Library, Wilmington, Del.)

TH&I-Bd Min: Minutes of the Board of Directors, Terre Haute & Indianapolis Railroad Company (Hagley Museum and Library, Wilmington, Del.)

TH&R-Bd Min: Minutes of the Board of Directors, Terre Haute & Richmond Railroad Company (Hagley Museum and Library, Wilmington, Del.)

TH Exp.: Terre Haute Express (microfilm, Vigo County Library, Terre Haute)

TH Gaz.: Terre Haute Evening Gazette (microfilm, Vigo County Library, Terre Haute)

1. Prelude

1. C. C. Oakey, *Greater Terre Haute and Vigo County,* 2 vols. (Chicago, 1908), 237.

2. Ibid., 178.

3. Ibid., 177, 185.

4. Ibid., 140.

5. Ibid., 140–41.

6. Samuel Hardin Church, *Corporate History of the Pennsylvania Lines West of Pittsburgh,* 15 vols. plus index (Baltimore, 1898–1927), 3: 101–104; for additional background on the Madison & Indianapolis, see Freda L. Bridenstine, "The Madison & Indianapolis Railroad" (Master's thesis, Butler University, Indianapolis, 1931), and Wylie Daniels, *Village at the End of the Road* (Indianapolis, 1938).

7. George S. Cottman, "Internal Improvements: Railroads," *Indiana Magazine of History* 3 (December 1907): 149–81; *ARJ* 20 (June 12, 1847): 381.

8. Oakey, *Vigo Co.,* 188.

9. Church, *Corp. Hist.,* 5: 79–81.

10. For background on Lanier, see J. F. D. Lanier, *A Sketch of the Life of J. F. D. Lanier* (privately printed, 1877).

11. H. C. Bradsby, *History of Vigo County, Indiana* (Chicago, 1891), 566; TH&R-Bd Min, August 3, 1852; "Genealogy and Benefactions of Chauncey Rose" (manuscript in files of the Vigo County Library, Terre Haute).

12. Oakey, *Vigo Co.,* 188.

13. George I. Reed, ed., *Encyclopedia of Biography of Indiana,* 2 vols. (Chicago, 1895), 1: 78–82; *A Biographical History of Eminent and Self-Made Men of the State of Indiana* (Cincinnati, 1880), 35.

14. Oakey, *Vigo Co.,* 192–95.

15. Ibid., 239; *A Biographical History,* 35.

16. TH&R-Bd. Min., January 3, 1853.

17. George W. Smith, *History of Illinois and Her People,* 6 vols. (Chicago, 1927), 2: 346–51.

18. Ibid., 2: 348–50; *ARJ* 24 (March 15, 1851): 170–71; 24 (May 3, 1851): 282.

19. Church, *Corp. Hist.,* 6: 614–16; *ARJ* 25 (December 11, 1852): 785–86.

20. *Gillinwater v. Mississippi & Atlantic Railroad,* 13 Ill. 1.

21. *People ex rel Gillinwater v. Mississippi & Atlantic Railroad,* 13 Ill. 66; William Henry Perrin, ed., *History of Effingham County* (Chicago, 1883), 112–13.

22. *ARJ* 25 (November 6, 1852): 716; 25 (November 13, 1852): 722–23.

23. Alvin F. Harlow, *Road of the Century* (New York, 1947), 348, 359–62.

24. *ARJ* 25 (November 6, 1852): 714–15; 27 (March 11, 1854): 165–66; 27 (March 25, 1854): 182–83; 27 (April 8, 1854): 212; 27 (May 13, 1854): 298–99; *People ex rel Janney* v. *Mississippi & Atlantic Railroad,* 14 Ill. 440.

25. Church, *Corp. Hist.,* 6: 614–16; *ARJ* 26 (May 7, 1853): 289–90; 28 (March 10, 1855): 154–55; 30 (April 4, 1857): 217–18.

26. *ARJ* 28 (May 26, 1855): 334; 29 (May 3, 1856): 284.

27. Perrin, *Effingham County,* 112.

28. 7th Annual Report of the Terre Haute & Richmond Railroad Company (1855) (cited).

29. Francis Hughes, "History of Terre Haute First National Bank" (undated manuscript in possession of Ms. Virginia Titus, Terre Haute), 92.

30. *Wabash Express,* January 2, 1856; *Wabash Weekly Courier,* January 5, 1856.

31. Oakey, *Vigo Co.,* 239; *TH Exp.,* October 3, 1881.

32. TH&R-Bd Min, April 14, 1857; John H. B. Nowland, *Sketches of Prominent Citizens of 1876* (Indianapolis, 1877), 314–15; B. R. Sulgrove, *History of Indianapolis and Marion County* (Philadelphia, 1884), 156–57.

33. 9th Annual Report—TH&R (1857); TH&R-Bd Min, January 3, 1859.

34. TH&R-Bd Min, January 4, 1858.

35. *ARJ* 31 (July 3, 1858): 419–20; 32 (October 1, 1859): 631–32; TH&R-Bd Min, April 13, 1858; December 23, 1858.

36. Church, *Corp. Hist.,* 6: 615; *ARJ* 32 (November 12, 1859): 723; TH&R-Bd Min, March 21, 1861; September 25, 1861.

37. 12th Annual Report—TH&R (1860) (cited).

38. 13th Annual Report—TH&R (1861); also the 14th Annual Report (1862); the 15th Annual Report (1863); and the 16th Annual Report (1864).

39. Oakey, *Vigo Co.,* 239; TH&R-Bd Min, January 7, 1862.

40. TH&R-Bd Min, March 20, 1862.

41. *A Biographical History,* 35; *Terre Haute Tribune,* March 7, 1922.

42. 4th Annual Report of the St. Louis, Alton & Terre Haute Railroad Company (1866).

43. TH&I-Bd Min, November 27, 1866; Church, *Corp. Hist.,* 5: 34.

44. Church, *Corp. Hist.,* 5: 86–87.

2. Executive

1. For a discussion of St. Louis's commercial situation, see Wyatt W. Belcher, *Economic Rivalry between St. Louis and Chicago, 1850–1880* (New York, 1947); Church, *Corp. Hist.,* 10: 29–35.

2. TH&R-Bd Min, April 4, 1862; June 23, 1864.

3. Pennsylvania Company, *Corporate History of the Pittsburgh, Fort Wayne & Chicago Railway Company* (Pittsburgh, 1875), 289–90; 6th Annual Report of the Pittsburgh, Fort Wayne & Chicago Railway Company (1867).

4. 6th Annual Report—PFW&C (1867).

5. *ARJ* 40 (January 12, 1867): 33; TH&I-Bd Min, January 28, 1867.

6. Penna. Co, *Corporate History of the PFW&C,* 290.

7. Church, *Corp. Hist.,* 6: 611–12; 6th Annual Report—PFW&C (1867).

8. Bradsby, *Vigo County,* 569.

9. TH&I-Bd Min, June 11, 1867.

10. TH&I-Bd Min, June 18, 1867.

11. TH&I-Bd Min, June 28, 1867.

12. Church, *Corp. Hist.,* 6: 611–12.

13. Ibid., 3: 45–47; B&K, *Cent. Hist.,* 188–92; Minutes of the Board of Directors of the Steubenville & Indiana Railroad Company, February 12, 1867; PC&StL-Bd Min, May 9, 1868.

14. James A. Ward, *J. Edgar Thomson, Master of the Pennsylvania* (Westport, Conn., 1980), 159–88.

15. Church, *Corp. Hist.,* 3: 36–37, 40; *ARJ* 33 (June 30, 1860): 555; 37 (November 26, 1864): 1139; C&C, *Const. Hist.,* 3: 464.

16. Ward, *J. Edgar Thomson,* 191–92; C. M. Woodward, *A History of the St. Louis Bridge* (St. Louis, 1881), 15–16.

17. 6th Annual Report—PFW&C (1867).

18. Church, *Corp. Hist.,* 5: 50–51; Ward, *J. Edgar Thomson,* 180 (plus note).

19. TH&I-Bd Min, July 3, 1867.

20. TH&I-Bd Min, October 23, 1867; Board Minutes of the Steubenville & Indiana Railroad, September 26, 1867.

21. TH&I-Bd Min, December 24, 1867.

22. 19th Annual Report of the Terre Haute & Indianapolis Railroad Company (1867); Messler Report.

23. *Dictionary of American Biography,* 10-1: 395–96.

24. StLV&TH-Bd Min, January 14, 1868; March 13, 1868.

25. TH&I-Bd Min, February 21, 1868.

26. TH&I-Bd Min, February 24, 1868.

27. TH&I-Bd Min, February 27, 1868.

28. Ibid. (cited).

29. TH&I-Bd Min, March 11, 1868.

30. For the complete documents, see Church, *Corp. Hist.,* 5: 44–49; 7: 325–26.

31. William E. McCaslin, ed., *History of Bond County* (Chicago, 1915), 628; Church, *Corp. Hist.,* 5: 15.

32. *A Biographical History,* 35.

33. Oakey, *Vigo Co.,* 238.

34. Dorothy Clark, *Historically Speaking* (Evansville, Ind., 1981), 244, 283; Bradsby, *Vigo County,* 514.

35. Clark, *Historically Speaking,* 277.

36. Denver Harper, *Coal Mining in Vigo County, Indiana* (Bloomington, Ind., 1985), 1; *ARJ* 22 (October 27, 1849): 678–79; *Exhibit of the Condition and Prospect of the Terre Haute and Richmond Railroad* (New York, 1851).

37. Oakey, *Vigo Co.,* 217–18.

38. TH&I-Bd Min, March 31, 1868; June 24, 1868; 21st Annual Report—TH&I (1869).

39. 12th Annual Report—TH&I (1860); 18th Annual Report—TH&I (1866); and 22nd Annual Report—TH&I (1870).

40. 21st Annual Report—TH&I (1869); see copy of proposed suit against I&StL in RWT/Lilly.

41. TH&I-Bd Min, March 31, 1868; April 17, 1869.

42. B&K, *Cent. Hist.,* 196–98.

43. *Logansport Pharos,* January 25, 1868—reprinted in *ARJ* 41 (February 8, 1868): 145–46; *ARJ* 39 (January 27, 1866): 81–82; 40 (May 11, 1867): 438–39.

44. *ARJ* 39 (January 27, 1866): 81–82.

45. 1st Annual Report of the Jeffersonville, Madison & Indianapolis Railroad Company (1866); 2nd Annual Report—JM&I (1867); Church, *Corp. Hist.,* 4: 606, 622–31.

46. Church, *Corp. Hist.,* 3: 64–86, 710–11; *ARJ* 37 (July 30, 1864): 747; 38 (December 30, 1865): 1237–38; 41 (June 6, 1868): 557; C&C, *Const. Hist.,* 3: 456.

47. 24th Annual Report of the Pennsylvania Railroad Company (1870); *ARJ* 41 (April 25, 1868): 390–91.

48. Julius Grodinsky, *Jay Gould: His Business Career, 1867–1892* (Philadelphia, 1957), 59–60; B&K, *Cent. Hist.,* 198.

49. Ward, *J. Edgar Thomson,* 143–47.

50. TH&I-Bd Min, June 23, 1869.

3. Owner

1. TH&I-Bd Min, April 1, 1869; April 17, 1869.

2. TH&I-Bd Min, June 23, 1869; January 1, 1867.

3. Church, *Corp. Hist.,* 5: 68–74 (see especially Section 23 of the TH&R charter on p.73).

4. Ibid., 5: 86–87.

5. *The Terre Haute & Indianapolis Railroad Company* v. *State ex rel. Ketcham,* 159 Ind. 438, 442–43; *State ex rel. Attorney General* v. *The TH&I RR Co.,* 64 Ind. 297; *TH Exp,* August 13, 1873; August 20, 1873; August 22, 1873; August 30, 1873.

6. TH&I-Bd Min, August 8, 1870.

7. Constitution of the State of Illinois, 1870.

8. George B. Roberts to Richard W. Thompson, January 14, January 25, January 27, February 8 (telegram), February 9 (telegram), and February 10 (telegram), all 1871 (RWT/IHSL); StLV&TH-Bd Min, February 15, 1871.

9. 22nd Annual Report—TH&I (1870).

10. Annual Report of the St. Louis, Vandalia & Terre Haute Railroad Company for 1871 and 1872; Roberts to Thompson, March 10, 1871 (RWT/IHSL) (cited).

11. PC&StL-Bd Min, April 27, 1871 (cited).

12. TH&I-Bd Min, July 1, 1871; Richard W. Thompson to William Thaw, June 21, 1871 (RWT/Lilly); RR Gaz 14 (July 1, 1871): 162; 14 (July 8, 1871): 174.

13. StLV&TH-Bd Min, April 29, 1871; July 26, 1870.

14. StLV&TH-Bd Min, June 26 and June 27, 1871.

15. Leland H Jenks, "Multiple Level Organization of a Great Railroad," *Business History Review* 35 (Autumn 1961): 336–43. The first president of the Pennsylvania Company was Thomas A. Scott, Thomson's vice president of the Pennsylvania Railroad. When Scott succeeded Thomson as president of the Pennsylvania Railroad in 1874, he would also retain the presidency of the Pennsylvania Company, a situation which would become normal policy thereafter.

16. Roberts to Thompson, January 24, 1872 (RWT/IHS) (cited).

17. TH&I-Bd Min, January 6, 1873; *TH Gaz.,* January 7, 1873; *TH Exp.,* January 8, 1873.

18. TH&I-Bd Min, January 16, 1873; March 25, 1873.

19. TH&I-Bd Min, January 12, 1874; July 16, 1873; December 30, 1873.

20. TH&I-Bd Min, August 8, 1870; August 13, 1870; 23rd Annual Report—TH&I (1871).

21. 26th Annual Report—TH&I (1874).

22. B&K, *Cent. Hist.,* 306.

23. 27th Annual Report—TH&I (1875); *RR Gaz.* 18 (June 6, 1874): 207.

24. *CFC* 18 (June 20, 1874): 622–23; *RR Gaz.* 19 (October 2, 1875): 411.

25. Church, *Corp. Hist.,* 6: 611–12.

26. 24th Annual Report—TH&I (1872); 25th Annual Report—TH&I (1873); 26th Annual Report—TH&I (1874).

27. TH&I-Bd Min, October 4, 1875; *RR Gaz.* 19 (November 27, 1875): 495; 19 (December 11, 1875): 513 .

28. *Pittsburg, Cincinnati & St. Louis Railway Company* v. *Columbus, Chicago & Indiana Central Railway Company,* 9 Biss. 456, 472–73; 7th Annual Report—Pittsburg, Cincinnati & St. Louis Railway Company (1874).

29. PC&StL-Bd Min, October 16, 1875.

30. Church, *Corp. Hist.,* 7: 327–28.

31. PC&StL-Bd Min, October 16, 1875.

32. 27th Annual Report—TH&I (1875).

33. 28th Annual Report—TH&I (1876) (cited).

34. *RR Gaz.* 20 (May 26, 1876): 235–36; *CFC* 24 (May 5, 1877): 419–20; 31st Annual Report—PRR (1877); PC&StL-Bd Min, October 16, 1876.

35. 29th Annual Report—TH&I (1877); 30th Annual Report—TH&I (1878).

36. TH&I-Bd Min, January 28, 1878.

4. The Strike

1. For a glimpse of the TH&I's rate-related problems, see McKeen's message in 26th Annual Report—TH&I (1874) and Simpson's comments in 27th Annual Report—TH&I (1875).

2. *RR Gaz.* 20 (April 21, 1876): 177; *CFC* 21 (April 22, 1876): 400; 29th Annual Report—TH&I (1877); 30th Annual Report—TH&I (1878).

3. *30th Annual Report—TH&I* (1878).

4. H. W. Schotter, *The Growth and Development of the Pennsylvania Railroad Company* (Philadelphia, 1927), 108–109; B&K, *Cent. Hist.,* 306–307, 314–15.

5. James A. Ward, "Power and Accountability on the Pennsylvania Railroad, 1846–1878," *Business History Review* 49 (Spring 1975): 37–59; *25th Annual Report—TH&I* (1873).

6. *TH Exp.,* July 22, 1877; *RR Gaz.* 21 (July 6, 1877): 310.

7. The single best source for an overall view of the strike is still Robert V. Bruce, *1877: Year of Violence* (Indianapolis, 1959).

8. *TH Exp.,* July 22, 1877; July 23, 1877.

9. *TH Exp.,* July 23, 1877.

10. Ibid.

11. *TH Exp.,* July 25, 1877.

12. Ibid.

13. Ibid. (cited).

14. Ibid.

15. Bruce, *1877,* 287; Matilda Gresham, *Life of Walter Quinton Gresham,* 2 vols. (Chicago, 1919), 1: 382.

16. Gresham, *Gresham,* 1: 379.

17. Ibid., 1: 385–86.

18. Ibid., 1: 387–89.

19. Ibid., 1: 391–92; *TH Exp.,* July 28, 1877.

20. *TH Exp.,* July 27, 1877.

21. *TH Exp.,* July 26, 1877; *TH Gaz.,* July 27, 1877; Gresham, *Gresham,* 1: 392.

22. Gresham, *Gresham,* 1: 384, 397; Bruce, *1877,* 287.

23. Gresham, *Gresham,* 1: 398–99.

24. *TH Exp.,* July 29, 1877.

25. Ibid.

26. Ibid.

27. Ibid.

28. Ibid.

29. Gresham, *Gresham,* 1: 399 (cited).

30. Ibid. (cited).

31. *TH Exp.,* July 30, 1877 (Extra Edition).

32. Ibid.

33. *TH Exp.,* July 31, 1877 (cited).

34. *TH Exp.,* August 1, 1877.

35. Ibid.

36. *TH Gaz.,* August 1, 1877; Bruce, *1877,* 308.

37. *TH Gaz.,* August 3, 1877.

38. Ibid.

39. *TH Exp.,* August 4, 1877; *TH Gaz.,* August 4, 1877.

40. Thompson to Thomas A. Scott, August 5, 1877 (RWT/Lilly) (cited).

41. *RR Gaz.,* 24 (April 16, 1880): 212; 24 (April 9, 1880): 201; Nick Salvatore, *Eugene V. Debs, Citizen and Socialist* (Urbana, Ill., 1982), 47.

42. *29th Annual Report—TH&I* (1877).

5. System Builder

1. Roberts to Thompson, August 12, 1879 (RWT/IHS).

2. Church, *Corp. Hist.,* 6: 613; *St. Louis, Alton & Terre Haute Railroad* v. *Indianapolis & St. Louis Railroad, et al.,* 9 Biss. 99, 112.

3. *St. Louis, Alton & Terre Haute RR* v. *Indianapolis & St. Louis RR, et al.,* 9 Biss. 99.

4. Roberts to Thompson, April 4, 1873; May 19, 1873 (RWT/IHS).

5. PC&StL-Bd Min, February 14, 1879; Roberts to Thompson, August 12, 1879 (RWT/IHS).

6. PC&StL-Bd Min, February 14, 1879 (cited).

7. *Pittsburg, Cincinnati & St. Louis Railway Co.* v. *Columbus, Chicago & Indiana Central Railway Co.,* 8 Biss. 456.

8. PC&StL-Bd Min, May 22, 1879.

9. William Thaw, J. N. McCullough, and Thomas D. Messler (PC&StL Ry Executive Committee) to W. R. McKeen, June 17, 1879 (in PRR-BF 30T).

10. Details of the proposal are included in PRR-BF 30T.

11. Roberts to Thompson, August 12, 1879; September 30, 1879; October 2, 1879 (RWT/IHS).

12. Roberts to Thompson, November 25, 1879 (RWT/IHSL); Messler Report.

13. Roberts to Thompson, November 25, 1879 (cited), December 11, 1879 (cited) (RWT/IHS).

14. Messler Report.

15. Oakey, *Vigo Co.,* 238; Church, *Corp. Hist.,* 4: 842–43; *Indianapolis News,* February 18, 1913.

16. Church, *Corp. Hist.,* 5: 147.

17. Ibid., 5: 7–10; *RR Gaz.* 16 (April 27, 1872): 187; 16 (August 10, 1872): 352; *TH Exp.,* November 28, 1872.

18. Church, *Corp. Hist.,* 5: 10; *Miltenberger, et al.* v. *Logansport, Crawfordsville & Southwestern Railroad Co.,* 106 US 286; *RR Gaz.* 21 (April 27, 1877): 187; *TH Exp.,* October 26, 1879.

19. Church, *Corp. Hist.,* 5: 11–13; TH&I-Bd Min, November 22, 1879.

20. *CFC* 31 (November 11, 1880): 547–48; 31st Annual Report—TH&I (1879); 32nd Annual Report—TH&I (1880).

21. B&K, *Cent. Hist.,* 383; *RR Gaz.* 24 (August 6, 1880): 421; *TH Gaz.* August 2, 1880; August 3, 1880.

22. Roberts to Thompson, August 23, 1880 (RWT/IHS) (cited).

23. PC&StL-Bd Min, September 29, 1880; *RR Gaz.* 25 (January 7, 1881): 7.

24. Compare 32nd Annual Report—TH&I (1880) and 33rd Annual Report—TH&I (1881).

25. *RR Gaz.* 25 (March 25, 1881): 173.

26. PC&StL-Bd Min, April 12, 1882.

27. *A Biographical History,* 35; S. B. Gookins, *History of Vigo County* (Chicago, 1880), 208–209; Hughes, "First National Bank," 93; *TH Gaz.,* October 12, 1896.

28. *TH Gaz.,* December 16, 1899 (Part 5 of Special Issue).

29. Frances E. Hughes, "McKeen Family Dates to Early 1800s," *The Spectator,* February 26, 1977, 13.

30. *Terre Haute Star,* February 18, 1913; *TH Exp.,* May 18, 1880; June 12, 1880; June 16, 1880; June 17, 1880; June 18, 1880.

31. 32nd Annual Report—TH&I (1880); 33rd Annual Report—TH&I (1881).

32. *RR Gaz.* 25 (December 30, 1881): 743.

33. *TH Gaz.,* October 4, 1881.

34. Messler Report.

35. Roberts to Thompson, December 7, 1880; March 6, 1882 (RWT/IHS).

36. Roberts to Thompson, March 6, 1882 (RWT/IHS) (cited).

37. Ibid. (cited).

38. *CFC* 34 (April 1, 1882): 366.

39. Timothy Edward Howard, ed., *History of St. Joseph County, Indiana* (Chicago, 1907), 239; Messler Report.

40. *TH Exp.,* February 1, 1882; January 1, 1883; *TH Gaz.,* March 31, 1883; 35th Annual Report—TH&I (1883); 36th Annual Report—TH&I (1884).

41. *RR Gaz.* 26 (December 29, 1882): 804–805; 27 (December 28, 1883): 852.

42. 37th Annual Report—PRR (1883); 38th Annual Report—PRR (1884).

43. *CFC* 33 (October 8, 1881): 370–71; *Agreement with Cleveland, Columbus, Cincinnati & Indianapolis Ry. Co.*, in *Indianapolis & St. Louis Railroad File* (PRR-BF 10); Church, *Corp. Hist.*, 3: 89–90, 94–95.

44. 36th Annual Report—TH&I (1884); 37th Annual Report—TH&I (1885).

45. 36th Annual Report—TH&I (1884).

46. George B. Roberts to William Thaw, May 1, 1885 (PRR-BF 17); Penna. Co.-Bd Min, March 4, 1885; Messler Report.

47. Messler Report (cited).

48. *Bradstreet's* 11 (June 6, 1885): 380; Roberts to Thaw, May 1, 1885 (PRR-BF 17).

49. *TH Gaz.*, December 12, 1887; *TH Exp.*, January 10, 1894.

50. *TH Gaz.*, December 12, 1887.

51. Messler Report.

52. Ibid.; TH&I-Bd Min, July 11, 1885.

53. Church, *Corp. Hist.*, 4: 605–607.

54. Ibid., 7: 689–92; *Biographical Memoirs of Greene County, Indiana* (Indianapolis, 1908), 302–303; *RR Gaz.* 29 (January 9, 1885): 32; 29 (January 23, 1885): 63; 29 (December 4, 1885): 781.

55. See *TH Gaz.*, June 3, 1887.

56. 38th Annual Report—TH&I (1886).

57. Margaret Wynn, "Natural Gas in Indiana," *Indiana Magazine of History* 4 (March 1908): 31–45; Bradsby, *Vigo County*, 514–16.

58. *RR Gaz.* 29 (January 23, 1885): 56; 37th Annual Report—TH&I (1885).

59. *RR Gaz.* 31 (April 1, 1887): 226.

6. Ives

1. *TH Exp.*, January 3, 1894; *RR Gaz.* 31 (October 7, 1887): 660.

2. Appellee Brief, 4–5; Master's Report, 5.

3. *TH Gaz.*, June 4, 1887; Edmund Clarence Stedman, ed., *The New York Stock Exchange* (New York, 1905; reprint, 1969), 330–32.

4. "Ives in Wall Street," *Bradstreet's* 15 (August 20, 1887): 552–53.

5. *CFC* 42: 752–53 (June 19, 1886); "Ives in Wall Street," *Bradstreet's* 15 (August 20, 1887): 552–53 .

6. *RR Gaz.* 30 (September 9, 1887): 590–91; *CFC* 45 (November 26, 1887): 692–93.

7. *Railway World* 31 (March 12, 1887): 247; 31(March 19, 1887): 266–67; *The Railway Times* 51 (March 12, 1887): 344.

8. *Railway World* 31 (March 26, 1887): 290–91.

9. Master's Report, 5–6; Appellee Brief, 5–6.

10. Master's Report, 5–6; Appellee Brief, 5–6.

11. *Terre Haute Star*, October 29, 1919; *Indianapolis Journal*, reprinted in *TH Gaz.*, January 9, 1888; *Proceedings of 24th Annual Meeting of the Indiana State Bar Association* (1920), 171–73; *RR Gaz.* 21 (April 27, 1877): 187.

12. Details of this meeting are found in Appellee Brief, 6–11; Master's Report, 6–8.

13. *Indianapolis Journal*, reprinted in *TH Gaz.*, May 18, 1887; Appellee Brief, 12–13 (cited).

14. Appellee Brief, 16.

15. Master's Report, 8; Appellee Brief, 16.

16. Details of the June 1, 1887, meeting in Appellee Brief, 17–21; Master's Report, 9–10.

17. Appellee Brief, 59; *TH Gaz.*, June 4, 1887.

18. *TH Gaz.*, June 1, 1887.

19. *TH Gaz.*, June 2, 1887; June 3, 1887.

20. Appellee Brief, 26.

21. Ibid., 26–27.

22. TH&I-Bd Min, June 4, 1887.

23. Appellee Brief, 28.

24. *TH Gaz.,* June 4, 1887; June 6, 1887; June 7, 1887; Appellee Brief, 46.

25. *TH Gaz.,* June 6, 1887.

26. 38th Annual Report—TH&I (1886).

27. 39th Annual Report—TH&I (1887).

28. *RR Gaz.* 31 (December 30, 1887): 846–47.

29. 41st Annual Report—PRR (1887).

30. *RR Gaz.* 31 (October 7, 1887): 660; 39th Annual Report—TH&I (1887); *Railway World* 31 (July 16, 1887): 686.

31. Appellee Brief, 32, 47.

32. *TH Gaz.,* September 27, 1883.

33. *TH Gaz.,* July 7, 1887; Appellee Brief, 30, 46; TH&I-Bd Min, June 25, 1887.

7. The Crash

1. *TH Gaz.,* June 9, 1887; July 8, 1887.

2. *TH Gaz.,* July 6, 1887; *Railway World* 31 (July 16, 1887): 686.

3. *St. Louis, Vandalia & Terre Haute Railroad Company* v. *Terre Haute & Indianapolis Railroad Company,* 33 F 440; *TH Gaz.,* July 7, 1887.

4. *TH Gaz.,* July 8, 1887.

5. *TH Gaz.,* July 7, 1887.

6. *TH Exp.,* July 15, 1887; July 16, 1887; *CFC* 45 (July 23, 1887): 113.

7. "Ives in Wall Street," *Bradstreet's* 15 (August 20, 1887): 552–53; Maury Klein, *The Life and Legend of Jay Gould* (Baltimore, 1986), 384.

8. TH&I-Bd Min, June 30, 1887; July 1, 1887; July 14, 1888.

9. Stedman, *The New York Stock Exchange,* 333; *TH Exp.,* July 15, 1887; July 16, 1887; 41st Annual Report of the Cincinnati, Hamilton & Dayton Railway Company (1887–88).

10. *RR Gaz.* 31 (July 22, 1887): 490; 31 (July 29, 1887): 504.

11. 41st Annual Report—CH&D (1887–88).

12. Ibid.; *TH Gaz.,* August 6, 1887.

13. *TH Gaz.,* August 8, 1887.

14. *Indianapolis Journal,* reprinted in *TH Gaz.,* August 8, 1887.

15. TH&I-Bd Min, August 8, 1887.

16. *TH Gaz.,* August 9, 1887.

17. Ibid. (cited).

18. Ibid.

19. Ibid.

20. TH&I-Bd Min, August 9, 1887.

21. *TH Gaz.,* August 10, 1887 (cited); Stedman, *The New York Stock Exchange,* 333.

22. TH&I-Bd Min, August 22, 1887.

23. 39th Annual Report—TH&I (1887); *TH Gaz.,* August 13, 1887; *CFC* 45 (August 20, 1887): 225.

24. 37th Annual Report—TH&I (1885); 38th Annual Report—TH&I (1886); 39th Annual Report—TH&I (1887).

25. *StLV&TH RR Co.* v. *TH&I RR Co.,* 33 F 440; *Railway World* 31 (October 29, 1887): 1046.

26. *StLV&TH RR Co.* v. *TH&I RR Co.,* 33 F 440.

27. *RR Gaz.* 31 (October 21, 1887): 692; Appellee Brief, 49–50.

28. *TH Gaz.,* December 6, 1887; Appellee Brief, 51.

29. *TH Gaz.,* December 6, 1887; December 7, 1887.

30. Appellee Brief, 52.

31. *TH Gaz.,* December 8, 1887 (cited); Appellee Brief, 52; *Cincinnati, Hamilton & Dayton Railway Company* v. *William R. McKeen,* 64 F 36.

32. *TH Gaz.,* December 9, 1887.

33. *TH Gaz.*, December 14, 1887; December 15, 1887; December 17, 1887.
34. Appellee Brief, 56.
35. Ibid.; *TH Exp.*, January 3, 1888.
36. TH&I-Bd Min, January 2, 1888; *TH Exp.*, January 3, 1888.
37. Appellee Brief, 55.
38. *TH Exp.*, January 4, 1888.
39. *TH Gaz.*, January 12, 1888; also see *StLV&TH RR Co.* v. *TH&I RR Co.*, 33 F 440.
40. *Railway World* 32 (January 21, 1888): 62.
41. Appellee Brief, 64–65.
42. *CH&D Ry Co.* v. *Wm. R. McKeen*, 64 F 36.
43. Ibid.; Appellee Brief, 66–67.
44. Appellee Brief, 74–75.

8. Caretaker

1. TH&I-Bd Min, July 14, 1888.
2. 40th Annual Report—TH&I (1888).
3. TH&I-Bd Min, July 14, 1888; 40th Annual Report—TH&I (1888).
4. 40th Annual Report—TH&I (1888).
5. *RR Gaz.* 32 (December 28, 1888): 854–55.
6. *RR Gaz.* 32 (September 28, 1888): 646.
7. 41st Annual Report—TH&I (1889).
8. *RR Gaz.* 33 (March 31, 1889): 150; 43rd Annual Report—CH&D (1889–90).
9. TH&I-Bd Min, January 6, 1890.
10. StLV&TH-Bd Min, August 4, 1890; Church, *Corp. Hist.*, 7: 327–30.
11. Church, *Corp. Hist.*, 7: 327–30.
12. Ibid.
13. StLV&TH-Bd Min, August 4, 1890.
14. See 42nd Annual Report—TH&I (1890); 43rd Annual Report—TH&I (1891); 44th Annual Report—TH&I (1892); also see President McCrea's statement in 48th Annual Report—TH&I (1896).
15. 44th Annual Report—TH&I (1890).
16. Reed, *Encyclopedia*, 2: 25–28; *A Biographical History*, 54–55; Bradsby, *Vigo County*, 706–707.
17. TH&I-Bd Min, May 27, 1889; Newton Bateman, J. Seymour Curwen, and Paul Selby, *Historical Encyclopedia of Illinois*, 2 vols. (Chicago, 1923), 2: 693–96.
18. TH&I-Bd Min, May 27, 1889; July 19, 1889; Church, *Corp. Hist.*, 7: 340–45, 5: 250–57.
19. 42nd Annual Report—TH&I (1890).
20. Ibid.
21. 44th Annual Report—TH&I (1892).
22. Ibid.; *TH Gaz.*, December 29, 1891; TH&I-Bd Min, January 15, 1896.
23. TH&I-Bd Min, January 15, 1896 (cited).
24. Loren Hassam, *A Historical Sketch of Terre Haute* (Terre Haute, 1873), 54; *A Biographical History*, 55–56; Church, *Corp. Hist.*, 5: 19.
25. *RR Gaz.* 15 (April 29, 1871): 58; 16 (April 27, 1872): 187; 16 (July 13, 1872): 302.
26. Church, *Corp. Hist.*, 5: 21.
27. *Union Trust Company* v. *Illinois Midland Railway Company*, 117 US 434.
28. Ibid.
29. *CFC* 29 (August 30, 1879): 225.
30. *Union Trust Co.* v. *Ill. Midland*, 117 US 434, 476–77; *TH Exp.*, March 24, 1882.
31. Church, *Corp. Hist.*, 5: 339–49.
32. Ibid., 5: 539–43; *The Railway Times* 50 (November 27, 1886): 696; *RR Gaz.* 30 (November 19, 1886): 804; 30 (December 3, 1886): 839; 30 (December 17, 1886): 879.
33. Church, *Corp. Hist.*, 5: 24–26.

34. Ibid.

35. Herbert J. Rissler, "Charles Warren Fairbanks, Conservative Hoosier" (dissertation, Indiana University, 1961), 33; Will Cumback and J. R. Maynard, *Men of Progress: Indiana* (Indianapolis, 1899), 506; *National Cyclopedia of American Biography*, 30: 531, 31: 279.

36. *Poor's Manual of Railroads: 1888*, 534; *Poor's Manual of Railroads: 1889*, 526.

37. *Indianapolis Journal*, reprinted in *TH Gaz.*, August 18, 1890.

38. Rissler, "Fairbanks," 74.

39. *TH Gaz.*, June 29, 1891.

40. *CFC* 55: 766 (November 5, 1892); TH&I-Bd Min, May 9, 1892; Church, *Corp. Hist.*, 7: 340.

41. Church, *Corp. Hist.*, 7: 330–40; 44th Annual Report—TH&I (1892).

42. 44th Annual Report—TH&I (1892); 45th Annual Report—TH&I (1893) (cited).

43. 45th Annual Report—TH&I (1893).

44. Ibid.

45. Ibid.

46. 46th Annual Report-TH&I (1894).

47. *TH Gaz.*, August 18, 1890.

48. TH&I-Bd Min, April 25, 1872; *Terre Haute Tribune*, November 30, 1924.

49. *TH Exp.*, July 9, 1890.

50. TH&I-Bd Min, January 5, 1891; *TH Gaz.*, August 7, 1890; August 15, 1893.

51. TH&I-Bd Min, January 5, 1891; *TH Gaz.*, August 15, 1893.

52. *TH Gaz.*, August 15, 1893.

53. *Terre Haute Star*, August 20, 1892; *TH Gaz.*, August 15, 1893.

54. *TH Gaz.*, August 15, 1893.

55. Ibid.

56. 45th Annual Report—TH&I (1893).

57. TH&I-Bd Min, July 1, 1887; Church, *Corp. Hist.*, 5: 6–7.

58. TH&I-Bd Min, January 8, 1889; January 5, 1891.

59. TH&I-Bd Min, May 9, 1892; August 10, 1892.

60. TH&I-Bd Min, January 2, 1893.

61. TH&I-Bd Min, August 10, 1892.

62. Ibid.

63. 44th Annual Report—TH&I (1892); 45th Annual Report—TH&I (1893).

64. *StLV&TH RR Co.* v. *TH&I RR Co.*, 145 US 393.

65. Church, *Corp. Hist.*, 3: 97–98.

66. *TH Gaz.*, December 21, 1889; *Ry Age*, (September 20, 1890), 667.

67. Penna Co-Bd Min, September 12, 1893.

68. Ibid.

69. Ibid.; TH&I-Bd Min, December 30, 1893.

70. *TH Gaz.*, January 2, 1894; *TH Exp.*, January 3, 1894.

71. *TH Gaz.*, January 2, 1894 (cited).

72. TH&I-Bd Min, January 1, 1894.

73. Ibid.; *TH Exp.*, January 6, 1894.

74. *CFC* 58: 9–19 (January 6, 1894).

75. 47th Annual Report—PRR (1895).

76. 45th Annual Report—TH&I (1893).

77. *Poor's Manual of Railroads: 1895*, 711–12; 46th Annual Report—TH&I (1894).

78. TH&I-Bd Min, January 1, 1894; 47th Annual Report—TH&I (1895).

79. TH&I-Bd Min, January 7, 1895.

80. *TH Exp.*, January 29, 1895; *TH Gaz.*, January 29, 1895.

81. 47th Annual Report-TH&I (1895).

82. Ibid.

83. *TH Gaz.*, December 31, 1895; *TH Exp.*, December 31, 1895.

9. Postlude

1. TH&I-Bd Min (Finance Committee), July 23, 1895; 47th Annual Report—TH&I (1895).

2. TH&I-Bd Min, January 15, 1896; B&K, *Cent. Hist.*, 517–18.

3. *CFC* 62 (January 25, 1896): 187; TH&I-Bd Min, January 13, 1897.

4. TH&I-Bd Min, January 13, 1897.

5. Ibid.

6. Ibid.

7. *Poor's Manual of Railroads: 1895*, 1125–26; *Poor's Manual of Railroads: 1896*, 1099; *Street Railway Review* 7 (March 15, 1895): 152–53; 7 (November 15, 1895): 793; *Poor's Manual of Railroads: 1898*, 972–73.

8. *Street Railway Review* 9 (May 15, 1899): 348; 9 (July 15, 1899): 506; 10 (September 15, 1900): 494; *Poor's Manual of Railroads: 1910*, 2003–2006.

9. Russel M. Seeds, ed., *History of the Republican Party of Indiana* (Indianapolis, 1899), 186–89; Harry J. Sievers, *Benjamin Harrison: Hoosier Statesman* (New York, 1959), 184–85.

10. Seeds, *Republican Party*, 65–66.

11. John Braeman, "The Rise of Albert J. Beveridge to the United States Senate," *Indiana Magazine of History* 53 (December 1957): 355–82; Seeds, *Republican Party*, 116.

12. Seeds, *Republican Party*, 77.

13. James H. Madison, "Charles Warren Fairbanks," in Ralph D. Gray, ed., *Gentlemen from Indiana: National Party Candidates, 1836–1940* (Indianapolis, 1977), 178–79.

14. Rissler, "Fairbanks," 74; Seeds, *Republican Party*, 80.

15. *TH Exp.*, January 13, 1897.

16. Seeds, *Republican Party*, 186–89.

17. 48th Annual Report—TH&I (1896).

18. Ibid.; TH&I-Bd Min, January 13, 1897.

19. 48th Annual Report—TH&I (1896); TH&I-Bd Min, January 13, 1897.

20. TH&I-Bd Min, January 13, 1897.

21. Ibid.

22. *CFC* 63 (July 18, 1896): 17; 63 (September 26, 1896): 561; *TH Gaz.*, November 14, 1896; *Terre Haute & Indianapolis Railroad Company* v. *Cox et al.*, 102 F 825; *Cox et al.* v. *Terre Haute & Indianapolis Railroad Company*, 123 F 439; 48th Annual Report—TH&I (1896).

23. *TH Gaz.*, November 14, 1896.

24. *TH Gaz.*, January 18, 1897; *Terre Haute & Indianapolis Railroad Company* v. *State ex rel. Ketcham*, 159 Ind. 438.

25. *TH&I RR Co.* v. *State ex rel. Ketcham*, 159 Ind. 438.

26. Church, *Corp. Hist.*, 5: 12, 28–29.

27. *Terre Haute & Indianapolis Railroad Company* v. *Indiana ex rel. Ketcham*, 194 US 579; *TH Gaz.*, May 31, 1904.

28. Church, *Corp. Hist.*, 11: 529; *CFC* 63 (December 5, 1896): 1011; 50th Annual Report—PRR (1896); *Poor's Manual of Railroads: 1901*, 738.

29. TH&I-Bd Min, October 17, 1904; 56th Annual Report—TH&I (1904).

30. TH&I-Bd Min, December 14, 1904.

31. Church, *Corp. Hist.*, 11: 529, 13: 201, 210–11.

32. Stock conversion calculated from Consolidation Agreement in Church, *Corp. Hist.*, 11: 625–32.

33. *CFC* 80 (April 1, 1905): 1243–45.

34. Hughes, "McKeen Family," 13; 54th Annual Report—TH&I (1902); Eric Hirsimaki, "Help from Above," *The Keystone* 31, no. 4 (Winter 1988): 36–40.

35. *Terre Haute Tribune*, February 18, 1913; *Terre Haute Star*, February 13, 1913; February 20, 1913; February 21, 1913.

36. *Terre Haute Star*, February 19, 1913; February 20, 1913; February 21, 1913; *Terre Haute Tribune*, February 20, 1913; *Terre Haute Evening Gazette*, October 13, 1902 (cited).

37. *Terre Haute Tribune*, February 20, 1913.

BIBLIOGRAPHY OF SECONDARY SOURCES

Bateman, Newton, J., Seymour Curwen, and Paul Selby. *Historical Encyclopedia of Illinois.* 2 vols. Chicago, 1923.

Belcher, Wyatt W. *Economic Rivalry between St. Louis and Chicago, 1850–1880.* New York, 1947.

Biographical History of Eminent and Self-Made Men of the State of Indiana, A. Cincinnati, 1880.

Biographical Memoirs of Greene County, Indiana. Indianapolis, 1908.

Bradsby, H. C. *History of Vigo County, Indiana.* Chicago, 1891.

Braeman, John. "The Rise of Albert J. Beveridge to the United States Senate." *Indiana Magazine of History* 53, no. 4 (December, 1957).

Bridenstine, Freda L. "The Madison & Indianapolis Railroad." Master's thesis, Butler University, Indianapolis, 1931.

Bruce, Robert V. *1877: Year of Violence.* Indianapolis, 1959.

Burgess, George H., and Miles C. Kennedy. *Centennial History of the Pennsylvania Railroad Company.* Philadelphia, 1949.

Clark, Dorothy J. *Historically Speaking.* Evansville, Ind., 1981.

Cottman, George S. "Internal Improvements: Railroads." *Indiana Magazine of History* 3 (December, 1907): 149–81.

Cumback, Will, and J. R. Maynard. *Men of Progress: Indiana.* Indianapolis, 1899.

Daniels, Wylie J. *The Village at the End of the Road.* Indianapolis, 1938.

Gookins, S. B. *History of Vigo County, Indiana.* Chicago, 1880; reprint, 1977.

Gray, Ralph D., ed. *Gentlemen from Indiana: National Party Candidates, 1836–1940.* Indianapolis, 1977.

Gresham, Matilda. *Life of Walter Quinton Gresham.* 2 vols. Chicago, 1919.

Grodinsky, Julius. *Jay Gould: His Business Career, 1867–1892.* Philadelphia, 1957.

Harlow, Alvin F. *The Road of the Century.* New York, 1947.

Harper, Denver. *Coal Mining in Vigo County, Indiana.* Bloomington, Ind., 1985.

Hassam, Loren. *A Historical Sketch of Terre Haute.* Terre Haute, 1873.

Hirsimaki, Eric. "Help from Above." *The Keystone* 31, no. 4 (Winter 1998): 36–40.

Howard, Timothy Edward, ed. *History of St. Joseph County, Indiana.* Chicago, 1907.

Hughes, Frances E. "The McKeen Family Dates to Early 1800's." *The Spectator,* February 26, 1977, p. 13.

———. "History of the Terre Haute First National Bank." Undated manuscript in possession of Ms. Virginia Titus, Terre Haute, Ind.

Jenks, Leland H. "Multiple Level Organization of a Great Railroad." *Business History Review* 35 (Autumn 1961): 336–43.

Klein, Maury. *The Life and Legend of Jay Gould.* Baltimore, 1986.

Lanier, J. F. D. *A Sketch of the Life of J. F. D. Lanier.* Privately printed, 1877.

McCaslin, William E., ed. *History of Bond County.* Chicago, 1915.

Nowland, John H. B. *Sketches of Prominent Citizens of 1876.* Indianapolis, 1877.

Oakey, C. C. *Greater Terre Haute and Vigo County.* 2 vols. Chicago, 1908.

Pennsylvania Company, The. *Corporate History of the Pittsburg, Fort Wayne & Chicago Railway Company.* Pittsburgh, 1875.

Perrin, William Henry, ed. *History of Effingham County.* Chicago, 1883.

Reed, George I., ed. *Encyclopedia of Biography of Indiana.* 2 vols. Chicago, 1895.

Rissler, Herbert J. "Charles Warren Fairbanks: Conservative Hoosier." Ph.D. dissertation, Indiana University, Bloomington, 1961.

Salvatore, Nick. *Eugene V. Debs, Citizen and Socialist.* Urbana, Ill., 1982.

Schotter, H. W. *The Growth and Development of the Pennsylvania Railroad Company*. Philadelphia, 1927.

Seeds, Russel M., ed. *History of the Republican Party of Indiana*. Indianapolis, 1899.

Sievers, Harry J. *Benjamin Harrison, Hoosier Statesman*. New York, 1959.

Smith, George W. *History of Illinois and Her People*. 6 vols. Chicago, 1927.

Stedman, Edmund Clarence, ed. *The New York Stock Exchange*. New York, 1905; reprint, 1969.

Sulgrove, B. R. *History of Indianapolis and Marion County*. Philadelphia, 1884.

Terre Haute & Richmond Railroad Company. *Exhibit of the Condition and Prospects of the Terre Haute and Richmond Railroad*. New York, 1851.

Ward, James A. *J. Edgar Thomson: Master of the Pennsylvania*. Westport, Conn., 1980.

———. "Power And Accountability on the Pennsylvania Railroad, 1846–1878." *Business History Review* 49 (Spring 1975): 37–59.

Woodward, C. M. *A History of The St. Louis Bridge*. St. Louis, 1881.

Wynn, Margaret. "Natural Gas in Indiana." *Indiana Magazine of History* 4 (March, 1908): 31–45.

INDEX

Note: Page numbers preceded by an asterisk (*) refer to photo captions.
Page numbers preceded by a double asterisk (**) refer to photographs.

RICHARD T. WALLIS, raised in a Pennsylvania Railroad family in New Jersey, studied history and found his soulmate at Oakland City College (now Oakland City University) in Oakland City, Indiana, before embarking on a career in broadcasting. It was in the Hoosier state that he rediscovered his railroad, and was introduced to the distinctive differences of its Lines West heritage. Wallis is a member of the Indiana Historical Society and the Pennsylvania Railroad Technical & Historical Society.